Women of the Western Frontier in Fact, Fiction and Film

Women of the Western Frontier in Fact, Fiction and Film

by

Ron Lackmann

McFarland & Company, Inc., Publishers
Jefferson, North Carolina, and London

For my favorite families—
the Pereiras
the Bretts
the Englishes
and
the Gelmans

The present work is a reprint of the illustrated case bound edition of Women of the Western Frontier in Fact, Fiction and Film, *first published in 1997 by McFarland*

Frontispiece: Calamity Jane, ca. 1895. (Library of Congress)

LIBRARY OF CONGRESS CATALOGUING-IN-PUBLICATION DATA

Lackmann, Ronald W.
    Women of the western frontier in fact, fiction and film / by Ron Lackmann.
        p.   cm.
    Includes bibliographical references and index.

    ISBN-13: 978-0-7864-2845-8
    ISBN-10: 0-7864-2845-7 (softcover : 50# alkaline paper) ∞

    1. Women pioneers—West (U.S.)—Biography.   2. Frontier and pioneer life—West (U.S.)   3. West (U.S.)—Biography.   I. Title.
F596.L33   2006
920.72'0978—dc21
[B]   97-34075

British Library cataloguing data are available

Cover photograph ©2006 Pictures Now

Manufactured in the United States of America

McFarland & Company, Inc., Publishers
  Box 611, Jefferson, North Carolina 28640
    www.mcfarlandpub.com

Table of Contents

Introduction   1

Chapter One
 Belle Starr and Calamity Jane: The Old West's Two Most Famous Women   5

Chapter Two
 Gunfighters' Wives and Lovers, and Female Outlaws   37

Chapter Three
 Female Entertainers Who Toured the Western Frontier   69

Chapter Four
 Prostitutes, Madams and Gambling Ladies of the Wild West   83

Chapter Five
 Remarkable Respectable Women of the Western Frontier   105

Appendix A
 Selected Western Silent Films Featuring Women in Prominent Roles   151

Appendix B
 Selected Western Sound Films Featuring Women in Prominent Roles   153

Appendix C
 Western Television Series Featuring Women in Prominent Roles   186

Appendix D
 Twelve Celebrated Locales of the Western Frontier   190

Bibliography   195

Index   199

Introduction

America's Western frontier has been so vividly depicted and so heavily exploited by writers and filmmakers that it is often difficult to draw a line between myth and reality. Clearly, the West has the stuff of which legends are made. Since Webster's Dictionary defines *legends* as "stories coming down from the past ... popularly regarded as historical although often not verifiable," a great deal of what has been written about the great American West can certainly be called "legendary." The American West of both fact and fiction—the vast areas of undeveloped land stretching from the Mississippi River to the Pacific Ocean—was an adventurous and often lawless place in the latter half of the nineteenth century, and the men and women who lived there had to be equally adventurous and frequently just as lawless in order to survive. They were not, however, the superheroes that pulp writers and filmmakers would have us think. They were real human beings, with all of the frailties of our species.

Romantic notions of what the American West must have been like were first promoted by the writers of adventure stories in the mid–1800s. Pamphlet-like little books, called "dime novels," and stories in such periodicals as *The New York Weekly*, *The Frontier Scout* and *The Police Gazette* were avidly read by millions of adventure-starved, city-dwelling Easterners. According to these fiction writers and the twentieth-century moviemakers who followed, the West's women were of three kinds: innocent and beautiful homesteaders' daughters; attractive, good-natured, mischievous tomboys (or "sports," as the dime novelists called them) or provocative saloon girls with hearts of gold under their gaudy taffeta gowns and quick wits under their dyed hennaed hair.

Our image of our Western heritage is also largely due to the work of nineteenth-century artists. Painters and etchers rendered romantic and panoramic images of the West and its inhabitants for such periodicals as *America Illustrations of Today*, which was widely distributed in the 1860s. These artists included George Catlin (1796–1872), who painted colorful Native American subjects, and landscape artists such as Albert Bierstadt (1830–1902) and Thomas Moran (1837–1926), who glorified the West's breathtaking natural scenery but never painted the muddy, dust-filled cow towns, the grime-covered mining camps or the hastily constructed shacks most Westerners lived in. Artist Frederick Remington (1861–1909) romanticized the American cowboy in his paintings and sculptures, but his creations could not depict the cowpokes as they actually were—overworked, saddle sore, and covered with cow dung.

In spite of what creative tale-spinners and fine artists have told us about the American West, most of its people were first and foremost survivors, albeit adventurous ones, who encountered numerous obstacles during their lifetimes. This was particularly true for the women. In the West in the years following the Civil War, women had few options. They could compete with men by wearing men's clothing and assuming masculine attitudes (sometimes even passing themselves off as men); they could become prostitutes; or they could bed down to lives of catering to men's needs as hard-working wives or servants. A few rare, enterprising women did manage to obtain a reasonable degree of independence as schoolteachers, waitresses or, if they had the resources, as independent businesswomen who owned ranches, stores, restaurants, or newspapers. One must remember, however, that women had not yet been granted the right to vote and in many states they were not even allowed to own property. Financially independent women were therefore few in number, though for sheer gutsiness and unconventionality, some of the West's most memorable women were certainly independent spirits. The celebrated Calamity Jane, for example, smoked cigars, cursed like the proverbial trooper, and wore baggy men's clothing 100 years before it became fashionable. She was also a hard-drinking, free-wheeling alcoholic most of her life, which may in part account for her unconventionality during that more "proper" century. The infamous "Bandit Queen of the Badlands," Belle Starr, far preferred diversified sexual activities to banditry and shared her bed with numerous men who happened to take her fancy, a century before it became a commonplace practice. Many other women of the Old West were just as unconventional and original as Calamity Jane and Belle Starr, and their stories certainly make for fascinating reading.

While researching this book, I often found it difficult to distinguish fact from fiction. Most historians, and certainly the fiction writers who used the great American West as the settings for their books, zeroed in on the westward expansion by the Euro-American settlers from the opening of the frontier in the late 1700s to its virtual closing in the late 1890s (the period of time covered in this book). The area is vast and varied in topography. The West as a single locality is impossible to pinpoint, except to say that it was the area west of the Mississippi River to the Pacific Coast. Few historians, and probably fewer Western fiction writers, had ever experienced the West's development firsthand, and therefore they had to depend upon whatever documentation others offered, and on the accounts of ordinary Westerners. These accounts were often less than reliable. Author Duncan Aiken's *Calamity Jane and the Lady Wildcats*, which includes accounts of many of the West's memorable women, was written 20 or 30 years after the subjects' heyday. Aiken interviewed Western celebrities, their relatives and their friends, and supposed eyewitnesses to the events he was reporting on. People's memories being what they are, one must assume that much of what Aiken recorded was mistaken, clouded or exaggerated, and that self-glorification may have been the aim of those interviewed. After all, people rarely shy away from becoming a part of recorded history, and sometimes they will stretch the truth a bit in a bid for immortality. It is therefore likely that much of what we know about the West's inhabitants and their activities is based on partial truths at best. The Old West's glory days have almost certainly been embroidered in order to add excitement to historical events.

In deciding which of the West's many remarkable women to include in this work, I read numerous retrospectives, journals, encyclopedias, biographies, autobiographies, newspaper articles, dime novels, magazine feature stories and books about the West as well as books about Western films and film stars. (Written material is listed in my bibliography; Western films featuring women in prominent roles are listed in Appendices A and B.) After making an initial list of the names of Western women I was already familiar with, such as Belle Starr, Calamity Jane, Annie Oakley and Lola Montez, I added the names of women I came across in my reading. The women I chose to include in this book are those who seemed to *demand* that they be included, not only because they were frequently mentioned, but also because they seemed to typify the image of the Old West which most people have. When I completed this list, most of the women I decided to include fell into one of four categories: the wives and lovers of gunfighters and female outlaws; prostitutes, madams, and gambling ladies; entertainers who toured the Western United States when it was still a wild, undeveloped frontier; and the "respectable" women who lived in the West (schoolteachers, army wives, ranchers, farmers, etc). I decided that this book should devote a chapter to each of these four categories. A separate chapter, however, seemed essential for the West's two most famous females, Belle Starr and Calamity Jane, whose names dominated all of the books I read and who, more than any of the others, epitomized the free-spirited women of the legendary West we have come to know and admire.

Here then are the remarkable women of the Western frontier, the way they really were, as well as the way Western mythmakers wanted us to believe they were.

Note: Birth and death dates are supplied where available. Most of the women mentioned in Chapter 5, *Respectable Women,* and Chapter Four, *Prostitutes, Madams and Gambling Ladies,* as well as a few women in other chapters, did not leave behind any documentation of their births and deaths. Dates I could not confirm are distinguished by question marks.

Chapter One

Belle Starr and Calamity Jane: The Old West's Two Most Famous Women

Without question, Belle "The Bandit Queen" Starr and Martha "Calamity Jane" Canary (aka Cannary) are the best remembered women of the Old West. Their names were well known throughout the United States during their lifetimes and their fame continued to grow long after they died. They became real legends of the Western frontier, equal in celebrity to such notable Western characters as "Buffalo Bill" Cody, "Wild Bill" Hickok, Kit Carson, Bat Masterson and Wyatt Earp. It seems therefore appropriate to begin with a separate chapter detailing the lives and reported adventures of these two truly remarkable women.

BELLE STARR (1846–1889)

The dubious distinction of becoming famous as the Old West's most notorious female outlaw, even though she barely qualifies for this title, certainly belongs to Belle Starr. Belle's status as a "bandit queen of the West" is actually based on very little evidence, since during her lifetime she was only arrested and tried for such minor crimes as stealing cattle and horses. Although it was said that she was a member of a gang of robbers for a short time, no documentation exists. Belle was, however, the friend, lover, consort, protector and confidante of many of the West's most infamous outlaws, including Frank and Jesse James, John Middleton, Jim Reed and the Younger brothers, and it is mainly because of these associations that she became world famous and earned her place in the Old West's history.

Belle Starr was born Myra Maybelle Shirley in Carthage, Missouri, on February 3, 1846. Her parents, John and Eliza Shirley, owned a hotel in Carthage which, according to some sources, they operated over a 25-year period. According to Belle's biographers, the Shirleys were among the leading citizens of Carthage, and because John Shirley had served as a minor judicial official in the town, he was affectionately called "the Judge" by members of the community. Apparently John Shirley was an intelligent, well read man and was said to have had one of the finest personal libraries west of the Mississippi River. His wife Eliza was a socially ambitious woman who, it seems, aspired to lead the refined life of a proper Southern lady (she had been born in the Deep South and migrated to Missouri when she was a young married woman). Eliza Shirley was said to have had a beautiful piano brought with her when she married and moved to Carthage from her family home. The piano, which was in the parlor of her house, was apparently the envy of every lady in Carthage. Mrs. Shirley is said to have kept the instrument highly polished at all times in order to dazzle visitors to her home. Eliza Shirley was also determined that her only daughter, Myra, would shine as brightly as her piano, and insisted she be "raised for a lady," as she put it. Myra Maybelle was given piano and horseback riding lessons, at which she is said to have excelled. She was also taught the polite manners and deportment of a proper Southern lady of quality, and she was always dressed in fashionable clothes. It's no wonder that Myra, like her mother's piano, became the envy of every woman in Carthage. Fortunately, Myra, like her father, was also intelligent and an avid reader—certainly no mere addlepated ornament. She was especially fond of the novels of William Gilmore, which often featured haughty, high-tempered, emotionally reckless heroines with whom she evidently identified.

Young Myra was "a hotel child" and grew up the center of attention at her parents' hotel. She was constantly surrounded by adoring adults who would prevail upon her to entertain them with her imaginative stories, or by playing the piano or dancing for them. From her earliest years, Myra delighted in all of the attention that was lavished on her.

Myra's introduction to lawlessness apparently occurred during the Civil War years, when she was in her teens. Her much-adored older brother Edwin (Ed) joined a band of renegade Southern sympathizers who raided towns in Missouri and neighboring Kansas whose citizens supported the Northern cause. The renegades robbed, killed, and generally terrorized the people who inhabited the Union-loyal towns. This guerrilla band served under a Kentucky-born captain named William S. Quantrill who originally fought with the regular Confederate Army but then became a partisan, leading his followers at such bloody massacres as the 1863 raid on Lawrence, Kansas, in which 182 townspeople, mostly Union supporters, were slaughtered. In addition to Quantrill and Ed Shirley, this band of ruthless rebels also included such Western outlaws as Jesse and Frank James and the Younger brothers. Because they were Southern sympathizers, and because their son Ed was serving under Quantrill, the Shirleys offered the mob a place to stay at their Carthage hotel whenever they needed a place to hide. It was at this time that Myra first became acquainted with many of the notorious outlaws who would later make her famous. When Quantrill was killed, the James and Younger boys continued their criminal ways, robbing banks, stagecoaches and trains, finding that crime was far more lucrative than trying to make an "honest" living at a respectable, low-paying town job, or toiling for little profit on some farm.

Belle Starr's biographer Duncan Aiken claims that Ed Shirley did not join the James and Younger brothers in their criminal activities; Shirley decided that he had had enough adventure and excitement to last a lifetime while serving under Quantrill, married a local Carthage girl and settled down to the life of a farmer in western Missouri. Glenn Shirley (who is apparently no relation to Myra Belle), in his biography *Belle Starr* (1982), says that Ed Shirley died in a gunfight shortly after Quantrill was killed.

Whatever the truth concerning Ed's fate, Myra apparently decided that there were greener pastures beyond Missouri, and left Carthage to seek her fortune in Texas, an area of the country she heard was overflowing with opportunities. With money that was given to her by her brother's bandit friends, Myra bought a run-down ranch near Dallas; biographer Glenn Shirley wrote that she moved there with her parents. Other sources, however, claimed that John and Eliza Shirley remained in Carthage and continued to operate their hotel until many years later when they did indeed move to Texas.

Myra's ranch became an ideal place for her outlaw friends to hide out when they were on the run from the law, and so their generous gift to Myra had apparently not been entirely without motive. Myra "Belle," as she began to call herself at this time, willingly offered her brother's former compatriots refuge at her ranch, but insisted on receiving additional financial compensation for her hospitality. When Cole Younger (1844–1916) needed a place to hide out after robbing a bank and killing several lawmen in 1866, he reportedly went to Myra Belle's place in Texas. Later reports claim that he became immediately attracted to the high-spirited and intelligent young Myra Belle, who was 20 years old at the time, and that the two had a tempestuous love affair, a fact that Cole later vehemently denied.

Cole eventually returned to Missouri and resumed his bank and stagecoach robbing. Myra Belle gave birth to a baby girl she named Rosie Lee but usually called her by her nickname, Pearl. (The child was always officially known as "Pearl Reed.") The same year Cole visited Myra Belle's place, another handsome young bandit named Jim Reed (1844–1874), who had also served under Quantrill and was a member of the Younger and James gangs, arrived at Myra Belle's ranch needing a place to hide when a bank robbery went wrong and made him a fugitive. Myra Belle was apparently attracted to the smooth-talking, good-looking young outlaw, and she was soon offering Reed more than a place to hide. She became his lover and eventually his wife, according to a marriage certificate that was issued to James C. Reed and Myra Maybelle Shirley on November 1, 1866, in Collin County, Texas. After a few months at Myra Belle's place, Reed was warned that he had been recognized in Texas and was about to be arrested and extradited back to Missouri. He persuaded Myra Belle to accompany him to Los Angeles, California, where he felt confident he would not be recognized; Belle took baby Pearl along with them. Myra Belle, however, returned to Texas in 1872 with Pearl and a new baby, whom she had named Ed in honor of her beloved brother. Belle later claimed that she strongly disapproved of Reed's continuing criminal activities and returned to her Texas ranch because she felt she could raise her children more properly there. In August 1874, Belle received word that her husband had been killed. A Paris, Texas, newspaper reported that on August 9, 1874: "Jim Reed, the San Antonio stage robber, was shot and killed by a J. Morris of McKinney (this evening) about 15 miles northwest of this city. Morris had followed Reed for three months and had succeeded in capturing him while he stopped at a farmhouse for dinner. Morris asked Reed to surrender, and he said he would; Morris told Reed to get up, but instead of doing so he ran under the table and raised it up between him and Morris and started out the door with it (the table). Morris shot two balls through the table. The third shot killed Reed almost instantly. Morris then brought the body to Paris."

Even though Myra and Jim had been married for eight years, she did not seem to mourn for long. In the December following his death, she testified in support of one of Reed's victims, Watt Grayson, who was trying to recover money taken from him in a robbery that Reed committed shortly before his death. Myra confirmed the fact that the money was indeed Grayson's and that her husband was the thief who had taken it. In spite of this, she wrote a long and chatty letter to Reed's mother and family who were living in Vernon County, Missouri. In the letter (composed two years after Reed was killed), Myra wrote:

> Dear Mother, Brothers and Sisters—I write you after so long a time to let you know that I am still living. Time has made many changes, and some very sad ones indeed. My poor father has left this world of care and trouble. He died two months ago today. It seems as if I have more trouble than any person. "Shug" [Myra's younger brother, Cravens or John Allison] got into trouble here and had to leave; poor Ma is left alone with the exception of little Eddie [Myra and Jim Reed's son]. She is going to move away from here in a few days [the Shirleys had obviously already left Carthage, Missouri, and were living in Texas by this time] and then I'll be left alone.
>
> Rosie [her daughter Pearl] is here in Dallas going to school; she has the reputation of being the prettiest little girl in Dallas. She is learning very fast. She had been playing on the stage here in the Dallas theater, and gained world-wide reputation for her prize performance. My people were very much opposed to it but I wanted her to be able to make a living of her own without depending on anyone. She is constantly talking of you all, and wanted to visit you, which I

intend she shall sometime [which was probably her real reason for her writing to her mother-in-law, since she had already taken up with a series of new lovers].

Myra's letter concluded with a statement obviously intended to gain sympathy: "I am far from well. I am so nervous this evening from the headache that I can scarcely write."

Visits from various outlaw friends continued and, as usual, her boarders always paid Myra handsomely for her hospitality. Whatever they paid her was apparently not enough for her, and so, in order to supplement her income, Myra Belle began to rustle neighbors' horses and cattle, selling them to fences.

In 1876, the law finally caught up to the James-Younger gang, who were ambushed during a bank robbery in Northfield, Minnesota. Gang member Charlie Pitts was killed, and the Younger brothers were seriously wounded and taken prisoner. The James brothers, however, escaped the ambush and continued their criminal activities for another ten years. The captured and jailed Younger brothers were sure the townspeople of Northfield were going to string them up to the nearest tree without benefit of a trial, but to their surprise, they were treated as if they were celebrities. The townsfolk, especially the women of Northfield, brought them gifts of food and flowers, eager to get a look at the handsome, dashing and daring young bandits who had attracted so much attention in the national press. It was little wonder that Myra Belle had fallen in love with the sweet-tongued, good-looking Cole Younger. While he was awaiting his trial, Cole granted numerous interviews to newspaper reporters, entertained visitors in his jail cell and generally endeared himself to the public, as well as to his jailers, who enjoyed their momentary glow in the spotlight. In the same seductive manner that had won over the impressionable young Myra Belle Shirley, Cole Younger told one reporter that his gang had been "drove to crime," adding that "circumstances sometimes makes men what they are." He also charmed a crowd of visiting ladies when he cooed, "I love flowers, because those I love loves flowers," as he was handed a bouquet of posies by an admiring young woman. Of course, a reporter from *The New York Times* was present to record that event for posterity with a photograph. Because of Cole's winning ways, the Youngers all managed to escape the hangman's noose, in spite of the fact that they were indeed cold-blooded killers. They were sentenced to life imprisonment, but after serving several years in jail, they were released for good behavior. Cole lived to the ripe old age of 78, and continued to bask in the glory of his infamous past, frequently granting interviews and generally holding court with anyone who wished to hear his stories about "the good old days" of the wild, wild West. He died in 1916.

In 1877, Belle and a female friend of questionable reputation, Emma Jones, were traveling from Myra Belle's home to a neighboring town to buy supplies when they were caught in a "Texas norther" (storm) and took shelter in a small village store. When evening came, the girls built a fire to warm a pot of coffee, using the rear wall of the building as a back log. The building burned to the ground and the next day Myra Belle found herself in a Texas jail charged with arson. At her hearing, her dignity and refinement so impressed an elderly, well-to-do local stockman named Patterson that he paid all of Myra Belle's legal fees and gave the owner of the store money to pay for the damage done to his property. Patterson also managed to have the charges against Myra Belle dropped by paying a nominal fine on a malicious-mischief charge. Myra spent a day or two being escorted about town by the elderly gentleman, but as soon as she could, she went home, leaving the dazzled, love-struck old man grieving at her departure. In 1878, Myra Belle was arrested for stealing a horse from a neighbor, but the charge could not be proven even though many of her neighbors had also been complaining that their livestock had been disappearing and that they were sure Myra Belle and the numerous "shady-looking" male guests who hung around her place were unquestionably

"Younger's Bend," Belle Starr's home in the Oklahoma Indian Territory. (Oklahoma Historical Society.)

responsible. Eventually the Dallas law authorities grew tired of the constant complaints being filed against her, and Myra Belle and her friends were ordered to leave Collin County once and for all. Realizing that it was probably only a matter of time before she would be held accountable for her criminal activities, Myra Belle sold her Dallas area ranch and began to ride the open ranges of the Texas and Oklahoma panhandle with a group of desperadoes and cutthroats, most of whom had already gained national reputations for their criminal activities. The band of outlaws "lived by villainy," according to writer Glenn Shirley, and were sought by the law after a succession of robberies and confidence schemes. Although it was only alleged that Myra Belle actively participated in any of these crimes, it *is* known that she did indeed travel around with these outlaws; several of these bandits, when later apprehended, claimed that Myra Belle Reed was "the brains of the band of thieves "and had actually planned most of their crimes.

Once again Myra Belle decided that, "for the sake of the children," it would be best to look for a place to settle down and "establish roots," so she bought yet another run down ranch, this time in the Indian Territory of Oklahoma. The ranch was situated on the Canadian River, and before long it too became a refuge for outlaws hiding from the law. The fugitives she harbored at her new home included several Indian outlaws, one of whom was Tom Starr, who had two sons (Sam and Jim) also involved in banditry. Many of the outlaws Myra Belle gave refuge to at this time apparently also became her lovers, and the roster of her notorious boarder-paramours included such sought-after criminals as Jack Spaniard, the suave but dangerous Jim French (who previously consorted with Myra Belle when he was a member of her Badlands gang) and the soft-spoken but treacherous John Middleton. Middleton was later ambushed by a posse in 1886 after being betrayed by the man who was to later become Myra Belle's second husband, Sam Starr; Starr was said to be jealous of Middleton's love affair with Belle. Middleton had been a member of the infamous "Regulars" gang with the murderous William "Billy the Kid" Bonney. This band of gunfighters had indiscriminately killed lawmen as well as innocent citizens in Lincoln, Nebraska, during a power struggle between two rival factions fighting for control of range lands and the politics of the county.

Myra Belle named her new home in the Oklahoma Indian Territory "Younger's Bend," in honor of the man she later told the press was her "first and one true love," Cole Younger. In Oklahoma, Myra Belle also became romantically involved with a series of Native Americans, including the attractive three-quarter Cherokee Sam Starr, whom she married on June 5, 1880. Her other Native American lovers included a muscular, good-looking young brave named Blue Duck, with whom she was photographed in 1884 to show her support when he was arrested for cattle rustling. Jim July, who was Sam Starr's brother and whose birth name was James Starr, later claimed that he was married to Belle at the time of her death.

Belle said in an interview with a Dallas newspaper that she had "fallen in love with Sam Starr the minute [she] laid eyes on him." Because of her marriage to Sam, who was entitled to full Cherokee Indian privileges, Myra Belle was made a member of the Cherokee nation, an honor few whites ever enjoyed, and she was even able to claim a parcel of free land in the Indian Territory for herself. After they were married, Myra Belle began using her middle name, "Belle," exclusively, telling a newspaper interviewer during one of her trials for horse stealing that she thought the name "Belle Starr" had "a nice ring to it." Belle and Sam's marriage license read, "On this 5th day of June 1880 by Abe Woodall-District Judge for Canadian Dist. C. N., Samuel Starr a citizen of Cherokee Nation age 23 years and Mrs. Bell[e] Reed a citizen of United States age 27 years." It was signed by H. J. Vann, Clerk.

Because of her past associations with the James and Younger brothers gang, Belle Starr was already the subject of considerable interest by the Eastern press from the time they had covered the trial of the Youngers in 1876. Her name had been frequently mentioned at their trial. The Youngers were by this time nationally known, and everything they did and said was duly reported in the newspapers. But it was during Belle's own trial for horse stealing that, like her friends Jesse James and Cole Younger, she became a legendary Western celebrity in her own right. The numerous reports about her close associations with many of the nation's most infamous outlaws once again resurfaced, and she was suddenly being called "The Bandit Queen of the Badlands" in the press. It was mainly because of these past relationships, rather than due to any actual criminal activities that she participated in herself, that Belle's reputation as a famous female outlaw was first bandied about in the press. The "Bandit Queen" label stuck. Of course, Belle had always been delighted by attention of any kind, and was thrilled by all the publicity and interest in her activities. She granted numerous interviews, posed for photographs and generally basked in the spotlight of her new-found celebrity.

At this time, Belle wrote a short biographical sketch for John F. Weaver of *The Fort Smith Elevator*, expressing her desire "to live a quiet life and be a credit to [her] sex and family." The biography read in part:

> On the Canadian River ... far from society, I hoped to pass the remainder of my life in peace.... So long had I been estranged from the society of women (whom I thoroughly detest) that I thought I would find it irksome to live in their midst. So I selected a place that few have ever had the gratification of gossiping around. For a short time, I lived very happily in the society of my little girl and husband ... but it soon became noised around that I was a woman of some notoriety from Texas, and from that time on my home and actions have been severely criticized. Notwithstanding some of the best people in the country are friends of mine. I have considerable ignorance to cope with, consequently my troubles originate mostly in that quarter. Surrounded by a low-down class of shoddy whites who have made the Indian Territory their home to evade paying tax on their dogs, and who I will not permit to hunt on my premises, I am the constant theme of their slanderous tongue.

Blue Duck and Belle Starr, 1884. (Oklahoma Historical Society.)

"My home," Belle admitted, "became famous as an outlaw's ranch long before I was visited by any of the boys who were friends of mine. Indeed, I never corresponded with any of my old associates and was desirous my whereabouts should be unknown to them. Through rumor, they learned of it. Jesse James first came in and remained several weeks. He was unknown to my husband [Sam Starr], and he never knew till long afterwards that our home had been honored by James' presence. I introduced Jesse as one Mr. Williams from Texas." Belle's brief autobiographical sketch is as interesting for what it left out as for what she chose to include.

In 1881, Jesse James' mother had her right arm blown off during a raid on her farm by Pinkerton detectives who were looking for her son. At the time, Jesse was laying low at Belle's Younger's Bend ranch. He should have remained at Belle's place, because one year later, on April 3, 1882, he was shot in the back in his Missouri home by a former member of his gang, Bob Ford, for the $10,000 reward money that was being offered for his capture "dead or alive."

When her horse-rustling trial ended, Belle and Sam Starr were found guilty of stealing a neighbor's property (horses) and selling them. Belle actually had the distinction of being the first woman who was ever sentenced by the infamous "Hanging Judge" Isaac Parker, who dealt much less severely with Belle and Sam than he had with others. Parker sentenced Belle and Sam to four years in prison. Belle was to serve her time at the Detroit, Michigan House of Correction. These were indeed very liberal sentences, considering Parker's customarily harsh judgments. While in prison, Belle wrote to her daughter, Pearl, about her incarceration:

> There is a great deal of difference in this place and a penitentiary; you must bear in mind and not think of mamma as being shut up in a gloomy prison. It is said to be one of the finest institutions in the United States, surrounded by beautiful grounds, with fountains and everything nice. Here I can have my education renewed, and I stand greatly in need of it. Sam will have to attend school and I think it will be the best thing that ever happened to him. And now you must not be unhappy and brood over our absence. It won't take the time long to glide by and as we come home we will get you [Pearl was staying with Belle's parents in Carthage], and then we will have such a nice time.

In reality, the prison was nothing like what she described to her daughter. It was actually a rather dismal and austere place; during her trial and subsequent incarceration, Belle appears to have aged drastically.

In 1886, Belle was released from prison and almost immediately resumed her former criminal activities, once again becoming a curse to her neighbors whose cattle and horses she continued to steal. In Don Cusic's book *Cowboys and the Wild West: An A–Z Guide from the Chisholm Trail to the Silver Screen*, a few months after his release from prison Sam Starr "was killed in a gunfight" with a lawman. A report in *The Muskogee Indian Journal* substantiates this fact, saying that an Indian policeman named John West, who had been tracking Sam Starr down after a series of robberies he committed immediately upon being released from prison, was informed that Sam had returned to his wife's ranch at Younger's Bend. An eyewitness reported that as John West approached the house, "Sam came outside and, seeing West, accused him of shooting his horse when the Cherokee officers were trying to arrest him several weeks before. A few hot words ensued, when Starr pulled his revolver, and West drew his as soon after as he could, but not until he had received a mortal wound, from which he staggered: but recovering, he sent a ball through Starr, and then fell dead. Starr staggered about ten feet and then he, too, fell a corpse." The next morning a heartbroken Belle took her husband's body in a wagon to Briartown, where he was buried in the Starr family cemetery overlooking the Canadian River.

Belle was deeply depressed by Sam's death and publicly announced that her home would "no longer be a place for outlaws to hide out." She failed to mention, however, that her cattle rustling activities were continuing in spite of her husband's death. Again, these activities became the source of numerous formal complaints filed against her by her neighbors.

As if the loss of her husband was not enough for her to cope with, Belle's daughter Pearl, who was 19 years old, was romantically involved with a young man and became pregnant. Belle sent Pearl to live with her grandparents, the Reeds in Missouri, where she gave birth to a baby girl. Belle's vow to "no longer harbor known criminals" was also soon forgotten and once Pearl was secured with Belle's in-laws in Missouri, that practice was also resumed. In

Belle Starr outside the courthouse in Fort Smith, Oklahoma, during one of her trials for horse stealing. (Oklahoma Historical Society.)

spite of her crimes, an acquaintance named Frederick Barde wrote about her sympathetically at the time:

> Even people who knew her to be merely a harborer of thieves had a bit of sympathy for her. She was human to the heart and in the thinly settled region where she lived, no woman was more generous to the sick and unfortunate…. When the women in the neighborhood were ill and unable to care for their families, Belle Starr went to their homes and ministered to them with her own hands…. Her voice was soft and pleasing, and her manner polite and engaging when she was in a good humor. Her language was not vulgar, nor was she profane when she was angry. There are still persons living in old Indian Territory who feel that she was more sinned against than sinning … the victim of surroundings from which she could not escape.

Other accounts of Belle's life, however, were in complete contrast to Barde's evaluation. An old miner named Mody C. Boatright told a tale, albeit a tall one, to author Joyce Gibson Roach, who included it in her book *The Cowgirls*. (The story had reportedly been told to Boatright by his father and told to Roach, whose book was published in 1977.) "The hotels were overflowing in San Antonio," Boatright said his father had told him, "when a cow puncher named Pete rode into town one evening. The proprietor of one small hotel agreed to house him in a room with another guest, provided the consent of the first guest was given. This was easily done and the two strangers shared a double bed. Pete and the roommate talked of many things that night, among them Belle Starr and her escapades. During the conversation Pete expressed his keen desire to meet this celebrated Western woman. The next morning," Boatright continued, "Pete found that his roommate had gotten out of bed before him and left. When he was leaving the hotel he saw a fine horse standing outside the hotel, saddled at the rack. His roommate of the evening before came out of a restaurant and mounted the horse.

"Did you say you would like to see Belle Starr?" Pete was asked.

"Yes, sirree," he replied.

"Well, you slept with her last night," he was told as Belle Starr herself galloped away.

Whatever Belle was up to at this time, on February 3, 1889, she was shot in the back and killed while traveling on horseback to Eufalia, Oklahoma. Newspapers all across the country made Belle Starr's death front page news. Three days after she was killed, even the respectable *New York Times*, under a headline that read "A Desperate Woman Killed," reported in a highly inaccurate news item:

> Word had been received from Eufalia, Indian Territory, that Belle Starr was killed there Sunday night. Belle was the wife of Cole Younger [she was never married to Cole].... Jim [actually Sam] Starr, her second husband, was shot down by the side of Belle [untrue] less than two years ago.... Belle was the most desperate woman that ever figured on the borders. She married Cole Younger directly after the war [untrue], but left him and joined a band of outlaws [unconfirmed] that operated in the Indian Territory. She had been arrested for murder [not so] and robbery a score of times [exaggerated], but always managed to escape.

One month after Belle's death, *The National Police Gazette* printed a lurid drawing of Belle on horseback at the moment of the mortal shooting, accompanied by a brief account of her demise. A disgruntled neighbor, Edgar Watson, who had openly complained about having had his horses stolen by Belle, was accused of her murder and placed on trial. Watson was acquitted since he could account for his movements at the time of Belle's death. Rumors then began to circulate that Belle was actually killed by her 18-year-old son, Ed, who was said to be furious with his mother for having beat him after he rode her favorite horse without permission. It was also whispered that Ed and Belle had been having an incestuous love affair and that the boy was jealous of Jim July. Whatever the actual circumstances of Belle Starr's death were, she was a full-fledged Western celebrity when she was murdered, and her death was big news all around the country.

Belle's oral will, which was filed in the Cherokee Nation, Canadian District office, left everything she had to Jim Starr (Jim July), and this became the basis for Jim's claim that he and Belle were married shortly after his brother's death. No documentation of such a union has ever been uncovered.

Belle's friends and her two children had a touching inscription placed on the headstone at her grave site at Younger's Bend. The stone, which had a bell and a star engraved on it in relief to represent her name, read:

> Shed not for her the bitter tear
> Nor give the heart in vain regret.
> 'Tis but the casket that lies here
> The gem that filled it sparkles yet.

Not long after Belle's death, her son Ed Reed was arrested for larceny and sentenced to five years by the same Judge Parker who had sent his mother to prison years before. Ed was later killed in 1896, while attempting to make a citizen's arrest of two men he accused of selling him bad whiskey. Belle's daughter Pearl married a man name Will Harrison, whom she later divorced after he deserted her. Pearl had three children by Harrison and eventually drifted into prostitution in order to support her children. She later became the madam of a five-dollar-a-night whorehouse in Fort Smith. In 1897, Pearl, who by this time was using her birth name of "Rosa," married a German musician named Arthur Erbach. She gave birth to a fourth child, a son, in 1902. Pearl died on July 6, 1925, and was buried in a sun-scorched cemetery with the name "Rosa Reed" engraved on her tombstone according to instructions she gave her family shortly before she died.

Biographies, Fictions and Films About Belle Starr

A book—actually little more than a pamphlet—about Belle Starr was written and published by Richard Fox and released shortly after Belle's death. The cover bore the title *Bella* [sic] *Starr: The Bandit Queen, or the Female Jesse James*, though an advertisement referred to it as *Life and Adventure of Belle Starr, the Noted Bandit Queen of the West*. It sold for 25 cents and became widely read in both the United States and abroad. The book was subsequently serialized in the *National Police Gazette* magazine. There were many other accounts of Belle Starr's life and activities written during her lifetime and shortly thereafter and these greatly added to her ever-increasing fame. Another book which certainly contributed to the Belle Starr folklore and her status as a true legend of the West was Samuel Herman's 1898 *Hell on the Border; He Hanged Eighty-Eight Men*, the story of "Hanging Judge" Parker. The author was a hotel owner and former newspaperman who had become acquainted with many criminals and marshals who lived in the Indian Territory and who knew Judge Parker and many of the famous criminals he had sentenced. It contained a 62-page chapter called "Belle Starr, the Female Desperado." Several subsequent biographies and accounts of Belle's activities certainly gave more detailed and accurate information than were supplied by either Fox or Herman. Duncan Aiken, in his 1927 book *Calamity Jane and the Lady Wildcats*, included a lengthy section on Belle's life, and even though it also contained several unconfirmed reports of her criminal activities, it was by far the most truthful telling of Belle's life published up until that time.

One of the most detailed and accurate accounts of Belle Starr's life was written by Burton Rascoe and published in 1941. In his book, Rascoe concentrated on several accounts of Belle's reported criminal activities, which he claimed included several murders and stagecoach robberies (charges that have never been substantiated). He also mentioned her associations with many known Western outlaws of her time. Like Fox, Rascoe avoided becoming involved in the more carnal aspects of Belle's life. Later biographies written by E. P. Hicks in 1968 and W. W. Breiham in 1970 were considerably less conservative in their accounts of Belle's activities, both criminal and sexual, since the United States was by then undergoing a sexual and social revolution, and the censors had begun to lose their control over written and filmed material. The authors of these two books openly discussed the numerous possible psychological Freudian manifestations of Belle Starr's unconventional behavior, attributing most of her activities to the fact that since childhood she "was always encouraged to be the center of attention." The most detailed account of Belle Starr's life is found in Glenn Shirley's *Belle Starr: Her Life and Times*, published in 1982. This is unquestionably the most comprehensive book about Belle Starr's life that has been published to date.

Considering Belle's censurable real-life activities, it is little wonder that her real story was never presented on the censor-controlled silver screen of the 1930s, '40s, and '50s. The first motion picture known to deal with Belle's life of crime was a silent film released in 1928. In this film, called *Court Martial*, silent screen star Betty Compson played Belle.

The first important motion picture about Belle's life, however, simply called *Belle Starr*, was released in 1941. Directed by Irving Cummings, this film starred the lovely motion picture actress Gene Tierney as Belle. Tierney's co-stars in this highly romanticized version of

Cover of a book published shortly after Belle Starr's death. (Author's collection.)

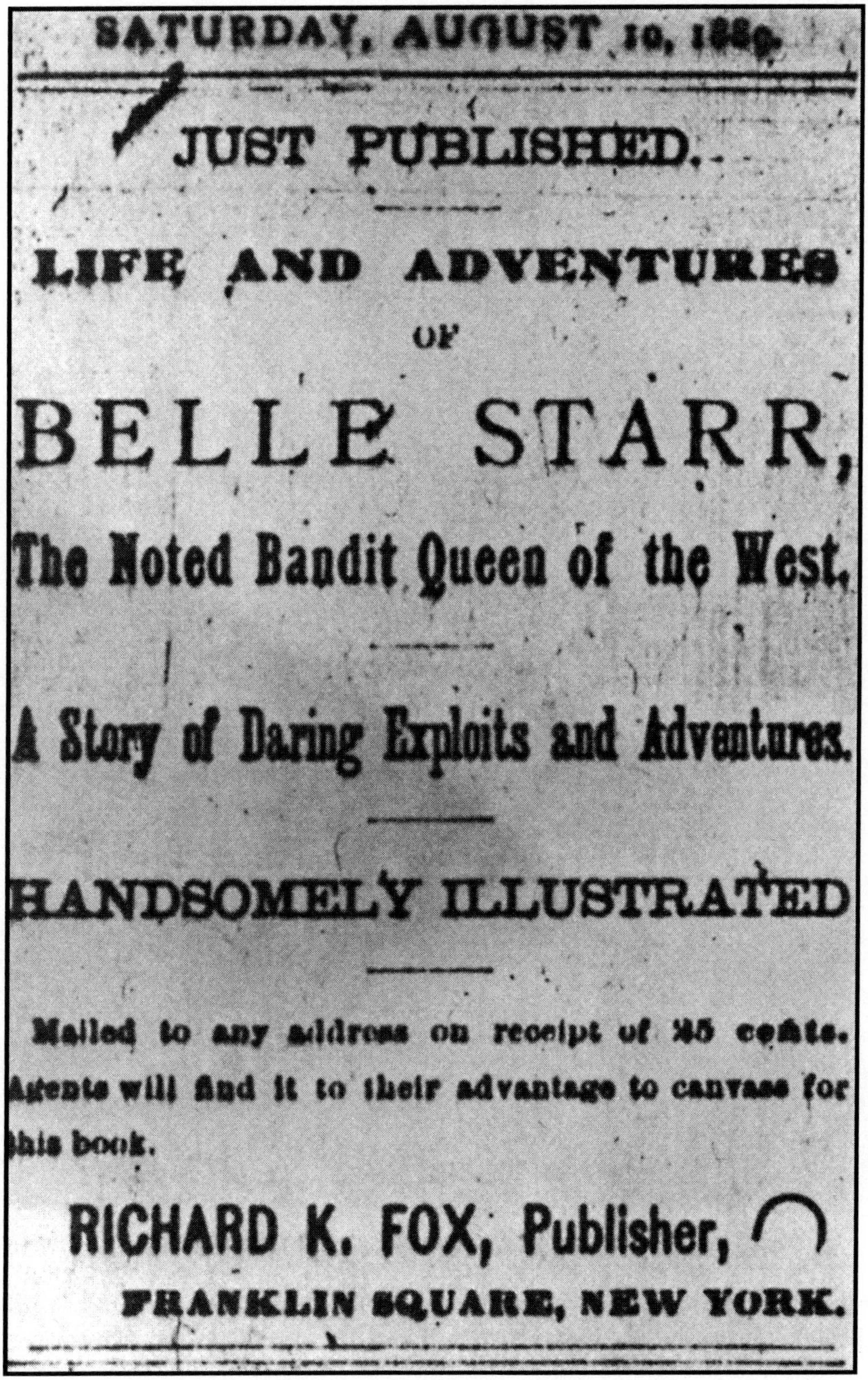

SATURDAY, AUGUST 10, 1889.

JUST PUBLISHED.

LIFE AND ADVENTURES
OF
BELLE STARR,
The Noted Bandit Queen of the West.

A Story of Daring Exploits and Adventures.

HANDSOMELY ILLUSTRATED

Mailed to any address on receipt of 25 cents. Agents will find it to their advantage to canvass for this book.

RICHARD K. FOX, Publisher,
FRANKLIN SQUARE, NEW YORK.

Ad for Belle Starr book. (Author's collection.)

Gene Tierney and Randolph Scott in *Belle Starr* (1941). (Author's collection.)

Belle's life included Randolph Scott, Dana Andrews, Elizabeth Patterson and Shepperd Strudwick. In this film, Belle was portrayed as a pretty, sensitive, and high-spirited Southern aristocrat who had a mammy like Scarlett O'Hara's and lived in an antebellum mansion as a girl. The plot suggested that most of Belle's criminal activities had been accidental affairs caused by an unfortunate set of circumstances. Although the real Belle's parents were

Ad for *Badman's Territory* (1946), in which Belle Starr (played by Isabel Jewell) was a minor character. (Author's collection.)

certainly comfortable, well-off Southerners, there was no Tara-like mansion, no mammy and definitely no Scarlett O'Hara lifestyle during Belle Starr's formative years.

Belle was a minor character in a feature called *Badman's Territory*, released in 1946. This film was directed by Tim Whelan and starred Randolph Scott, Ann Richards, George "Gabby" Hayes, Ray Collins and Isabel Jewell as Belle Starr. In 1948, Jewell once again played Belle in a film of pure fiction called *Belle Starr's Daughter*. Although Jewell had a considerably larger role in this film, its star was actress Ruth Roman, who played the title role of Belle's daughter. Also appearing were George Montgomery and Rod Cameron. Neither of these screenplays attempted to relate the actual story of Belle Starr's life to the movie-going public.

In 1952, the buxom screen star Jane Russell played Belle in RKO's *Montana Belle*. Directed by Allan Dwan and featuring Forrest Tucker, George Brent, Scott Brady and Andy Devine in the supporting cast, this sexist joke portrayed Belle as a "reformed bandit queen" who spent most of her time trying to convince the outlaw Dalton brothers to turn themselves in to the law (which in reality most assuredly never happened). The film's inept script, and Miss Russell's obvious lack of histrionic ability, did little to make *Montana Belle* the least bit credible as a biography of Belle Starr.

In 1980, Elizabeth Montgomery portrayed Belle in a decidedly more accurate made-for–TV film biography that was directed by John A. Alonzo. Also appearing in this production were Cliff Potts, Michael Cavanaugh, Fred Ward, Jesse Vint and Geoffrey Lewis as Belle's various lovers and outlaw friends. Although Montgomery played a complex woman with a definite criminal bent and certain psychological problems, the many sexual encounters the real Belle engaged in during her lifetime were definitely downplayed in order to conform to the censorship that still prevailed to "protect" young television viewers. The film *The Long Riders*, also released in 1980, featured Pamela Reed as Belle and starred James and Stacy Keach as Jesse and Frank James and David Carradine as Cole Younger.

Belle Starr has also been the subject of poems, novels and stageplays. One of the best-known poems in which Belle was glorified was George Riley Hall's "The Last Ride of the Bandit Queen," which was originally published in the *Muskogee Daily Phoenix* in 1898 and was subsequently included in several poetry anthologies. George Appell's novel *Belle's Castle*,

Ad for *Belle Starr's Daughter* (1948). (Author's collection.)

Stoney Hardcastle's *The Legend of Belle Starr*, Speer Morgan's *Belle Starr* and Glenn Shirley's *Outlaw Queen* perpetuated many of the myths that had been growing since the days Belle was still roaming the West.

Two plays, John Woodworth's *Cheat and Swing: A Legend Based on the Life of Belle Starr*, presented at the University of Oklahoma in 1938, and *The Missouri Legend*, presented on Broadway in 1939 and starring actress Elizabeth Gentry as Belle, centered around the legendary character that Belle Starr had become by the mid-twentieth century. In the early 1970s, TV personality, musician and composer Steve Allen wrote a musical comedy called *Belle Starr* that was based on the life of the famous bandit queen of the badlands. Presented in London's Palace Theater, the musical starred the former film musical leading lady Betty Grable as Belle. Unfortunately, the production, which Allen had hoped to transport across the Atlantic to Broadway, did not prove popular enough with either the British critics or the public, and the project was abandoned after a relatively short run in London's West End.

MARTHA "CALAMITY JANE" CANARY
(A.K.A. CANNARY) (1852–1903)

Like Belle Starr, Martha "Calamity Jane" Canary also became a legend in her own time due to the considerable amount of publicity she received in Eastern publications. Calamity was also the heroine of several fictional dime Western adventure stories written by Edmund Whelan during her lifetime. Her appearance in *Buffalo Bill's Wild West Show* from 1893 until 1895 greatly added to her status as one of the Old West's living legends.

Calamity Jane was born Martha Jane Canary in Princeton, Missouri, on May 1, 1851. Martha was the eldest daughter of farmers Bob and Charlotte Canary, who had four other children. Court records in Princeton reveal that Martha Jane's grandfather James Canary bought a 280-acre parcel of land in the Collins' church district in 1855, and it is believed that her father also farmed this land. As a young woman, Martha's mother was said to have been a high-spirited girl whose unconventional behavior included smoking cigars and drinking alcohol in public places, and whose salty language shocked the conservative farm community residents of Princeton. Her daughter Martha Jane often mimicked her mother's shocking behavior, and later in her life, she also picked up her mother's habit of drinking whiskey. The good citizens of Princeton later claimed that they thought Charlotte was a very poor mother for having set such a bad example for her impressionable daughter. By the time she was ten years old, Martha Jane had established the reputation of being a real "wildcat," like her mother. When the Canarys announced that they had decided to leave Princeton "to take up the land out west," their neighbors were apparently relieved to be rid of them. Bob, Charlotte and their eldest daughter Martha Jane headed West, leaving their other children in the care of Bob's more prosperous brother Thornton in Princeton.

The Canarys reportedly arrived in Virginia City, Montana, in 1865. A Virginia City laundress named Mary Kelly was interviewed many years later and claimed that she had known Martha Jane long before she had become well known as a Western character called "Calamity Jane." Kelly said that Martha Jane's father was not a particularly healthy man, and died during a smallpox epidemic in 1867. She also said that Charlotte Canary died shortly after her husband.

In her book *Old Deadwood Days*, Estelline Bennett, who had grown up in Deadwood and knew Martha Jane Canary, said that Bennett's uncle, General Dawson, had a different version of Martha Jane's early life out West. An old bull-whacker who knew Martha Jane Canary when she was a small girl in Fort Laramie told General Dawson that Martha Jane was born at the La Pont's trading post in 1860, and that when she was two years old, her father was killed and her mother wounded by a band of renegade Sioux Indians. The young Martha was taken to Fort Laramie, according to the bull-whacker, and adopted by an army sergeant and his wife. He claimed that even though the couple loved the little girl and spoiled her outrageously, they let her "run wild." Her mother Charlotte, the bull-whacker added, had become involved in an affair with an army lieutenant named Hart after her husband's death, and eventually married him. The bull-whacker said that the Harts and Martha Jane moved to Salt Lake City for a while, but when Martha Jane was in her early teens she ran away from home and went to Rawlins, Wyoming, where she became a scout for the army.

A Western adventure periodical of the 1930s, *The Wild West*, printed a different account of Martha's younger days. The magazine claimed that Martha's father did indeed die in 1867, but said that Charlotte Canary became the owner of a popular saloon in Virginia City,

Martha Jane Canary in her teens. (Montana Historical Society.)

Montana, and later moved to Salt Lake City, Utah, with her new husband, leaving Martha behind. Whatever the truth is, all mentions of Charlotte Canary ceased around 1867. Considering her desire to be the center of attention wherever she was, it seems unlikely that Charlotte lived beyond 1867 or she would have remained in the spotlight. Martha was, at any rate, only 15 years old when she was left to fend for herself. According to laundress Mary Kelly, the uneducated and inexperienced girl wandered around Virginia City looking for work in order to support herself. Kelly described Martha as "looking like a lost soul" at this time. There were few "decent" jobs available for a young single girl in an untamed Western boom town in the 1800s, and the only places willing to hire inexperienced girls like Martha were the local saloon's whorehouses. The idea of becoming a prostitute did not appeal to Martha, who had since childhood preferred the company of males only as friends, and thought of herself as being more like a boy than a girl. By this time, she had already begun to assume a decidedly masculine demeanor. Unable to find suitable work in Virginia City, Martha hitched a ride on a supply wagon to Bancock, Montana, where she heard the mines were hiring workers. Once again, however, she met with rejection, since the mining company officials did not care for the idea of hiring females to work in their mines, no matter how masculine their appearance. Soon Martha was destitute and the pangs of hunger had begun to overtake her, so she took to begging on the street. It was during this low point in her life that Martha Jane met the notorious Madame Mustache, a well-known gambler and whorehouse madam, in a Bancock saloon. "La Mustache," as the madam was called, had arrived in Bancock with her stable of girls to take advantage of the easy money by offering sexual diversions and games of chance to the hundreds of men, who had arrived in the West mostly womanless, longing for female company. Madame Mustache believed that she had discovered a marketable product in the earthy, high-spirited young Martha Jane Canary, and convinced the desperate young woman that selling her body to miners was certainly preferable to starving to death. Martha reluctantly gave in to the madam's overtures and began her training in the fine art of prostitution as taught to her by the expert Madame Mustache herself.

Within less than a year, the strong-willed Martha became disenchanted with the bossy madam, and with the physically demanding requirements of prostitution. She became increasingly uncooperative with the Madam's clients and eventually she began to drown her shame and unhappiness by drinking ever-increasing quantities of whiskey. Martha left the madam's brothel by mutual consent, and once again found herself looking for work. Feeling Montana was not the right place for her, Martha left in 1868 for Wyoming, where once again she heard that jobs were available to anyone who was willing to perform a hard day's work. This time, she applied for a job as a muleskinner—a job she felt she was better suited for than prostitution. The big and strong-looking Martha had little trouble convincing Wyoming stagecoach company officials that she would be as capable as any man of driving a team of horses, especially after she made an impressive trial run. In addition to muleskinning, Martha also worked as a construction worker, a railroad trackman and, according to her autobiography (written while she was touring in Buffalo Bill's Wild West Show), a scout for the United States Army. In this less-than-reliable biography, Martha, who was usually inclined to exaggerate the details of her life, claimed that she went out on her first military expedition in 1870, which might have been true. She wrote, however, that she performed "thousands" of scouting missions for the army and "participated in many pitched battles with wild Indians." There is little documentary evidence to support these claims. It is true that she was at Fort Saunders, Wyoming, during the winter and spring of 1872, when the United States army was fighting hostile Indians in a skirmish called the Muscle Shells War, and that she did scout for the army at this time, since her name appears on the pay rosters of the fort. But whether she ever actually fought in any battles is certainly questionable.

Biographer Duncan Aiken says that in Dodge City in 1872, a cowboy ballad singer with the insinuating name of "Darling Bob" Mackay "presumed on his talents for the risqué, and asked Martha Jane an intimate question about her lower lingerie." Martha Jane promptly "filled the air with shrill and slightly obscene rebukes for his bawdiness, and fired several warning bullets into the singer's sombrero."

Calamity Jane as General Crook's scout. (Library of Congress.)

According to the same supposed eye-witness who relayed this amusing anecdote to a reporter, Martha (temporarily out of work as a muleskinner in 1874) found herself without female attire and, wanting to apply for a job as a waitress, borrowed a dress from a Cheyenne woman. That same year, it is said that Martha "married" a railroad brakeman named Rawlins, but no marriage certificate has ever been produced to prove that such a union ever took place. About this same time, a family who had known Martha since she first arrived in Wyoming were interviewed by author Duncan Aiken in 1926 for his book *Calamity Jane and the Lady Wildcats*. They claimed Martha Jane Canary was "an extraordinarily nice girl to have grown up on the plains and in the mining camp." They also stated that she "was always agreeable and witty, as well as intelligent and kind hearted." They recalled that when a little girl in their family became ill during an epidemic of "black diphtheria," Martha ignored the dangers of the contagious disease and diligently nursed the little girl until the child eventually died.

In her autobiography, Calamity claimed that she was still working for the U. S. Army as a scout in 1876 and that she arrived on the scene of Custer's Last Stand "only minutes after the last soldier had been killed." Other sources indicate that she was working as a cattle driver in Wyoming and was ill at the time of Custer's demise. Martha, always ready to stretch the truth a bit, had actually contracted pneumonia several weeks before the massacre and was confined to a hospital and nowhere near Little Big Horn when Custer and his troops put up their last fight.

One amusing and somewhat bizarre story that appeared in the *Deadwood Dispatch* newspaper in 1877 does have a ring of truth to it, considering Martha's uninhibited, unconventional and often shocking behavior. It was reported that Martha was out on a scouting mission for the Army one hot summer day when she "came upon a group of soldiers bathing in

Calamity Jane. (Montana Historical Society.)

Illustration from *The Coming of Empire* by H. Maguire, showing Calamity Jane in action. (Author's collection.)

a creek, as naked as jaybirds." An officer later coming upon the scene was shocked to see a very nude Martha frolicking in the creek with the men. He discharged her on the spot, charging her with "indecent behavior and conduct unbecoming a United States Army military scout." Once again, Martha was unemployed. When interviewed about this incident, Martha Jane Canary began to call herself "Calamity Jane" "because," as she said, "of all of the trouble I always seemed to get mixed up in." In an era of such grotesque female nomenclature as "Pickhandle Nan," "Madame Mustache," "Kitty the Schemer," "Rowdy Kate," *et al.*, Martha, apparently not wishing to be outdone, was shrewd enough to grasp the "Calamity Jane" label's merit. Her scandalous but often amusing activities had begun to attract the attention of sensation-seekers back East who enjoyed reading about Buffalo Bill and Jesse James' escapades, and Calamity became a minor celebrity. In the 1870s, Horatio N. Maguire wrote a book about his Western observations (*The Coming of Empire*) and devoted considerable attention to military scouts; "Calamity Jane" Canary was prominently mentioned in this section. He also included an engraving of Calamity labeled "Miss Martha Canary, the Female Scout." The book was widely read by the public and certainly contributed to Calamity Jane's celebrity status.

In her highly questionable autobiography Calamity claimed that she met and immediately fell in love with the Western celebrity James "Wild Bill" Hickok in 1876 (it is almost certain that she had met Wild Bill several years earlier). Hickok was already a famous gunfighter and lawman and had also been a much-publicized Union Army scout during the Civil War, gaining nationwide attention for his heroism and devotion to the Union cause. The publicity-seeking, post–Civil War hero Hickok had begun to capitalize on his wartime and Western adventures as a buffalo hunter by selling stories about his experiences (both real and exaggerated) to various Eastern newspapers and he had thus been able to increase his fame as well as his fortunes. Hickok even toured in a play called *Scouts of the Plains* with his old friend Buffalo Bill Cody, whose adventures had also become as well known throughout the country. Both Hickok and Buffalo Bill's names became familiar to millions of people as the heroes of several fictional Western dime novels that were written by a man named Nichols and published in *Harper's* magazine.

According to Calamity Jane's biographer Duncan Aiken, "Wild Bill Hickok was the real thing in Western derring-do and had no doubt killed upwards of a dozen men, probably in self-defense, as a gambling *punticello*, and as a peace officer—but he had certainly never killed the 'hundred or more men' whose deaths had been sensationally attributed to him." Apparently, Wild Bill became intrigued with the idea of having a colorfully mannish, female "sport"—one who had already gained quite a bit of notoriety of her own—as part of his entourage. It is highly doubtful, however, that he had any sort of an intimate relationship with Calamity. "Wild Bill," Aiken wrote, "was the sort of person who would be grimly amused" by the antics of characters like Calamity, but he was a happily married man at the time that he and Jane were associated with each other. Hickok had married popular circus proprietress Alice Lake in 1875, and she had been largely instrumental in increasing his fame, since she was well aware of the value of good publicity. His so-called "romance" with Calamity Jane, therefore, was simply good self-promotion and most likely had been planned by an impresario named Charlie Utter—but more about Utter later in this book.

Stories soon began to appear, however, in the country's periodicals about Wild Bill and "his new paramour, 'Calamity Jane' Canary, the tough-as-nails-yet-adventurously glamorous wildcat of the West." The Eastern pulp writers reported on Wild Bill and Calamity's every action, actual and fabricated, such as their "triumphant entrance into the town of Deadwood" during which time, according to Deadwood newspapers, "they hooted and hollered and shot off their six-shooters to let the people in town know that they had arrived." Because of the publicity she was receiving, Calamity Jane's name also began to be used by dime novelist E. L. Wheeler as the heroine of a series of soft-cover Western adventure books. Wheeler had written many other books using fictional Western "sports," which was what Western women such as Calamity Jane were called, as their major characters. By the late 1880s, the Calamity Jane character was one of Wheeler's most popular sports. Dime novels were widely distributed in the United States throughout the latter part of the nineteenth century. These slender novelettes were approximately 30,000 words in length, that had lurid, brightly colored paper covers and were sold for "one thin dime." They were mostly read by adventure-starved Easterners and were best-sellers because of their inexpensive cover price and because of the exciting tales of adventures out West. In addition to Westerns, these books also featured mysteries, science fiction stories and historical fictions. The first series of dime novels were launched in 1866 by Ernest Beadle, who had printed similar adventure books, with much less success, in Boston in 1844. Five million copies of these dime novels (an unprecedented number of books for a time when illiteracy was commonplace) were sold between 1860 and 1865 alone, and they continued to sell well beyond the turn of the century. These books often used real-life adventurers such as "Buffalo Bill" Cody, Jesse James, "Wild Bill" Hickok and Calamity Jane as their major characters. Because of these well-read fictions, these Westerners' names became widely known to the general public. Hundreds of dime novels glorified, and most often fabricated, events in the lives of these celebrated Westerners. Dime novels, perhaps more than anything else, helped popularize the wild and woolly image of the West most Americans, and indeed people all around the world, have to this day.

E. L. Wheeler's Calamity Jane stories painted a colorful portrait of this most unusual lady sport. Wheeler's Calamity Jane books included (among others) *Deadwood Dick on Deck; or, Calamity Jane, the Heroine of Whoop-Up*. In this novel, Wheeler has someone ask if Jane is "a hard case" (a loose woman), and another character in the book explains that "Jane is just a daredevil. Some say a man deserted her and she took up a roving life to hunt him down," the character says. "Others tell that she is married to a brute," the character continues, "and she ran away from him. Jane has a pretty but hard face. She wears buckskin pants met at the knee by fanciful beaded leggins, dainty slippers, a velvet vest and a boiled shirt. Her jacket is of velvet and her Spanish broad-brimmed hat is slouched upon one side of a regally beautiful head. Jane wears a revolver around her waist and carries a rifle strapped to her back. She rides a black pony richly equipped in Mexican style." When asked why she always dresses like a man in the story, Calamity replies, "I don't allow ye ken beat men's togs much fer handy locomotion an' so forth, an' then, ye see, I'm as big a gun among the men as any of 'em." Another Wheeler book that featured the Calamity Jane character as its heroine was *Deadwood Dick in Leadville; or, A Strange Stroke for Liberty* in which Jane saves a man's life when he becomes involved in a crooked card game and she challenges his cheating opponent to a gun duel.

At the same time Wheeler's Calamity Jane dime novels were being published, an English periodical also published a fictional story about Calamity. It was written in a tone of solid British decorum and referred to the locale of her reported wildcat activities, Deadwood, as "the goal."

In 1876, Wild Bill was shot and killed in Deadwood by a glory-seeker named Jack McCall while he was playing cards, only months after Hickok had arrived in Deadwood with Calamity and friends. Jane was said to have been devastated by his death. Some believed that she was merely disappointed that her time in the spotlight as Wild Bill's sidekick had been too short, but her gambler-friend Poker Alice Tubbs said that Jane was actually extremely fond of Wild Bill and mourned pitifully after his death. Whatever she was feeling at the time of his death, Calamity once again turned to whiskey to drown her sorrows.

After this period of continual inebriation, lasting just short of a year, Calamity's desperate financial situation forced her to sober up long enough to attempt to earn some money by selling stories about her friendship with Wild Bill, both factual and fictional, to anyone who was interested in buying them. Sometimes all she was paid was the price of a drink, a dinner or a room for the night.

In 1877, in the town of Spearfish in the Black Hills, Calamity reportedly warned a wagon train boss that hostile Indians had murdered a family on the northwestern trail, and that they had better watch out for an ambush. No Indians ever attacked the wagon train, but the lady who had identified herself to the trail boss as "Calamity Jane" Canary had certainly told the wagonmaster the truth about the murdered family, which meant that she must have gained at least a certain degree of sobriety by this time in order to have been able to warn him of the possible attack.

In the winter of 1878, Calamity returned to nursing the ill back to health when a disease called "mountain fever" struck a large number of miners who were working under unhygienic conditions near Deadwood. Later that year, when a smallpox epidemic struck miners in South Dakota, she was also on hand to do what she could for the stricken miners and their families. She apparently was fearless as far as infections were concerned and nursed victims of the disease back to health. At this time, a Deadwood newspaper quoted her as saying, "I'm Calamity Jane, by God, and them sick boys I'm lookin' out for up here in the hills don't get no grub 'til they get good and able. Get that?" This earned her the admiration of the mining community and the attention of anyone who read about her selflessness in the nation's newspapers.

Duncan Aiken, in his *Calamity Jane and the Lady Wildcats*, related an incident that reportedly took place on a train in 1879 and certainly typifies her behavior. A young graduate

Calamity Jane at Wild Bill Hickok's gravesite. (Library of Congress.)

of New York's Columbia Law School was traveling on the Union Pacific railroad heading for San Francisco where he planned to set up his law practice. He met a weather-beaten, obviously drunk woman who was wearing a cowboy hat and a coarse-materialed riding skirt. The woman, whom he took to be about 45 years old even though she was actually only 28, had taken a seat next to him on the train. The lady lit a pipe and, according to the young lawyer, asked him what he was doing on the train. He told her, and the woman exclaimed, "Now what the hell do you think of that? Going to San Francisco when the town's already gone to the business damnation, and he might be coming to Deadwood. You look like an honest and smart young fellow," the harsh-voiced woman continued. "You come on up to Deadwood with me and start practicin', and if there ain't enough law business to begin with, I'll make it for you." The youth politely rejected the woman's invitation and when she departed the train, he was thrilled to learn from the conductor that he had just been talking to "the famous female Western scout, Calamity Jane." The young man eagerly told this story to a newspaper reporter the moment he arrived in San Francisco.

Around this time, Calamity reportedly joined a troupe of mining camp burlesque artists who were called "Al Swerringer's Lady Entertainers" as an actress. Even this somewhat loose profession had too many restrictions for Calamity to handle, and it is said that she was dismissed for improvising lines and "using postures on stage which were beyond the limit" of what was considered "acceptable behavior." It was also said that Calamity appeared at a number of performances in Deadwood impossibly drunk.

Calamity Jane was, according to many other newspaper reports that chronicled her comings and goings, in Montana and Wyoming for the greater part of the 1880s. When a reporter was in the town of Billings, Montana, which was only a Northern Pacific Railroad construction camp that contained two stores and a half-dozen saloons with rooms above for ladies of the evening, he wrote that he saw Calamity Jane leaning out of one of the upper story windows, cursing a defaulting teamster. It is, however, highly unlikely that Calamity would have returned to prostitution, an occupation she found repellent, as a means of making a living, no matter how desperate she might have become. Another reporter wrote that he had seen Calamity being bodily thrown out of "a house of peculiarly riotous fame" (a saloon) for drawing two guns on patrons one summer night, and making them dance as she fired bullets at their feet. This certainly sounds much more likely than the previous story.

When he was in his late 70s in the 1920s, a former cowboy named Teddy Blue claimed that he "knew practically every celebrated Westerner who had ever roamed the West." Blue said that he met Calamity Jane at a stagecoach stop in the late 1880s, and his account of this meeting certainly is credible since it underlines Calamity's independent, self-reliant nature. Teddy said that he was temporarily out of funds and asked to borrow 50 cents from Calamity in order to buy himself a meal. Without hesitation, Blue says Calamity gave him the money and Blue claimed he said, "Someday I'll pay you." Calamity replied, "I don't give a damn if you never pay me." Several years later, Blue says he came across Calamity Jane once again in Gilt Edge, Montana, and walked up to her and asked if she remembered him. She said that she "most certainly did," and he handed her the 50 cents he had borrowed. "I told you, Blue," Calamity said, "that I didn't give a damn if you never paid me," and the two went into the nearest bar and had a drink together.

When the town of Carthage began to thrive in 1890, the town's newspaper reported that Calamity's ever-present urge to fight "sent her to jail after a violent, drunken display of anger during an argument with a cowboy."

Nine years after Wild Bill's demise in 1876, Calamity thought she had found the perfect solution to her persistent financial problems. She married a wealthy, alcoholic, celebrity-worshipping playboy named John (or Clinton) Burke (or Burk), whom she had met in a saloon while in Carthage. The marriage, which was said to be Calamity's third, lasted for less than a year, since Burke's socially prominent San Francisco family were apparently repulsed by the masculine, crude and poorly educated Calamity, and told Burke that if he didn't have his marriage annulled, his inheritance would be cut off. Burke decided to retain his inheritance and left Calamity, but not before a child had been conceived. Seven months after the marriage was dissolved, Calamity gave birth to a baby girl whom, like Belle Starr, she called "Pearl." For several years Calamity tried to raise the child by herself, but she eventually accepted the fact that she was not able to support a child on her own, especially when the little girl reached school age, and she turned the child over to Burke's wealthy family "so that she could receive a proper education." Many years later, in her Buffalo Bill Cody Wild West Show autobiography, Calamity rather insensitively claimed that the child was actually Wild Bill Hickok's illegitimate offspring, but dates totally disprove this claim, since Wild Bill had long been dead before the child was conceived. The story did, however, prove good copy for the Eastern press, and managed to put a few dollars in the desperate Calamity's pocket when the story appeared in various periodicals.

According to Estelline Bennett's book *Old Deadwood Days*, Calamity returned to Deadwood in the late 1800s. She was shabbily dressed and her seven-year-old daughter, whom she had not yet given up to her in-laws, was with her. Most of Calamity's old friends from Deadwood's boom days were gone, but the citizens of that town were well aware that they had a legendary Western character in their midst and treated her like a celebrity. Estelline Bennett, who was a young girl when Calamity was visiting Deadwood, wrote that one day she was walking down Main running an errand for her mother when her father came up to

Calamity Jane in later life. (Montana Historical Society.)

her and told her that her uncle, General Dawson, wanted to introduce her to the famous Calamity Jane. When General Dawson saw Estelline approaching, he made his way through a group of people who were gathered on a street corner surrounding Calamity, and escorted Estelline up to a rather plain woman who looked considerably older than she probably was. "She wore a shabby, dark cloth coat that had never been good," Estelline wrote in her book, "and a cheap little hat, a faded frayed skirt and arctic overshoes although the sidewalks were perfectly clear of snow and even the crossings were not muddy. It was late in fall, but it hadn't snowed since the last chinook. 'Miss Jane,' the General announced in a voice that sounded as if he were presenting Estelline to royalty, 'this is my niece, Estelline Bennett.' Calamity Jane held out her hand and said she was pleased to meet me."

When the opportunity arose to go on tour with *Buffalo Bill Cody's Wild West Show* as a novelty act in 1893, Calamity jumped at the chance. Originally called *Buffalo Bill's Wild West Congress of Rough Riders of the World*, the show toured the United States and Europe for over 30 years. It was a three-hour extravaganza that featured shooting exhibitions, military demonstrations, dramatic spectaculars and pageants, parades of cowboys and famous Indians such as Sitting Bull himself, horse races and numerous specialty acts. William "Buffalo Bill" Cody (1846–1917) had been a Pony Express rider as a young man, a cowboy and then a celebrated buffalo hunter before he became a showman after discovering the value of capitalizing on his Western adventures by selling stories to the Eastern press. Like Belle Starr, Calamity Jane and Wild Bill Hickok, Buffalo Bill had also become a major character in bestselling dime novels which contributed to his fame. In Buffalo Bill's show, Calamity was little more than a curiosity and certainly not an actual performer. Her "act" consisted of shooting blanks from a pair of six-shooters and riding around the arena waving her hat at the crowd of spectators. In spite of her obvious lack of performing talent, the crowds always cheered her wildly as she made her entrance since she was well known to them. Her fame increased during her years with Buffalo Bill's show, one of the most popular entertainment attractions in America in the late 1800s. Unfortunately, Calamity, in addition to lacking any talent, also lacked the discipline needed to remain with the show for longer than two years. By the time she left the Buffalo Bill show, she was drinking more heavily than ever and was missing most of the show's performances. Because of her habitual, unprofessional hijinks, Buffalo Bill claimed that he had "no other choice but to let her go with great regret."

For the remaining eight years of her life, from 1895 until her death in 1903, Calamity wandered from one Western town to another, pathetically telling her life's story to anyone who was interested enough to buy her a drink. Eventually she drifted back to Deadwood, the scene of her greatest glories, in time to die.

Twenty-seven years after her friend Wild Bill Hickok's death, a drunk and derelict Calamity Jane's life ended in a boarding house in Terry, a gold-mining camp in the mountains above Deadwood. A funeral service was held for Martha Jane Canary in the Deadwood Methodist Church and a sermon was delivered by one of the Black Hills' most eminent clergymen, C. B. Clark, who never mentioned any of the more unsavory aspects of Calamity's life. Instead he stressed her kindness and unselfishness towards others who were less fortunate. Calamity had always said that she wanted to be "buried next to Bill" (Wild Bill Hickok), who had been killed in Deadwood, and so the women of Deadwood, determined to grant one of their most famous citizens her last request, made sure that her body was carried to the small cemetery on the outskirts of Deadwood and laid to rest next to Wild Bill, whom she called her "one true love." Right up until her end, Calamity Jane, it seems, knew the value of good publicity.

Calamity Jane as a Character on Radio, in Films and on Television

Any resemblance between the real Calamity Jane, the actresses who played her in the various entertainment media and the depictions in the dime novels, was purely coincidental. Throughout the twentieth century, Calamity Jane remained as well known as she had been during her lifetime.

Calamity was spoofed on radio, which was the "queen of the entertainment industry" in the 1930s and '40s when she became a running character on the popular *Red Skelton*

Calamity Jane when she was touring in Buffalo Bill's Wild West Show. (Library of Congress.)

Program. On this half-hour weekly series, the Calamity Jane character was usually featured in sketches with comedian Skelton playing an amusing Western character named "Dead-eye." The part of Calamity was played by actress-singer Harriet Hilliard, who was also the show's vocalist and later became famous as Harriet on *The Adventures of Ozzie and Harriet* radio and television series. On the Skelton radio show, Hilliard spoke in a tough, cracking voice when she played Calamity, and provided the program with many of its laughs.

The delightful film comedienne Jean Arthur played Calamity on the silver screen in the 1936 epic *The Plainsman*, which was directed by Cecil B. De Mille and also starred Gary Cooper as Wild Bill Hickok. The film, more fiction than fact, finds Wild Bill rescuing Calamity from a band of renegade Indians, which most certainly never happened. But that did not deter filmmaker De Mille. *The Plainsman*, however fictional, proved immensely popular with the moviegoing public, and Arthur's portrayal of Calamity Jane as a pert and cute tomboy became the prototype for several on-screen Calamity Janes that followed.

In 1949, sexy screen siren Yvonne DeCarlo played a tough Calamity in a film called *Calamity Jane and Sam Bass*, which was directed by George Sherman and co-starred Howard Duff, Dorothy Hart and Lloyd Bridges. Screenwriters often invented relationships between well-known celebrities in order to guarantee "name" recognition at the box office. It didn't matter whether or not the famous people being depicted had actually been connected in any way. It is highly unlikely that the real Calamity Jane ever met, much less fell in love with, the legendary Western outlaw Sam Bass, as in this film.

The best-remembered of all of the Calamity Jane screen portrayals, however, was essayed

Top: Jean Arthur as Calamity Jane, with Gary Cooper as Wild Bill Hickok in *The Plainsman* (1936). *Bottom:* Yvonne de Carlo was Calamity Jane in *Calamity Jane and Sam Bass* (1949). (Both from author's collection.)

The 1953 Doris Day film *Calamity Jane* is probably responsible for Calamity Jane's cute, perky image in the public mind today. (Author's collection.)

by the saccharin darling of movie musicals and comedies of the 1950s, Doris Day, in a film called *Calamity Jane*. Perter, cuter and sassier than Jean Arthur, Doris made Calamity seem more fun than a pen of freckled pigs in this 1953 release, which was directed by David Butler. The film co-starred Howard Keel as Wild Bill Hickok and featured Allyn McLerie, Phil Carey and Gale Robbins in the supporting cast. Big old Calamity Jane must have squirmed about in her grave at the thought of being portrayed as adorably as Doris dared to play her. The film was, like *The Plainsman*, popular with the public and unquestionably added to the Calamity Jane mystique.

A much more authentic depiction of Calamity Jane's life and times was offered in a made-for-TV movie filmed in 1985. This film starred actress Jane Alexander as Calamity. She was, however, depicted as a pathetic, vulnerable victim of life, an image Calamity certainly would not have approved. Calamity had always thought of herself as a free-spirited, fun-loving woman who "lived and loved hard and enjoyed every minute of [her] life."

In 1994, Anjelica Huston played Calamity in a TV mini-series adaptation of Larry McMurtry's successful novel *Buffalo Girls*. Huston's performance was both sensitive and realistic, but once again Calamity was seen as a tragic figure.

In 1995, Ellen Barkin played Calamity Jane in the film *Wild Bill* which co-starred Jeff Bridges as Hickok. Barkin probably came closer than any other actress to playing Calamity as she most likely was in real life. The romantic aspects of her relationship with Wild Bill were certainly exaggerated, but the film is well acted and realistically gritty. Bridges makes the character of Wild Bill come to life, but apparently makes Hickok a much more sensitive and lovable man than he actually was.

In this author's estimation, one the best of the Calamity Jane biographies is Duncan Aiken's *Calamity Jane and the Lady Wildcats* (1927). Aiken's book also chronicles the lives and adventures of several of the West's other celebrated females, including Belle Starr, Madame Mustache and Lola Montez. Aiken's writing is somewhat Victorian and stilted in style, and he carefully skirts the issue of Calamity's questionable sexual inclinations, but he does provide generous amounts of information about her other activities.

In 1949, R. J. Casey wrote a book called *The Black Hills and Their Incredible Characters*, which included a lengthy section about Calamity and her adventures. A 1959 biography written by Glenn Claimont is informative and fact-filled and contains many incidents that were only briefly covered in the other books, such as details of her two-year stint as a member of Buffalo Bill's Wild West Show troupe. But none of these books presented Calamity Jane as she apparently would have truly liked to have been remembered—as a woman who lived the life she wanted to live and miraculously survived, in spite of alcoholic excesses and physical neglect, until her death at the age of 52.

Chapter Two

Gunfighters' Wives and Lovers, and Female Outlaws

Gunfighters of the Old West, whether lawmen or outlaws, were certainly among the most flamboyant characters to inhabit the quickly developing area during the latter half of the nineteenth century.

In the twentieth century's motion pictures, gunfighters' female friends were usually relegated to strictly supporting roles, and the same was actually true in real life. Outlaws' women, and often the wives and girlfriends of gunfighting lawmen, for the most part just held the reins of their menfolk's horses as the boys robbed the banks, stagecoaches and trains, or chased the bad guys. Occasionally gang girls scouted possible locations for a heist, and they often fenced goods such as jewelry or other stolen valuables for their robber-lovers. But for the most part, the women mainly helped their menfolk relax after a hard day of banditry or bandit chasing and, of course, cooked and kept house for them. There was nothing, it seems, these ladies wouldn't do for their men, including kill for them if necessary. On rare occasions a gang girl did manage to obtain full-fledged outlaw status, as was the case with the Wild Bunch's Laura Bullion a.k.a. Della Rose. Occasionally they were instrumental in promoting their husbands into legendary status, (for example, Wyatt Earp's wife Josie)— but this was the exception rather than the rule. The Old West was, after all, a male-dominated society. Very little film fiction, however, lives up to the real-life adventures and experiences these gunslingers' women actually lived through.

QUANTRILL'S WOMEN (1863–1865)

The first major Western outlaw gang to achieve any sort of public recognition was a group of Civil War Rebels who became renegade outlaws and called themselves "Quantrill's Raiders." Their leader, William Clark Quantrill, was a commander under General Robert E. Lee at the beginning of the War between the States, and then led a band of guerrilla-warriors on rampages of lawlessness against Union loyalists in and around the border state of Missouri. Quantrill was a strikingly handsome man who had "fair hair the color of wheat, baby blue eyes, a manly physique, a fine Romanesque nose and a most pleasant complexion." He was, supporters rhapsodized, "designed to set female hearts aflutter at the mere sight of him, and inspire members of his own sex to absolute devotion due to his heroic posture." During the final year of the Civil War, the South was demoralized by its deteriorating military position and was desperately in need of a heroic daredevil to soften the humiliation of its impending defeat. Quantrill and his Raiders, for a short time at least, seemed to fill this bill.

Quantrill appeared as a major character in several films in the 1930s, '40s and '50s, sometimes being depicted as a misunderstood, misguided hero. He was also portrayed, however, as a black-hearted villain, according to the screenwriters' whims. Typical of the devoted loyalty of the women who walked in the shadows of celebrated gunfighting desperadoes were the camp-following wives and girlfriends of Quantrill's infamous rebel-raiders. Surprisingly, none of the films made about Quantrill and his men included a dramatic event that involved Quantrill's female followers, even though it is certainly one of the most poignant incidents that occurred during Quantrill's notorious career. After a particularly bloodthirsty attack by the Raiders on the town of Lawrence, Kansas, in which most of that town's Union sympathizers were mercilessly slaughtered, women known to be associated with the Quantrill gang were rounded up by law authorities for questioning. Seventeen women were jailed and interrogated, but not one shred of information could be extracted concerning the Raiders' possible whereabouts. During a heavy rainstorm, the walls and roof of the jail collapsed and came crashing down on their unfortunate heads. At least half of the women were killed and most of the others were badly injured. When news of the disaster reached the public, a loud cry of outrage erupted, especially in the South, and many people not sympathetic to Quantrill and his renegades began to offer this fair-haired hero and his men comfort and support, hiding them out and making the Union Army's job of tracking them down more difficult than ever. In 1865 most of the Raiders, including Quantrill, were tracked down and killed after one of their raids in Kentucky, thus ending their notorious careers.

In 1958, Edward Bernds directed a film called *Quantrill's Raiders* that centered around the renegade band and its leader. It was mainly concerned with the group's raid on Lawrence, Kansas. Steve Cochran, Diane Brewster, Leo Gordon and Gale Robbins appeared in the film, which did not even attempt to be accurate and was carelessly acted and produced. Prior to this film, Quantrill's Raiders had merely been thinly disguised villains, usually not identified by name in order not to offend the many Southerners who still thought of them as war heroes. Unfortunately, none of these films, e.g. *The Desperados* (1943, 1969) and *The Desperados Are in Town* (1956), told the real story of Quantrill or his Raiders, and all were decidedly anti-Southern in their approaches.

CELSA GUITERREZ (1856–?) AND BILLY THE KID'S OTHER GIRLFRIENDS

According to Paulita Maxwell, the sister of Billy the Kid's friend Pete Maxwell, "The Kid fascinated many women. In every *placeta* in the Pecos, some little senorita was proud to be known as his *querida*." Although she denied it, Paulita herself was said to be one of Billy's "*queridas*." Another of Billy's girlfriends was Celsa Guiterrez, a Mexican-American girl who it seems was married to a man named Sabal Guiterrez. According to the census of 1880, she was 24 years old at the time she was Billy the Kid's lover. Celsa was the mother of a baby boy, fathered by her legal husband, but she was said to have been absolutely devoted to Billy the Kid (in spite of being married) and was, according to Paulita Maxwell, "Billy the Kid's favorite girlfriend." The amorous Billy was also intimate with three other Mexican-American women: Abrana Garcia, who reportedly mothered two illegitimate daughters of Billy's (both of whom died in early infancy); Narsaria Yerby, an 18-year-old housekeeper of a friend of Billy's; and Manuella Bowdre, the wife of another friend.

Billy the Kid (1858–1881), a.k.a. William Bonney and Henry Antrim and Kid Antrim, was one of the Old West's most notorious outlaws. In spite of his more celebrated aliases, Billy was actually christened Patrick Henry McCarty in New York City where he was born. One of Billy's boyhood teachers, questioned after Billy had become an outlaw, said, "Billy was no more of a problem than any other boy his age and was always quite willing to help with chores around the schoolroom." Something apparently happened to Billy as he was growing into young manhood which turned him from a quiet, well-behaved young man into a killer-desperado, who it is said murdered 21 men during his 21 years on earth. (In spite of what people might believe, Billy was a killer and outlaw for only the last four years of his life. He killed six men during those years, not the 21 he was reported to have murdered.)

Billy the Kid's name first became known to the public when he was hired as a cowboy-gunfighter and became involved in the much-publicized Lincoln County Wars. These "wars" were struggles between two power-hungry cattle and political factions in Lincoln County, Nebraska, who were fighting for control of town and range. Billy chose to fight on the wrong side of the law, and when he killed Lincoln County's sheriff, he became a fugitive. The Lincoln County Wars were widely covered in the press, especially in the well-read *National Police Gazette*, and these articles brought Billy his first taste of celebrity. Billy was further glorified (and became one of the Old West's legends) when a man named Pat Garrett, who had been his friend during the Lincoln County Wars, killed him in an ambush. Garrett then wrote about it in a book called *The Authentic Life of Billy the Kid*, which was published only months after Billy's 1881 demise.

The Kid's first brush with the law had actually occurred several years before his Lincoln County involvement. Billy's widowed mother had taken Billy and his brother West when their father died, and the family settled in the New Mexico Territory in 1873. The 15-year-old Bill Bonney (Bonney was his mother's maiden name) was arrested for stealing clothes from two Chinese railroad workers. He escaped from jail before he was placed on trial for this crime and went to Arizona, where he obtained work as a cowboy. Shortly afterwards, he became involved in the Lincoln County wars and began his career in crime.

The Lincoln County sheriff was not the first man Billy killed. His first victim was a blacksmith named F. P. Cahill, who Billy claimed taunted and bullied him when he was a 17-year-old cowboy. He was arrested for this killing, but again managed to escape before his trial. Once he became a fugitive, Billy assumed the name of "Kid Antrim," Antrim being his stepfather's name, and went on his notorious crime spree as a bank and stagecoach robber. Billy was eventually arrested, placed on trial and found guilty of murdering several people during one of his crimes. Again he managed to escape the hangman's noose, tricking his prison guards and fleeing from prison.

In 1881, while Billy was hiding out from law authorities in New Mexico, he was reunited with his pretty Mexican-American girlfriend Celsa Guiterrez at Fort Summer, where she was living. Billy had met Celsa at a dance in 1879, and he had visited her often during his fugitive years. Celsa was the daughter of a prosperous Mexican-American sheepherder who, understandably, strongly disapproved of his married child's relationship with the wild, young "gringo" outlaw. Celsa's husband, however, apparently did nothing to discourage her affair with the young outlaw and was said to have had his own lover to keep him occupied. Celsa and Billy, ignoring her father's protests, continued to meet secretly and corresponded with each other whenever they had the opportunity.

On July 14, 1881, while Billy was visiting Fort Summer, he spent the day with Celsa. Unknown to the young outlaw, a posse led by Pat Garrett had already tracked him to Fort Summer, where they knew Celsa lived, and were waiting for him to make an appearance. On the evening of his first day at Fort Summer, Billy and Celsa decided that they were hungry, and the Kid went to the house of his friend, butcher Pete Maxwell, to ask him for the key to his meathouse. By chance, Garrett's posse was at Maxwell's house when Billy showed up at his door and Garrett shot the Kid when he turned to go toward the meathouse, killing him with a single bullet hole through his heart.

When Celsa and Billy's other friends at Fort Summer heard about his death, they became extremely distraught. According to author Robert Utley in his book *Billy the Kid*, Celsa cursed Garrett and "pounded on his chest as others tried to pull her away." Billy's other lady friends at Fort Summer—Nasaria Yerby, Abrana Garcia, Paulita Maxwell and a Navajo woman named Deluvina Maxwell, Pete Maxwell's wife—gathered around Celsa consoling her "as they wept and talked softly among themselves."

The next day, the entire town was buzzing with talk about Garrett's dastardly ambush of their friend "The Kid," and there was even talk of a vigilante hanging of Garrett, whom they felt was merely an opportunist and betrayer.

The women who loved Billy the Kid took charge of his burial. His body was laid out on a workbench in a carpenter's shop for friends to view. Celsa and Paulita placed candles around the body, according to their idea of properly conducting a wake for the dead, and people filed by his corpse crying and praying.

"Neatly and properly dressed," Garrett later wrote, "Billy's remains were placed in a coffin which was borne to the old military cemetery that served the community." There, on the afternoon of July 15, 1881, the people of Fort Summer paid their final respects to Billy the Kid, as Celsa Guiterrez and the other women who loved him wept uncontrollably.

Billy the Kid has been the central character of several films and plays throughout the twentieth century. As early as 1907, stage actor-director Sidney Olcott toured the country with Joseph Stanley and Marion Leonard in a production called *Billy the Kid*, which was immensely popular wherever it was performed. Billy was also the major character of several films. In 1930, King Vidor directed an early sound film called *Billy the Kid* which featured Johnny Mack Brown, Wallace Beery and Kay Johnson. In this film, Billy was depicted as a decent boy gone bad due to circumstances beyond his control. Robert Taylor played Billy in the 1941 film, *Billy the Kid*, directed by David Miller. Also in the cast of this film was Brian Donlevy as Garrett.

Billy turned up once again as a title character in a ridiculous second feature called *Billy the Kid Versus Dracula*. This foolish effort was directed by William Beaudine and starred Chuck Courtney as Billy and John Carradine as Dracula.

By far, the best of the many films that have been made about Billy the Kid is Howard Hughes' production of *The Outlaw* (1941), which starred Jack Buetel as Billy. This highly publicized "sex western" received an inordinate amount of pre-release publicity which mainly centered around a buxom young actress named Jane Russell, who was making her film debut. This film is actually a rather compelling dramatization of Billy the Kid's life; although filled with fictional events, it features especially effective performances by Buetel and veteran character actor Walter Huston.

ETTA PLACE, ANNIE ROGERS AND LAURA "DELLA ROSE" BULLION

According to author Pearl Baker's informative book *The Wild Bunch of Robber's Roost*, several members of this infamous gang of thieves that included Butch Cassidy and the Sundance Kid "formed alliances with women, some of considerable significance and duration. The Sundance Kid had the lovely, refined Etta Place as a loyal and loving companion for many years; gang member Elzy Lay fell in love with and married a woman named Maude Davis; and another Wild Bunch outlaw, Ben Kirkpatrick, consorted with and reportedly married, a pretty young woman named Laura Bullion alias Della Rose, who often joined the gang in their criminal activities."

This group of Western bandits managed to attract the attention of adventure-starved

The Sundance Kid and Etta Place. (Author's collection.)

periodical readers during the latter part of the West's heyday. The Wild Bunch were cattle rustlers and bank, train, and stagecoach robbers, and its members, in addition to Cassidy, Sundance, Lay and Kirkpatrick, also included a cold-hearted killer named Kid Curry, among others. The mob operated from 1886 until 1901 from places with such typically Western names as Hole in the Wall, Brown's Hole and Robber's Roost, where they often hid out in between robberies. According to Don Cusic's Facts on File encyclopedia, *Cowboys and the Wild West*, The Wild Bunch "was a loosely organized band and approximately 100 different outlaws rode with the group at different times. They were responsible for well publicized robberies at such places as Castle Gate, Utah; Belle Fourche, South Dakota; Wilcox, Wyoming; Tupton, Wyoming; and Malta, Montana (a train robbery which was their last known job in the United States)."

In the 1969 film *Butch Cassidy and the Sundance Kid*, which was produced by John Foreman and directed by George Roy Hill, these outlaw-killers (played by actors Paul Newman and Robert Redford) were just fun-loving, good-natured boys who, like Billy the Kid, were dealt an unfortunate hand. Nothing could have been further from the truth. In reality, Butch Cassidy (1866–1907), whose real name was Robert or George LeRoy Parker, or possibly William T. Phillips, and the Sundance Kid (1861–1908), born Harry Longabaugh, were ruthless, cold-hearted criminals whose disregard for the law placed them with the worst of the West's bad men. This fact was far more realistically depicted in director Sam Peckinpah's 1969 film *The Wild Bunch*, which starred William Holden, Ernest Borgnine, Robert Ryan and Edmond O'Brien.

In the Newman-Redford film, the boys had a female companion named Etta Place (played by Katharine Ross) who accompanied them on many of their escapades. This was certainly true, and Etta Place (c. 1880–?) was definitely as attractive in real life as film star Ross, as can be seen in a photo taken of her with her boyfriend Sundance. Etta was said to have been a respectable schoolteacher before she met Sundance at a dance and fell in love with the handsome charmer. Don Cusic's book, however, claims that Etta was a prostitute when Sundance first met her, but this author could find no documentation of either version. At one point during their outlaw days, Etta was identified as having participated in a train robbery that took place between Rawlins and Rock Springs. It was later definitely established that the woman who participated in this particular robbery was actually gang member Ben Kirkpatrick's wife Laura Bullion a.k.a. Della Rose. Laura strongly resembled Etta, which may have accounted for misidentification. The Sundance Kid was said to have been totally devoted to Etta Place, and when she became ill, Sundance and Butch reportedly risked arrest when they traveled to New York City, where she could receive treatment at a hospital, before they left the country for South America in 1907. Don Cusic, however, claims that Sundance and Butch took Etta to Denver to be treated for appendicitis *after* the three of them had already been in South America, and then returned to South America without Etta. In Argentina, Butch and Sundance are said to have operated a cattle ranch, worked for a mining company and then returned to bank robbery before both were killed in an ambush in Bolivia by law authorities. Eyewitnesses, however, claimed that Butch Cassidy returned to the United States and was seen in Arizona by former acquaintances, including an old girlfriend, as late as the 1930s.

In addition to appearing as a character in the film *Butch Cassidy and the Sundance Kid*, Etta Place was also the title character in a 1976 movie called *Wanted: The Sundance Woman*, in which Katharine Ross once again played Etta. This film also starred Steve Forrest and Stella Stevens and apparently had absolutely no basis in fact. In it, Etta runs guns for the Mexican rebel Pancho Villa. No documents have been uncovered to prove what eventually happened to Etta Place

Butch Cassidy and the Sundance Kid (1969): Paul Newman (seated), Katharine Ross, and Robert Redford. (Photofest.)

Another member of the Wild Bunch gang, Kid Curry (a.k.a. Harvey Logan, 1876–1904), also had a devoted girlfriend whose name was Annie Rogers (c. 1877–?). Annie was not depicted in either film about the Wild Bunch, even though her contributions to their criminal activities were serious enough to land her in jail. Annie was a pretty, if somewhat dim-witted, Irish immigrant who fell deeply in love with Kid Curry and followed him about, cooking meals for him and the gang and generally caring for the Kid's other needs as required.

Annie Rogers of the Wild Bunch. (Author's collection.)

She was apparently totally devoted to Curry and did anything and everything she could to please him. Annie often acted as the gang's fence and was arrested during one of these assignments in 1899, placed on trial and sentenced to serve several years in jail. By the time Annie was released in 1904, Kid Curry had committed suicide during a gun battle with a posse after participating in a failed train holdup near Parachute, Colorado. It is not known what Annie's feelings about Kid Curry's death were; like Etta Place, she disappeared from the public's eye after she was released from prison.

Another woman who became entangled in the Wild Bunch's criminal activities was the attractive Laura Bullion (c. 1876–?). Laura, who used the alias "Della Rose" during her criminal career, was the girlfriend, or possibly the wife, of Wild Bunch gang member Ben Kirkpatrick. Born in Knickerbocker, Texas, Laura grew up on a sheep ranch in Concho County, where she had apparently met Kirkpatrick when he worked there. In 1895, Laura accompanied Kirkpatrick to Brown's Hole, Colorado, which was a Wild Bunch hideout. Unlike Etta Place and Annie Rogers, Laura took an active part in many of the Wild Bunch's robberies, usually dressed as a man. During the Great Northern train robbery at Wagner, Montana, in 1901, Laura and Kirkpatrick were apprehended and put on trial. Laura was sentenced to serve time at the Jefferson City, Montana, penitentiary. When Kirkpatrick was released, one year after Laura, the couple resumed their outlaw careers. Kirkpatrick was killed during a 1912 train robbery and Laura, who was not with him at the time, reportedly retired from crime. People who claim to have known Laura many years after she was a Wild Bunch gang member, said that after mourning her dead husband for several years, she remarried and spent the rest of her life as the wife of a law abiding rancher.

Wild Bunch gang member "Elzy" Lay (William Ellsworth Lay—1862-1934) was born on a farm in Ohio, but grew up in Colorado where his parents moved when he was a

Laura "Della Rose" Bullion of the Wild Bunch. (Author's collection.)

small boy. Lay became a cowboy and, while working on a Colorado ranch, he met Maude Davis, the sister of Albert Davis, a cowboy who worked with Lay. Sixty years after they had met and married, Maude stated in an interview that she knew Elzy was the man for her. "It was love at first sight for both of us," Maude sighed as she began to recall her years with Elzy.

Elzy Lay was a very handsome young man. He was tall and slim and had a dark complexion. He was also said to have had "beautiful dark eyes and possessed an outstanding gracefulness in a land where riding and outdoor activity made every man a demigod," according to Maude. In her book *Colorado's Historical Journal*, Cattle "Queen" Ann Bassett of Brown's Hole wrote, "Lay married Maude on a mountainside after he kidnapped a preacher from a nearby town, and the couple dramatically departed on their honeymoon on horseback."

In 1896, in the town of Green River, Utah, a man named Jim McPherson said that a woman he identified as Maude asked him when the wagon would be leaving for "the Roost" (a Wild Bunch hideout). Maude had been told to go to the Green River and wait to be picked up by Lay so that she could be with him while he was hiding out at the Roost. McPherson assured Maude that the wagon was usually on time and that she wouldn't have long to wait. The next day, Maude did indeed join Elzy at Robber's Roost. She remained at the Roost for several months, even after the Wild Bunch resumed their criminal escapades. Neighbors later reported that in addition to Maude, they had also seen another woman at the Roost, but could not say for sure who she was. Some people claimed that the woman in question was Sadie Moran, gang member Jack Moran's daughter. Others said that she was a woman they knew as Nancy Ingalls. But in 1970, the Sundance Kid's son by a woman he had known years before turning to crime said that the mystery woman was his father's girlfriend Etta Place, whom he had met while he was visiting his father there that summer. In a late-in-life interview, Maude remembered that it was indeed Etta Place who was with her at the Roost when she was there. Maude said that she had "loved and admired Etta" and thought that "she was the most beautiful woman" she had ever seen.

The girls left Robber's Roost that spring, one month before the Wild Bunch's notorious Castle Gate holdup. Maude said that she had been trying to get Elzy to give up his life of crime and that Elzy refused to listen, so the couple decided to separate. Maude was understandably grief-stricken at their split-up, but in time she filed for divorce and returned home to Brown's Hole. Maude later married a respectable farmer named Orrin Curry, had a child by him and led "a normal life" as an ordinary housewife.

LITTLE BRITCHES AND CATTLE ANNIE, AND THE ROSE OF THE CIMARRON

One of the West's most treacherous Western outlaw mobs of the late nineteenth century was the Bill Doolin Gang. Like Quantrill and the "Kids" (Curry and Sundance), Doolin was a very good-looking man who was popular with the ladies. Described as "a tall, redheaded Irish-American," Doolin had "a robust sense of humor," "a pleasant personality," and, according to a girl called Rose of the Cimarron who knew him, "possessed an endearing smile." Doolin's criminal activities attracted considerable attention in the nation's press from 1891 until 1896.

William M. "Bill" Doolin (1858–1896) was born on a farm in Arkansas and worked as a cowboy when he was in his teens. In 1891, Doolin joined the infamous Dalton brothers Jim, Grattan (Grat) and Emmett, who had formed a gang of thieves and killers called "The Oklahombres." The gang robbed banks, stagecoaches, and trains, and indiscriminately murdered lawmen and innocent bystanders. The Dalton brothers were the sons of the eldest sister of the infamous Younger brothers but, before they turned to lives of crime, the Daltons were lawmen and deputy marshalls. Grat and Bob Dalton were killed in an ambush as they attempted to rob two banks in Coffeyville, Kansas, on October 5, 1892, but Bill Doolin managed to escape capture. Bob Dalton had a girlfriend named Eugenia Moore who worked as the gang's advance agent, but she had apparently died of cancer weeks before Coffeyville; the fact that she was no longer around to help was supposedly one of the reasons the gang wasn't prepared for the ambush that awaited them. The Coffeyville disaster made Bill Doolin as infamous as his former gang members the Daltons, and he soon became one of the West's "Most Wanted" outlaws. Doolin went into hiding after Bob and Grat Dalton were killed, and in 1893 he married a preacher's daughter. But not long after the ceremony, he formed his own gang and resumed his criminal activities.

In 1896, Doolin's luck finally ran out and he was arrested during a robbery attempt. His smooth talk, however, managed to get him sentenced to serve his time in a hospital in Eureka Springs, Arkansas, instead of being incarcerated in a jail cell. The judge at Doolin's trial, totally taken in by his charm, ruled that the outlaw was to receive treatment for the chronic rheumatic condition which Doolin claimed was the cause of his criminal ways since it was "a source of constant pain." Soon after he was released from the hospital, Doolin resumed his bank and train robbing, but he was ultimately gunned down by a posse member named Bill Dunn in 1896, while he was on the run after robbing a bank.

Shortly before he was killed, Doolin enlisted the services of two teenaged girls who were apparently as charmed by the outlaw as everyone else who met him. They agreed to work for the Doolin gang as lookouts while the boys were hiding out in an Indian Territory cabin in between robberies. The girls' job was to warn Doolin and his gang members if anyone approached their hideout. A posse did learn of Doolin's whereabouts when neighboring ranchers reported seeing "unfamiliar men, including a tall Irishman with a hearty laugh, obviously Doolin, who were hiding out in a remote, deserted cabin" in the area. As the posse approached Doolin's hideout on horseback, they came upon a young girl (no older than 15) sitting on a horse at the side of the road. The girl fired a rifle shot into the air and then galloped off. By the time the posse reached the Doolin gang's cabin, it was deserted (the girl had fired a warning shot to let Doolin and his men know that the posse was approaching). Upon questioning ranchers in the area and describing the girl, the sheriff learned that she was a young woman her neighbors had nicknamed "Cattle Annie," because they suspected that she had been rustling cattle from them. Annie, the ranchers told the posse, had a close friend who was her constant companion—a girl they called "Little Britches" since she always wore a pair of men's trousers which were many sizes too large for her. Questioning the neighbors further, the lawmen learned that the girls were poor, uneducated orphans whose real names were Annie McDougal and Jennie Metcalf. They were told the girls were living in a shack on a deserted ranch on the Indian Reservation near the Doolin hideout. When the lawmen approached the shack, they found several of the neighbors' missing steers corralled in a fenced-in area next to the shack. After a few shots were fired from inside the cabin, and the lawmen fired back, Annie and Jenny surrendered and were arrested. During their trial for cattle theft and harboring fugitives, the girls stated that they had always been great admirers of one of their former neighbors, the famous "Bandit Queen" Belle Starr. They also admitted that they were actually flattered when Doolin asked them to act as lookouts.

Annie and Jennie were convicted and sentenced to serve five years in the Women's Prison at Framingham, Massachussetts. Instead of being angry, the girls were thrilled by the thought that they would be traveling East to serve time. As they boarded the prison train, Annie and Jennie giggled like students on a school outing. Neither Jennie nor Annie had ever been more than ten miles away from their birthplaces, and traveling East by train was the most exciting thing that had ever happened to them—besides, of course, meeting and working for the infamous Bill Doolin.

Annie and Jenny proved model prisoners and in 1899, less than three years after they began serving their time, they were released for good behavior. Jenny returned to the West and eventually married a poor-but-honest rancher, preferring to stay out of the spotlight for the remainder of her life. She apparently lived to a ripe old age, although the date of her death remains unknown.

Annie was not as fortunate. Upon her release from prison, she decided she wanted to remain in the East and went to New York City, where she joined the Salvation Army. While on one of her angel-of-mercy missions in 1899, Annie contacted pneumonia and died after a brief illness.

Director Lamont Johnson filmed an appropriately gritty made-for-television film called *Cattle Annie and Little Britches* in 1980. The film starred Amanda

"Cattle Annie" McDougal and Jennie "Little Britches" Metcalf of the Doolin Gang. (Author's collection.)

Plummer and Diane Lane as Annie and Jenny and featured Burt Lancaster, Rod Steiger, John Savage, Scott Glenn and Michael Conrad. Although the facts were somewhat distorted in this film, it was naturalistic and thoughtful, and contained several excellent performances.

Another female member of the Doolin Gang who could rustle cattle as well as any male was the lovely Rose (Rosa) Dunn, who was given the nickname "The Rose of the Cimarron" by members of the press. Rose had gone west with her parents in 1889, when the Dunns made the run for land when the Oklahoma Indian Territory was opened up for development. Her parents were law-abiding, God-fearing people and Rose was educated in a convent school when the family lived in Wichita, Kansas. In all probability, Rose first met the Doolin gang through her brothers, who (when ranching did not work out for the family) became cattle thieves. Rose became an expert rider and excelled in roping as well as sharpshooting. She crossed the border into Mexico several times to assist her brothers in their cattle rustling activities in Pawnee Country and participated in a cattle drive to Guthrie, where a dishonest butcher was waiting to receive the stolen steers. Rose met, and fell desperately in love with, a good-looking young outlaw named George "Bitter Creek" Newcomb (1867–1895), who was given his nickname by friends because he was always singing and whistling a popular cowboy song of the day that contained the lyric, "I'm a wolf from Bitter Creek, and it's my night to howl." Since Newcomb was a member of the Bill Doolin gang, Rose joined the gang, becoming their nurse, courier, fence and scout. Members of the gang who were captured

"The Rose of Cimarron," Rose Dunn. (Author's collection.)

by the law said that Rose Dunn was "no loose woman" and insisted that she "always conducted herself as a proper lady should." Had anyone suggested otherwise, Doolin and the rest of the gang "would have killed them on the spot."

After one of the gang's robberies, the Doolin mob were tracked down by a posse in Ingalls and surrounded. The women who traveled with the gang, including Rose, had checked into the Pierce Hotel, a boarding house run by Mary Pierce, a woman who fed and housed (and provided sexual favors to) womanless boys. The boarding house was a crudely constructed building, and instead of an indoor staircase leading to the upper floors, a ladder had merely been placed against the building for patrons to ascend into the bedrooms on the second floor. When Rose, who was standing at one of the bedroom windows, saw her boyfriend Bitter Creek fall wounded in front of the town's livery stable during a gun battle with lawmen, she buckled two cartridge belts around her waist, put two guns in her belt, grabbed a rifle and climbed down the ladder. Running into the line of fire between her boyfriend and the posse, Rose gave Newcomb the loaded guns and began firing at the posse with her

rifle. The couple managed to escape, and Rose nursed Newcomb back to health. Unfortunately, the very next time the Doolin mob robbed a bank, Rose (according to writer Everett Nix's book *The Oklahombres*) was arrested and spent a short time in a federal prison.

At the time of her reported arrest, Rose became the center of press attention. She granted numerous interviews and even had her photograph taken holding a six-shooter. Author Nix later claimed that the photograph of "The Rose of the Cimarron" was actually that of another young woman who happened to be visiting the jail at the time and had been substituted for the temporarily unavailable Rose. Others claimed that the woman in the photo was indeed Rose, and that her family had invented the other story in order to downplay her involvement with the gang. According to James Horan, author of the book *Desperate Women* (1952), Nix was also wrong about Rose's arrest. Horan claims that Rose was never arrested or required to spend time in prison, although the photograph (if the woman in it is indeed Rose Dunn) would disprove this claim. In all probability, the truth is that Rose was arrested but that charges were never filed against her, since a short time later, she was staying with her brothers at their ranch when Bitter Creek Newcomb went to visit her and to collect $900 which the Dunn boys owed him. There was a $5,000 reward for Newcomb's capture, dead

Ella "Cattle Kate" Watson. (Denver Public Library.)

or alive, and to Rose's horror, her brothers ruthlessly shot her lover for the reward money. The next morning, the Dunn brothers were taking Newcomb's body to Guthrie to collect the reward money when Newcomb, who was not dead, awoke and asked for water. The Dunn boys shot him again, making sure that he was dead. It was said that Rose never forgave her brothers and did not speak to either one of them again. Rose later married a member of a well-to-do Oklahoma ranching family and reportedly lived a long and comfortable life as a respectable member of her Oklahoma community.

ELLA "CATTLE KATE" WATSON (C. 1862–1889)

The sexist attitudes prevalent in Victorian England also existed in the United States during the latter half of the nineteenth century. These attitudes sometimes worked to the advantage of female outlaws. Women bandits were seldom, if ever, as severely punished as males, even when they committed similar crimes. The infamous "Hanging Judge" Parker, who usually condemned criminals to death for even the slightest infraction, sentenced Belle "The Bandit Queen" Starr to a mere four years for her numerous outlaw activities instead of dealing out his usual fatal judgment. One exception to this, however, was the vigilante hanging of a cattle-rustling prostitute named Ella "Cattle Kate" Watson, whose neighbors decided they had certainly had enough of Kate's thievery and immorality. Her murder became front page news in most of the newspapers in the United States, and eventually made "Cattle Kate" Watson one of the Old West's legendary characters.

The unfortunate Miss Watson was born in Lebanon, Kansas. By 1882, she was one of the most popular prostitutes in Johnson County, Wyoming, and ran a prosperous brothel there. In 1886, Ella met James "Jim" Averill (or Averell), an enterprising, well-educated, good-looking Bostonian who worked as a surveyor and eventually bought a store and a saloon in Johnson County. Averill managed to charm the people of the county into voting for him as justice of the peace, in spite of the fact that he appeared to be involved in an inordinate amount of criminal activities. Ella and Jim were married the year they met, and whether their marriage was based upon love, or was just a matter of "good business," is certainly open to speculation. People who claim to have known the couple said that Ella was very much in love with Averill (he was, after all, quite a catch in a place where education and good manners were in short supply among the local males). To a woman like Ella, who had been born to poor parents, and spent her formative years working in various cow town saloons and bawdy houses, the match must have seemed heaven-sent. The marriage proved beneficial and they thrived financially and bought adjoining ranches in Johnson County. Trouble began to surface, however, when Ella began to accept stolen cattle as payment for her sexual favors from the local males. (Her prostitution seems to have continued even after she married Averill.) Ella willingly accepted the cattle in lieu of money, since livestock was considered as good as cash by most people in Johnson County. Ella earned her nickname "Cattle Kate" because of her practice of accepting cows instead of cash from customers.

Before long, the respectable ranchers whose cattle were being stolen began to resent Mr. and Mrs. Averill's obvious prosperity which, they justifiably felt, mostly came from the theft of their cattle by Ella's patrons. In 1889, wealthy rancher Albert J. Bothwell publicly accused Ella and Jim of accepting, and then fencing, property stolen from him. The literate Mr. Averill immediately wrote articles (published in *The Casper Weekly Mail*) proclaiming his innocence. He then attempted to turn public opinion against Bothwell and the other large ranch owners by calling them "aristocratic despots." This infuriated the ranchers. Ultimately, Averill's writings backfired due to the fact that Bothwell and his friends had more money and influence than Averill and were, of course, the county's major employers. Averill's fate was sealed when a young woman who was working at Ella's "hog ranch" (her house of prostitution) was found badly beaten, her clothes in tatters, tied to a wagon wheel on a snowy morning. The woman, near death from exposure, accused Jim Averill of mistreating her because she wanted to leave Ella's employ and find more respectable work. The church-going citizens of Johnson County became enraged, and began to talk about driving out "the wicked Averills." In spite of these threats, Averill and Ella arrogantly continued their questionable activities and added insult to injury by continuing to accept stolen cattle as payment.

In 1889 Bothwell formed a group of vigilantes to deal with the couple. Throughout the West, Vigilance Committees were commonplace. These groups consisted of ordinary citizens who decided to take the law into their own hands when they felt little or no law enforcement was forthcoming. Thieves, cattle rustlers, and killers were dealt with severely by these self-appointed groups. Even though there was often a need for this type of justice in a frontier where lawmen were in short supply, these vigilante groups went beyond what can fairly be called "justice" and often did more harm than good to their communities' reputations. At times, vigilantes hindered justice, especially when the land barons' financial interests were at stake. A. J. Bothwell was a member of the powerful Wyoming Stock Growers Association, which had been formed to control cattle rustling. The group later became involved in the Johnson County War, which pitted ordinary citizens and small-time ranchers and cowboys against Bothwell and other land barons whose control over the politics and economy of Wyoming's cattle industry was choking them. These accounts were documented in *The Cheyenne Daily Leader*, and after several rather bloody battles between the two factions, the U. S. Military was called in to restore law and order.

Led by Bothwell and John Durbin, a wealthy cattleman and pillar of the Methodist church in Johnson County, about 30 vigilantes descended upon Ella's ranch, cut the wire fence of a corral and drove off the cattle that were enclosed. The herd did indeed include several of Bothwell's calves, which were set out to pasture with the other "rescued" cattle. When Ella came out of her cabin to see what the commotion was about, she was alarmed to see the large group of angry men, all pointing six-shooters in her direction. Her first impulse was to run, so she jumped on a horse which was tied up outside her cabin and attempted to get away. Ella was overtaken by two of Bothwell's ranch hands, Bob Connor and Ernest McLain. The vigilantes ordered Ella to get into a wagon, but she convinced them to allow her to go into her cabin to dress herself in "more appropriate attire for traveling." When she emerged from the house, she was wearing a fetchingly seductive gown which apparently failed to serve its purpose—to charm and calm down the angry ranchers. When she was secured in the wagon and headed toward town, Ella—still unaware of the seriousness of her situation—joked with, and even cursed at, her captors in good-natured defiance.

Averill was overtaken by the vigilantes a half hour later as he was headed for Casper to conduct business. The vigilantes told him they had a warrant for his arrest (which they did not), and when Averill asked to see their warrant, Bothwell and Durbin drew their six-shooters and told him that their guns "were all the warrant they needed." Averill was taken to the wagon in which Ella was being held on the outskirts of town. When Ella and Averill were told to either leave town immediately or face the consequences, they merely laughed at their captors, still unaware that they were in danger of losing their lives. Their light-heartedness turned into terror when ropes were slung over the lower branches of a nearby tree. The suddenly frightened Ella began to scream and thrash about as a noose was placed around her neck. She begged for mercy and wildly thrashed about trying to free her hands, which had been tied behind her back, and pull her head free from the noose. Jim was apparently too frightened to protest, and merely sat, white-faced and frozen in place, as he too was prepared for hanging. The wagon horses were slapped on their rear ends and galloped off, pulling the wagon behind them, leaving the struggling couple dangling helplessly at the end of the ropes. Observers later said that it seemed like an eternity before the death throes of Ella and Jim stopped and they swung motionless.

The idea of hanging a woman was repugnant to most late Victorians, who regarded women as objects of innocence, or simply "victims," and believed them incapable of any real criminal mischief (unless coerced into such behavior by a villainous male). Because of this attitude, newspapers reporting the details of Ella's death did so with a great deal of moral indignation. The life of a member of "the fair sex" had been brutally taken. The news of Ella's violent end was followed by numerous protests by members of the general public, in spite of her sordid occupation and her criminal activities, and it is mainly because of these sympathetic news editorials and protests that Ella "Cattle Kate" Watson is remembered today. In spite of Ella's posthumous celebrity, nothing was ever done to punish her murderers. One year after their deaths, Ella and Jim's ranches were seized for nonpayment of taxes and sold to a homesteader. Soon after, A. J. Bothwell purchased the properties from the homesteader and made them part of his vast ranch-empire.

In 1980, United Artists produced the film *Heaven's Gate*, which was directed by Michael Cimino and starred Kris Kristofferson and Isabelle Huppert as Jim Averill and Ella Watson. The film, which was pure fiction, was more interested in establishing Averill as the hero of the Johnson County range war than revealing the truth about him and his paramour. *Heaven's Gate* was one of the most costly films ever made—and one of Hollywood's most colossal box office failures. Interestingly, Jim and Ella were not hanged at the film's end, which was certainly the most dramatic event of their lives. According to the film's writers, Ella and Jim continued to live well after the cattle wars. Also featured in the colossal film failure were such talented performers as Christopher Walken, John Hurt, Sam Waterston, Joseph Cotten, Jeff Bridges and Terry O'Quinn, but neither their performances nor the breathtaking scenery and impressive cinematography could save this expensive, confusing production from box-office failure.

TWO MORE CATTLE-RUSTLING FEMALES

Anne Richey and Grace Newton were two other women who rustled cows, but they did not end up being hanged for their crimes like the unfortunate Cattle Kate Watson.

Richey attracted considerable attention when, in 1919, she became the first woman actually convicted of cattle rustling in the state of Wyoming. Though Anne was unquestionably aided by an accomplice, she refused to implicate anyone else in her crimes. According to an article titled "The Cattle Queen of Wyoming Must Serve Her Sentence" which appeared in *The Denver Post* in 1921, Richey was shot in the arm by a masked rider (perhaps her accomplice) while she was on trial for cattle rustling. The Wyoming Supreme Court ruled that she was to serve time for her crimes, but she was granted the opportunity to make her ranch ready for the coming winter before going to prison. Richey was mysteriously poisoned and died before she could begin serving her sentence or name her partner in crime.

Grace Newton's cattle-rustling activities were infamous in La Plata Valley, New Mexico, where Grace and her son Orlando ("Sonny") stole hundreds of steers from the open range and sold them to the highest bidders. When they were arrested, Grace claimed she knew nothing about Sonny's activities and said that she had never stolen anything, leaving Sonny to take the rap for both of them. Sonny did indeed go to prison, and Grace was never prosecuted. She was later caught rustling steers on her own, and this time she was placed on trial, convicted of grand larceny and sentenced to spend three years in prison. Sonny was still serving his time for their first crime when Grace was released from prison.

THE EARP WOMEN

Lawmen, gunfighters, peacemakers, cold-blooded killers—the West's celebrated Earp brothers were apparently all of these things. The close-knit, clannish Earps, who were reportedly led by Wyatt (1848–1929), included Virgil (1843–1905), Morgan (1851–1882), James (1850–?), Newton (1846–?) and Warren (1855–1900). Hired because of their expertise as gunfighters, the Earp brothers worked together as marshalls, sheriffs and deputies in such well-known Western locales as Dodge City and Tombstone, where (in addition to serving as law enforcement officers) they also opened and operated saloons and hotels which were also whorehouses. The brothers also owned several mines in the Tombstone area. It was in Tombstone that Wyatt, Morgan and Virgil participated in the gunfight at the O.K. Corral

on October 26, 1881. The Earps were determined to rid Tombstone of a bunch of rowdy cattle-rustling cowboys led by the Clanton and McLaury brothers and their friend Billy Claiborne. These cowboys began threatening vengeance after the Clanton brothers' father was
killed by Wyatt during a skirmish. Virgil was the U.S. Marshall of the territory and Morgan and Wyatt were his deputies. In the O.K. Corral showdown between the Earp brothers and the Clanton-McLaury gang, Virgil and Morgan Earp were wounded and Tom and
Billy Clanton and Frank McLaury were killed. Ike Clanton, who encouraged the feud
between his family and the Earps, escaped before the gunfighting erupted. Wyatt and his
friend Doc Holliday, who had joined the gunfight, also escaped injury. The remaining members of the Clanton-McLaury mob claimed that the gang was getting ready to peacefully
leave Tombstone when the Earps and Holliday ambushed them at the corral. Sheriff John
Behan was known to be envious of the Earps' career as gunmen, as well as jealous that Wyatt
had stolen his girlfriend, Josie Marcus. Behan arrested the Earp brothers and Holliday and
charged them with murdering his friends Tom and Billy Clanton and Frank McLaury. On
December 1, 1881, a justice of the peace ruled that the Earps were innocent since their lives
had been threatened by the Clantons and they were merely acting in their capacity as marshalls. Morgan Earp was later shot and killed while playing billiards at Campbell and Hatch's
Billiard Parlor by a revenge-seeking member of the Clanton-McLaury mob. This led to retri-
butions by the Earp clan, in which all of the cowboys who sided with the rustlers were brutally gunned down by Wyatt Earp and his supporters.

The Earp brothers were born in Illinois, but grew up in Missouri and Iowa. They
migrated to California with their parents as young men. Their mother was a firm believer
in family unity and apparently was a strong influence on her sons' lives. She encouraged her
boys "to always stick together," which they most certainly did (at least until the tragic events
at the O.K. Corral forced them to go their separate ways). After leaving their parents comfortably settled in California, the brothers returned to Missouri, where Wyatt worked as a
buffalo hunter. The brothers eventually moved to Dodge City where they became lawmen,
even though they had previously been on the other side of the law and were even said to
have robbed a stagecoach at one time. Wyatt's fame, which far exceeded that of his equally
adventurous brothers, seems primarily due to the fact that he simply lived longer than any
of his brothers, and also because he became the hero of a popular book, *Wyatt Earp: Frontier
Marshall*, which was written by Stuart Lake and published shortly before Wyatt's death in
1929. The book was widely circulated throughout the United States and abroad and almost
certainly added to Wyatt's reputation as one of the West's most famous characters.

Like their family-minded mother, the Earp brothers' various wives and consorts were
fiercely loyal to their menfolk, and certainly as strong-willed as their mother. Little is known
about Virgil's first wife, but his second wife Alvira (Adelia), or "Allie" as everyone called her,
became well known when her nephew Frank Waters wrote a book about her and the Earp
brothers called *The Earps of Tombstone*. In this book Allie told her nephew that Virgil's first
wife had remarried another man when Virgil was reported "killed in action" during the Civil
War. Allie was Virgil's faithful and devoted companion until the day he died, and was with
him in Tombstone when he was badly injured during the O.K. Corral gunfight. In his book,
Waters gives an account told to him by his Aunt Allie about what happened when she first
learned about the gunfight. "Lou (Morgan Earp's wife) and me was sewin' that carpet
together," Allie recalled, "when all of a sudden guns started roarin'. The noise was awful, it
was so close—just a couple of short blocks up Fremont [Street]. Lou laid down her hands
in her lap and bent her head. I jumped up and ran out the door. I knew [the showdown
between the Earps and the Clanton mob] had come at last. Mattie [Wyatt's second wife]
was outdoors. Her hair was done up in curlers and she was ashamed to have people see them

so she ran back inside the house. I flew up the street. People all over were runnin' toward the O.K. Corral. The butcher's wife as I ran past caught me by the arm and slapped a sunbonnet on my head. One of the McLaury brothers was lyin' dead on the corner of Third Street. Was he the one Hattie [Morgan's stepdaughter] had kissed and hugged in the moonlight? I never stopped runnin' past him. All I had in mind for was Virgil. Bunches of people were collectin' in front of the corral. One of them was carryin' Billy Clanton across the street. He was a young boy, only 19, and he was dyin'. … I knelt down beside Virge. The doctor was bendin' over his legs probing for the bullet. Behind us was another one, I never asked which one was inside. I seemed to know it was Morg."

After Allie nursed Virgil back to health, she convinced him to retire from gunfighting and to leave Tombstone. When Morgan was killed, Virgil and Allie took his body to Colton, California, for burial near the Earp home. In Frank Waters' book, he quotes his Aunt Allie as saying, "Well, it was all over for us at last. After just two years and three months in Tombstone, we all got ready to leave Arizona." Allie and Virgil departed Tombstone on March 24. Morgan's wife Lou, Jim Earp's wife Bessie and Wyatt's wife Mattie left Tombstone soon after Allie and Virgil. Wyatt remained behind to "get even with" his brother's killers. Some time later, Virgil and Allie returned to Arizona where Virgil panned for gold, and by 1900 the couple was living in Wilcox, Arizona, and in several mining camps. In 1905, Allie and Virgil joined Wyatt in Goldfield, Nevada, for a brief period of time, but friction between Allie and Josie Earp (Wyatt's new wife) caused them to move on. Virgil, who was never well after the gunfight in Tombstone, died of pneumonia shortly afterwards. He was buried by Allie and Jane (his daughter from his first marriage) near Wilcox. When Stuart Lake's book was published in 1929, Allie publicly declared that it was just "a lot of hogwash." She then faded from the public spotlight. She died in Los Angeles in 1947, shortly before her one hundredth birthday (her name at the time of her death was Alvira Packingham). Her nephew said that her funeral was held in downtown Los Angeles on "Funeral Row" on a dreary day. Only a handful of old-timers and a small crowd of her neighbors attended. Frank Waters wrote an obituary which he attempted to have printed in the Los Angeles papers, but no one was interested in running it. Waters claimed that many years before she died, Allie had composed an epitaph she hoped would be placed on her tombstone. It read: "Here lies the body of Alvira Packingham; She's dead as hell and she don't give a damn!"

The other Earp women, who all apparently worked as prostitutes before marrying the Earps, continued to manage the Earp family's saloons and brothels after they married. Like Allie, the wives of Jim, Morgan and Warren proved themselves as loyal and loving, even though they continued to prostitute themselves. Wyatt Earp is known to have had at least three wives. His first wife (whose name remains unknown) died in a fire with their infant daughter three months after the marriage. In 1879, Wyatt is said to have remarried (although there is no documentary evidence). His second wife Matilda ("Mattie") was in all probability his common-law rather than his legal spouse and, like her sisters-in-law, was a prostitute. The first time Mattie surfaced was when Wyatt and his brothers were working as lawmen at Fort Griffin. Some people in Fort Griffin later said that Mattie was the stepdaughter of James Earp from his wife's previous marriage and that her family name was Blaylock. When Wyatt, Jim and his wife Bessie, Virgil and Allie, Morgan and his wife Lou and Doc Holliday and his girlfriend (wife?) Kate Elder went to Dodge City, Mattie went with them. In 1879, after only two short months in Dodge City, the Earp clan packed up their suitcases and moved on again, taking Mattie with them. *The Dodge City Globe* reported at the time: "Mr. Wyatt Earp, who had been on our police force for several months, resigned his position last week and took his departure with his family for Las Vegas, Nevada." The entire family next turned up in Tombstone, where the Earp women continued to operate the family's various businesses. Interestingly, they also took in sewing in order to supplement their incomes. The Earp boys immediately obtained employment as lawmen. According to Allie Earp, 22-year-old Mattie Earp "was a young, modest woman and a good worker. She was a fine girl!"

By the time the Earps left Tombstone after the gunfight at the O.K. Corral and the subsequent murder trial, Wyatt had fallen in love with another woman. When Mattie left Tombstone, it was the last time she ever saw Wyatt. She went from one town to another working as a prostitute, and finally ended up in Globe, Arizona, where Doc Holliday's mistress Kate Elder (deserted by Doc) ran a boarding house brothel. Mattie lived with Kate for one year, "eking out a miserable existence by any means she could" (according to Kate Elder). Mattie eventually committed suicide in Pinal, Arizona, after telling anyone who would listen that Wyatt Earp had "wrecked [her] life" by deserting her and that she "didn't want to live." A simple notice in *The Silver Belt*, a Globe, Arizona, newspaper, stated, "Mattie Earp, a frail denizen of Pinal, culminated a big spree by taking a big dose of laudanum on Tuesday and died from its effects. She was buried on the 4th." No mention was made of the fact that she had once been Wyatt Earp's wife.

The woman for whom Wyatt deserted Mattie was a lovely young actress named Josephine Sarah Marcus. Born in Brooklyn, New York, Josie (whom Wyatt affectionately called "Sadie") was the daughter of wealthy Jewish parents who had relocated to San Francisco in the 1860s. In 1879, the high-spirited, stage-struck Josie ran away from home and joined Pauline Markham's *H.M.S. Pinafore* troupe which was touring the West. "Josie," according to Allie Earp, "had a small, trim body and a meneo [*sic*] of the hip that kept her full, flounced skirts bouncing." When Markham's troupe was appearing in Prescott, Arizona, a friend of the Marcus family recognized Josie on the stage and convinced her to return to her parents in San Francisco. But Josie had already met and fallen in love with a handsome young lawman named John Behan in Prescott, and after a short visit with her parents, she went to Tombstone where Behan was town sheriff. Josie began to call herself "Mrs. Behan," even though the couple were never married. When Josie met deputy marshall Wyatt Earp, however, the two were immediately attracted to one another. Josie's strange New York accent sounded exotic to the ears of the Western gambler-lawman, but it was Josie's beautiful face and figure that totally captivated him. Wyatt's good friend and fellow lawman Bat

This photo appeared on the cover of *I Married Wyatt Earp: The Recollections of Josephine Sarah Marcus*. (Arizona Historical Society.)

Masterson described Josie as being "an incredible beauty," and an Arizona newspaper once described her as "a lady anywhere." Masterson also called Josie "the belle of the honky tonks, the prettiest dame in 300 or so of her kind," which suggests that Josie might not have been averse to working as a prostitute when she had to. The pretty actress, however, always managed to present a respectable image. She lived with an upstanding, religious Tombstone couple when she was being courted by both Behan and Earp. When Josie became Earp's mistress, events were apparently set in motion that eventually led to the famous O.K. Corral gunfight. The Earps' enemies (the Clantons and McLaury's) were, after all, good friends of Sheriff Behan.

The fact that Wyatt was a deacon of the Union Protestant Church and Josie was Jewish did not seem to affect their relationship, which lasted over 30 years. When Wyatt finished his business in Tombstone, he was reunited with Josie in Los Angeles and the couple went to Dodge City in 1884, where Wyatt once again became a law enforcement officer. Josie and Wyatt apparently prospered as saloon keepers in Dodge City, and also made a great deal of money jumping other miners' claims, thus adding to their income. The Earps eventually moved on to Wyoming and then Texas before they turned up in San Francisco, where they bought a saloon which they operated from 1886 until 1890. In 1890, the Earps bought a horse ranch and raised thoroughbreds in the San Diego area until 1897.

In 1897, Josie and Wyatt migrated to Nome, Alaska, to participate in the gold rush, but instead of panning for gold, they bought another saloon which they operated until 1901. The Earps returned to the Southwestern United States that year and bought saloons in Tonopath and Goldfield, Nevada. By the time he died in 1929, Wyatt Earp was a world-famous Western celebrity. He even visited Hollywood a year before his death to discuss a possible movie biography which was to star filmdom's most famous silent screen cowboy star, William S. Hart. It was said, however, that Josie was the real driving force behind Wyatt's becoming a legendary western character.

Over the years many movies featured Wyatt Earp as a major character. Among the most notable are *My Darling Clementine* (1946) and *Gunfight at the O.K. Corral* (1957). *My Darling Clementine*, which was directed by John Ford, was an unusual Western in that it introduced many techniques that had not been used in Westerns before that time. It also had an excellent storyline that contained action and also attempted to explain the characters' motivations in an intelligent, sensitive manner. *My Darling Clementine* starred Henry Fonda as Wyatt and Victor Mature as Doc Holliday, and featured Linda Darnell as saloon girl Chihuahua and Cathy Downs as the Clementine (a fictional character) of the film's title.

Gunfight at the O.K. Corral (1957), directed by John Sturgis, is considered one of the best Westerns ever filmed. It starred Burt Lancaster as Wyatt Earp and Kirk Douglas as Doc Holliday. Although highly romanticized, it features one of the most exciting and suspenseful gunfights ever put on film. The Earp women are, however, depicted as much softer and more gentle than they probably were in real life, considering their occupations. The film also includes an effective performance by Jo Van Fleet as hard-bitten prostitute Kate Fisher, Doc Holliday's girlfriend.

In 1993, two big-budget films about Wyatt' life and times were released. They were *Tombstone*, which starred Kurt Russell as Wyatt, Val Kilmer as Doc Holliday and Dana Delany as Josie Earp, and *Wyatt Earp*, which starred Kevin Costner and Dennis Quaid as Wyatt and Doc and featured Isabella Rossellini as "Big Nose" Kate Fisher (Holliday's girlfriend), Catherine O'Hara as Josie Earp and Jobeth Williams as Allie Earp. Both films were fairly accurate, as far as details of the Earp brothers' lives are concerned, but *Tombstone* emerged as the better of the two as far as dramatic action and acting is concerned.

In 1955, Wyatt Earp became the major character of a popular weekly television series called "The Life and Legend of Wyatt Earp." The series starred Hugh O'Brian as Wyatt and featured Denver Pyle and Hal Baylor as the Thompson brothers (fictional characters), Gloria Talbott as a saloon girl (Abbie Crandall), Douglas Fowley as Doc Holliday and Carol Stone as Kate Holliday. It was one of television's longest-running and most popular western series and remained on the air until 1961. Scripts for this series were written by Frederick Hazlitt.

Besides the previously mentioned book by Stuart Lake, which was written during Wyatt Earp's lifetime and certainly glamorized his activities, there have been excellent accounts of his life included in Kent Alexander's *Heroes of the Wild West* (1992) and Don Cusic's *Cowboys and the Wild West* (1994). One of the most detailed books about the Earp brothers, however, is Martin Douglas's *The Earps of Tombstone* (1959), which includes articles that appeared in *The Tombstone Epitaph*, a newspaper which was in business when Wyatt and his brothers were patrolling the streets of Tombstone. This book reprinted many of the actual reports of the Earps' activities while they were in Tombstone. Two other informative books about the Earps' gunfighting careers and personal lives were written by E. Bartholomew and are titled *Wyatt Earp: The Man and the Myths* and *Wyatt Earp: The Untold Story*.

MARY CATHERINE "BIG NOSE KATE" ELDER, A.K.A. KATE HOLLIDAY AND KATE FISHER (1850–1940)

Mary Catherine Elder, unflatteringly called "Big Nose Kate," claimed she was "the one and only wife" of the famous gunfighter John Henry "Doc" Holliday (1819–1887), good friend of Wyatt Earp and his brothers Morgan, Virgil, James and Warren. Allie Earp reported in her nephew Frank Waters' book, *The Earp Brothers of Tombstone*, that "Doc was Wyatt's favorite crony. He was a tall and thin man, with blonde hair, cold gray-blue eyes and a pasty white face. I never could stand him, and he didn't have any use for me either." Holliday was the son of well-to-do Southern parents who lived in Griffin, Georgia. He was encouraged by his father to attend dentistry school in Baltimore, but when he developed chronic, pulmonary tuberculosis, he moved to Texas and then to Arizona, hoping the dry, warm climate would improve his health. Holliday met the Earp brothers, as well as the woman who would become his mistress-wife, Kate Elder, in Fort Griffin. Doc and Kate joined the Earps when they went to Dodge City, and then accompanied them to Tombstone where they eventually fought the Clanton and McLaury brothers and Billy Claiborne at the O.K. Corral and became national celebrities.

Mary Catherine "Big Nose Kate" Elder claimed she was born in Hungary and immigrated to the United States in 1853, settling with her family in Davenport, Iowa. Allie Earp, however, said that Kate was born in Davenport and that she married Doc in the Planter's Hotel, St. Louis, in 1870, shortly after she met him in a brothel. (According to Justice of the Peace J. C. Hancock of Davenport, he officiated at the ceremony, confirming Allie Earp's claim.) The couple found themselves in rather bleak financial circumstances and Kate returned to prostitution shortly after they were married. The nickname "Big Nose Kate" was apparently given to her not because she had a particularly large proboscis, but because she had a habit of sticking her nose into other people's business. Kate, it seems, accepted the nickname good-naturedly. At Holliday's insistence, Kate joined the stable of girls working at Bessie Earp's house of ill repute in Wichita, Kansas, in 1874, where a black woman named Madame Sperber ran a rival brothel.

In 1875, Kate relocated to Tom Sherman's dance hall in Dodge City, and then left Dodge in 1877 and went with Doc to Fort Griffith, Texas, which is where they met Wyatt. Frank Waters wrote in *The Earp Brothers of Tombstone* that when Doc killed a man during

"Big Nose Kate" Elder, Doc Holliday's girlfriend. (Author's collection.)

a card game and was about to be lynched, Kate set fire to a hotel and, during the confusion that ensued, rescued Doc from jail; the two rode away on horses which she had waiting for them at the back door of the jailhouse. After they left Fort Griffin, the couple and the Earps traveled to Las Vegas, Nevada, where they remained for a few months, and then moved to Dodge City and then on to Tombstone. In Tombstone, Doc and the Earps became entangled in a battle with Sheriff Behan, even though the Earp brothers were sworn-in town marshalls, and eventually fought their famous gunfight at the O.K. Corral.

According to Allie Earp, Doc was a heavy drinker and when he drank, Allie said, he often became violent. During these binges, Doc was especially hard on Big Nose Kate. Allie said that she "came upon Kate on a Tombstone street one day and she looked as if an ore wagon had run over her. She had a black eye, one lip was swelled up, and her clothes looked like the wind had blown 'em on her ever' which way." Allie, as she usually did, blamed Wyatt for Doc's behavior. "That God-damned foxy con-man [Wyatt] had cast a spell of evil over Doc that was his ruin. Not that Doc was a saint. But he was such a sick man, and drank to keep alive and he couldn't help himself. Wyatt encouraged Doc's drinking 'cause it amused him to see what he'd do when he was drunk." After another violent fight with Doc, Kate went to Sheriff Behan and accused Doc of participating in the Benson stagecoach robbery in which two men were killed. She even intimated that the Earp brothers had also been involved. Behan arrested Holliday, but did not have enough evidence to bring charges against the Earps. Before Doc could be convicted, Kate recanted her accusation, claiming that she said what she did because she was "mad at Doc" for having beat her up.

When Doc died of tuberculosis in 1887, Kate married a man named George M. Cummings, with whom she lived until 1930. Big Nose Kate Holliday entered the Pioneer Home in Prescott in 1931 and resided there until her death in 1940.

In 1941, a story appearing in the Western adventure magazine *Wild West Adventures* claimed that Kate was killed in 1887, two years before Holliday died. This story reported that Kate was working in a Tombstone saloon when Holliday became involved in a gunfight with a fellow gambler whom he said was cheating him at cards. The man, badly wounded by Holliday, began firing his six-shooter indiscriminately at anyone who happened to be in the saloon. According to this story, Kate was leaning over the bar, trying to jump over it to get out of the line of fire, when she suddenly slumped to the floor, dead. At first, no bullet hole could be found, but later it was discovered that a bullet had entered her rectum while

Madam Sperber and her girls of Wichita, Kansas. (Author's collection.)

she was bending over the bar and had killed her. Of course, this ridiculous story simply made good copy for the numerous Easterners who adored sensational adventure yarns. Amusingly, Kate Holliday's obituary had appeared in the very same magazine one year before the story was printed.

Kate Elder (called Fisher) appeared as a character in the classic Western *The Gunfight at the O.K. Corral*, which was released in 1957. She was played by the talented character actress Jo Van Fleet. In the film *Tombstone* (1993), Kate appeared as a minor character and in *Wyatt Earp* (1993), she was played by Isabella Rossellini in three major scenes.

TWO NOTORIOUS KILLERS

Although they cannot technically be labeled "gunfighters," the murderous ways of Sally Skull (a.k.a. Scull) and Laura Fair certainly qualify them for inclusion in this chapter. Sally was a true "wild woman" of the frontier. She was described by contemporaries as being a "merciless killer when aroused" and it seems it did not take much to ruffle Sally's feathers. The first mention of Sally Skull appeared in print when she divorced her husband, which was a rare occurrence in the 1850s. No record of Sally's birth or marriage has ever been uncovered. When she was divorced, Sally was left with two children to support. Believing it was in their best interest, Sally sent her daughter to a boarding school in New Orleans and her son to live with his father. The children became understandably indifferent about their mother. In a letter the son wrote to his sister when he was in his teens, he briefly mentions that he saw his mother "at King's Ranch" on December 1, 1863, and that he "did not speak to her but a few minutes." Sally felt that the only way she was going to survive as a single woman in the untamed West was to perform a man's work, and so she became a horse trader. Sally had probably learned about horses from her first husband Jesse Robinson, a horse rancher and trader in Live Oak County, Texas. Sally conducted her business in the dangerous areas along the Texas-Mexican border, where she bought and stole horses and then sold them for a profit. This area was famous for the large number of bandits who lived there, and one self-proclaimed Mexican "governor" of the area once arrested Sally and put in her in jail for a few days to discourage her from rounding up livestock in territory he considered his domain. Sally spoke fluent Spanish and hired several Mexicans to work for her. Of course, they were also useful when she went on one of her many raiding parties across the border into Mexico. With their help, Sally continued taking wild horses and stray cattle from the area, in spite of its governor's protests. Sally was known to use salty language which amused men and shocked ladies, and she was also well known as an excellent markswoman and for always wearing men's clothing. Sally carried a rifle slung under her arm and a pair of pistols in a cartridge belt. She was never without a whip, and cut flowers from their stems with it in order to amuse herself and others. But it was for her use of guns that she was best remembered. Horse trader Ben Kinchlow recalled seeing Sally whirl a gun around one finger, catch it and then fire, using either her left or right hand and always hitting her target (which was often anyone who stood in the way of what she wanted). Skull also had a reputation for killing without remorse. The exact number of competitors she killed remains unknown, although it is said to have been well in excess of three score. Late in life, Sally married a man named "Skull," whose named she retained, and when Skull died, she married another man named Bill Hornsdoff, whose surname she never assumed. Sally and Bill never really got along very well and argued frequently. One night, after a violent fight, Sally took out her rifle and fired several shots at Bill. The bullets missed, which unquestionably meant that Sally had no intention of actually killing him. It was rumored that when Bill asked for his share of the money that Sally had made during their marriage, she flatly refused to give him one cent of what she felt was hers and hers alone.

While the couple was on a horse trading trip across the Mexican border, Sally disappeared. Bill returned home alone and claimed that Sally "had simply wandered off after an argument." Of course, their neighbors suspected that Bill had done away with Sally and dumped her body somewhere in Mexico. No charges were ever brought against Hornsdorff, however, since Sally's body was never found. Bill later left the Refugio area where he had lived with Sally and was never heard from again. In 1962, long after she had disappeared, her fame had become such that a marker was placed on U. S. Highway 183 and State Highway 202 near Refugio:

> Sally Skull—Woman rancher, horse trader, champion "cusser." Ranched NW of here. In civil war Texas, Sally Scull freightwagons took cotton to Mexico to swap for guns, ammunition, medicines, coffee, shoes, clothing and other goods vital to the Confederacy. Dressed in trousers, Mrs. Scull bossed armed employees. Was sure shot with the rifle carried on her saddle or the two pistols strapped to her waist. Of good family, she had children cared for in New Orleans school. Often visited them. Loved dancing. Yet during the Mexican war, did extremely hazardous "man's work."

No films were made about her life and adventures. Two excellent articles were written about Sally Skull published in the November 1928, issue of *The Frontier Times* and in the March 4, 1937, issue of *The Corpus Christi Caller.*

Laura Fair was a wild Western woman of an entirely different sort. She was a murderess. Laura left a trail of dead lovers and husbands that earned her a reputation as one of the West's most notorious killers. Laura Fair was a woman who apparently lacked any sense of

morality and certainly had little con-
science. She was born in Mississippi
in 1835. When she was 16, she married a much older man. Her husband
died under mysterious circumstances
only one year after their marriage and
it was widely rumored that Laura had
poisoned him because she had found
another man who interested her more.
No charges were brought against
Laura since no proof of her involvement was ever uncovered.

Her second husband was a man
named Thomas Grayson. A short six
weeks after they were married, Grayson began to arrive home miserably
drunk every night. When he shot a
gun over his sleeping wife's head, and
then went outdoors and shot hundreds of chickens in the yard, Laura
fled in terror and filed for a divorce,
which was promptly granted.

In 1855, Laura became the mistress of prominent California lawyer
Colonel William D. Fair, with whom

Murderess Laura Fair. (Author's collection.)

she lived for five years and whose last name she began using as her own. It was said that Mr.
Fair committed suicide when he learned of Laura's numerous affairs with other men, but the
circumstances of his death were highly suspicious, and people once again believed that Laura
had probably poisoned him. Again, no charges were brought against her, however, since there
was absolutely no evidence.

In 1863, Laura went to Virginia City, Montana, where she ran a boarding house. Never
a woman to be without a man in her life, she soon became the mistress of Alexander Crittenden, a wealthy Virginia City businessman. Although she remained Crittenden's mistress,
Laura married a man named Jesse Snyder. Ironically, the couple divorced after Laura accused
Snyder of adultery. When Crittenden refused to leave his wife and marry Laura, she decided
to confront him while he was on a ferryboat with his wife and daughter in 1870. Shouting
"You have ruined me," Laura fired a fatal shot into Crittenden's heart.

Crittenden was a member of a prominent Kentucky family, and they were determined
not to allow his murderer to go unpunished. They pressed authorities until Laura was finally
arrested and placed on trial for murder. Throughout her trial, Laura appeared unconcerned
about the possible consequences of her murderous actions. Her trial became one of the most
widely publicized events of the time. When the jury returned a verdict of "guilty of murder
in the first degree," Laura was genuinely shocked. The judge condemned her to hang for her
crime, but his decision was challenged (since most people were still reluctant to hang women)
and Laura was eventually granted a new trial. To the Crittenden family's horror, Laura was
acquitted on the grounds that she was "emotionally unstable" at the time of the killing.

An Englishwoman named T. B. H. Stenhouse was visiting California in 1876 and wrote
a book called *An Englishwoman in Utah* (1882) about her experiences in America. Stenhouse
wrote that she met "the accused murderess Laura Fair" at a party and that she was a local

celebrity. "She lives in style, gives balls, and speculates in stock," Stenhouse wrote. "Few ladies are so often named at dinner-tables, and the public journals note her doings as the movements of a duchess might be noted in Mayfair." Laura Fair had obviously gotten away with murder.

PEARL HART (1872–1937?)

Since her brief career as a lady bandit took place in the year 1899, Pearl Hart (née Taylor) certainly qualifies for inclusion in this section. She was one of the last of her breed, and her brush with lawlessness was rather minor compared to other notorious Western women's activities. But Pearl was active at a time when readers of Western adventure stories were popular; this unquestionably accounts for the fact that Pearl Hart is remembered at all.

Pearl Taylor was born to middle-class, respectable parents in Lindsay, Ontario, Canada. In 1888 the unruly 16 year old was sent off to a Canadian boarding school for young ladies where her mother hoped she would obtain a degree of self-control and learn the proper deportment of a British colonial schoolgirl. Unfortunately, the strong-willed Pearl spent more time running away from school than she did in classrooms. She frequently traveled into town to carouse with a group of young ruffians. It was during one of these forays into town that she met a good-looking young punk named John Hart. Leaving her schoolmasters to explain to her parents what had become of their daughter, Pearl eloped with Hart in the spring of 1889, but frequently returned to her parents' home in Lindsay when she became disenchanted by the behavior of her irresponsible young husband. Hart enjoyed having a good time and was especially fond of drinking and gambling. In spite of her annoyance with him, Pearl consistently returned to Hart, undoubtedly excited by the wild life her young husband led.

In 1893, the couple decided to leave Canada and go to Chicago to take in the wonders of the *World Columbian Exhibition*. At the Fair, Hart gambled away what little money the couple had managed to extract from their parents. Penniless, Pearl decided to leave her husband and return to Lindsay and her parents. She became bored with life in the provincial Canadian town and returned to the excitement of life in the big city, Chicago. Hearing that there were fortunes to be made in the West by people who liked to take chances, Hart convinced Pearl to accompany him to Trinidad, Colorado, a prospering mining town where he hoped to pursue a career as a professional gambler.

"Bandit" Pearl Hart. (Author's collection.)

The card-playing of the other professional gamblers, however, proved too competitive for the relatively inexperienced Hart, and in time, he had Pearl selling herself to those same men in order to pay the rent. Pearl, it seems, was not entirely opposed to working as a prostitute, and later admitted she enjoyed "the sociability, conversation and good times" she had in the brothels of Colorado.

Pearl soon grew tired of this life as well, and claimed that she had become embarrassed by the way the respectable citizens of Trinidad (who were so much like her own parents) treated the ladies of the evening. Pearl once again decided to leave her husband. She moved from one Western town to another, drinking, gambling and consorting with unsavory characters. She also made the acquaintance of "the few veteran killers and road agents who had not been slaughtered or jailed, learning from them a good deal about their trade operations," according to Duncan Aiken's book *Calamity Jane and the Lady Wildcats*. In 1895, Pearl ran into her husband in Phoenix, Arizona, and against her better judgment decided to take him back, but insisted that he settle down and get a job. Hart went to work in various saloons and gambling houses as a bartender, and the couple eventually had a child. When a second child arrived Hart became alarmed, withdrew the couple's meager savings from the bank and revived his gambling habit. He caroused, occasionally beat his wife and eventually deserted her once again. Realizing that her children would be better off living with her mother (who had moved to Ohio), Pearl packed them up and sent them off. She obtained a job as a cook in a private home and then worked in various mining camps. Just as Pearl was beginning to get her life under control, Hart, true to form, turned up again. When the Spanish-American War broke out, Pearl convinced her husband to join the Army, later stating that she was hoping that he would become one of the war's casualties. The war proved to be brief, and when it ended, Hart again returned to Pearl, who by this time had become a rather worn-out, tired-looking woman, although she was only in her mid–20s. Pearl decided that she had finally had enough of Hart and told him to get out of her life once and for all. It was at this time that Pearl decided she was going "to make society pay" for her misfortunes by pursuing a life of crime.

When a stagecoach from Benson was headed to the Globe mining camp on May 30, 1899, the driver was suddenly commanded to halt by a mounted outlaw who (passengers said) looked more like a boy than a man and pointed a revolver at them. As the passengers got off the stage, the "boy" dismounted and began going through their pockets while a second bandit (who was taller and more mature-looking) sat on his horse nearby, pointing a rifle in their direction. When the passengers arrived in Globe later that day, they described the younger assailant as "a terribly little fellow to be dragged into this criminal business." One of them added that he "almost wished there was some way of letting him off with a good spanking." Of course the "boy bandit" was actually Pearl Hart. The older man was a friend of Pearl's named Joe Boot. Pearl had been cooking at a mining camp called "Mammouth" and became friendly with Boot, a happy-go-lucky prospector working at the mine site. When the mining camp suddenly closed down, Pearl and Joe found themselves without jobs. Pearl had heard that her mother was critically ill in Toledo, Ohio, and desperately in need of money, she convinced Joe to join her in robbing the stage, which she had heard "was always used by well-to-do eastern passengers who were doing business with the mine owners in Mammouth."

Unfortunately, the stagecoach robbery yielded little more than $350 worth of jewelry and cash; Pearl, who felt sorry for her victims, even returned one dollar to each of the passengers "to take care of [their] food and lodgings for the night when [they] reached Globe." After the robbery, Pearl and Joe headed northeast toward the New Mexico border and the Santa Fe railway line. On the way, they decided to spend a few days in the Cane Spring Canyon, where they thought no one would think to look for them. But a posse had already been formed to track them down and was hot on their trail. Through the stagecoach passengers' description of the "boy" robber, everyone in town knew that the thief could be no one other than Pearl Hart, who had been bragging that she was going to rob a stagecoach. The posse eventually caught up to Pearl and Joe in the canyon while they were sleeping behind a clump of cactus. Pearl and Joe surrendered without so much as a sigh.

By the time they were brought back to Benson, female bandit Pearl Hart had already become a minor celebrity. The press, ever eager to write about female wildcat-outlaws, had not seen her likes for quite some time, and eagerly pounced on the story of this latest lady road agent. Delighted by the attention, Pearl posed for photographs dressed in male attire, holding a rifle, looking as hard-boiled and as menacing as she could and generally enjoying her newfound fame. Soon reporters from the Eastern newspapers began to arrive in Benson to interview her. Somewhere along the way, Pearl managed to obtain a pronounced Western drawl, which she began to use to answer interviewers' questions. As reporters took notes and cameras clicked, Pearl basked in the spotlight. She soon began to make appearances wearing all manner of colorful attire; she sometimes appeared in sombreros, holding two or more six-shooters and a rifle, and always looking right at the camera with the studied cold stare of a real desperado. The residents of Benson thoroughly enjoyed all the excitement Pearl was generating and began to visit Pearl in jail to hear her talk about her life and adventures (which became more and more exciting with each retelling).

Joe and Pearl were eventually taken from Benson to Florence, where they were to be incarcerated until they were placed on trial. Late in June, Pearl was parted from Joe and given a separate trial in Tucson. In a rather pathetic attempt to keep publicity coming her way, Pearl faked a suicide. She had apparently become so used to receiving attention that she would do anything to remain in the spotlight, even risk her own life. The jury convicted her of robbery and the judge sentenced her to ten years in prison. After serving only a few years, however, she was released for good behavior and immediately headed East to visit her children and mother in Ohio. "She was," according to author Duncan Aiken, "still a regional celebrity at the time of her release from prison, and when she stopped at a Texas city to change trains in the 1920s, she was, according to a letter she wrote to a friend, 'annoyed at the slightly ribald curiosity of the multitude.'"

In time, Pearl's moment in the spotlight faded and she became just a footnote in Western history and legend. Considering the rather minor nature of her single brush with the law, she received more notoriety than she deserved. Pearl reportedly lived the life of a comfortably well-off woman after her parents died, settling down to a quiet existence in her parents' Ohio home. Her husband was said to have joined her once again, this time remaining at her side until she died in 1937.

Of all of the many books this author read while doing research, one of the best for information about women outlaws was *The Women's West*, edited by Susan Armitage and Elizabeth Jameson. Also helpful and certainly full of information about female outlaws was Joyce Roach's book *The Cowgirls*.

Western Outlaw Women in Song

Two popular cowboy songs reportedly written by Jack Thorp (a collector and author of many songs of the Old West) are about renegade Western females. One of these songs tells the story of a girl traveling in the Overland Stagecoach; she is "slim and girlish, but has the devil in her eyes." The beauty, the ballad says, "is the kind of woman every man wants to protect." During the trip, the girl pulls out a gun, robs the passengers and, cutting a horse loose from the stage, rides off with her booty. Thorp calls the lady desperado "Broncho Sue";

From *Cat Ballou* (1965). Left to right: Dwayne Hickman, Michael Callan, Jane Fonda, Lee Marvin and Tom Nardini. (Author's collection.)

she was probably fashioned after "Broncho Sue" Yonkers, an infamous lady bandit who lived near Tularosa, New Mexico, raised fine horses, swore like a trooper and spent a lot of time in the company of cowboys and unsavory characters. In his songs, Thorp also mentions such notorious females as Belle Starr and Rose of the Cimarron. In one of his other songs he rhapsodizes:

> Hunted by many a posse,
> Always on the run.
> Every man's hand against them,
> They fought, and often won.
> With a price upon each head,
> They'd have to fight and stand,
> And die as game as any man
> With a gun in either hand.

Even the venerable world of classical music managed to capitalize on the popularity of all things Western when Giacomo Puccini composed an opera called *The Girl of the Golden West* in 1910. In this piece, the central character is a colorful woman of the West who becomes involved with an outlaw who meets with a tragic end.

In *The Beautiful Blonde from Bashful Bend* (1949) Betty Grable plays a gun-toting saloon girl. (Author's collection.)

Fictional Gang Girls in Films

Fictional Western female outlaws were sometimes the major characters of big-budget Hollywood films. A few of these films are worth highlighting in this chapter.

The film *Cat Ballou* was a major success in 1965. It was adapted from a series of stories called "The Ballad of Cat Ballou" and were written by Roy Chanslor and published in 1956. A comedy, *Cat Ballou* starred Jane Fonda as an inept lady bandit who hires an over-the-hill, drunken gunslinger (who even has a drunken horse) to eliminate her chief nemesis, a vicious killer who wears a metal nose cap. Both the gunslinger-drunk and the villain were played by Lee Marvin, who won an Academy Award for his efforts. The film was directed by Elliot Silverstein and featured Mike Callan, Dwayne Hickman, Tom Nardini and Reginald Denny in the supporting cast. Stubby Kaye and Nat King Cole were also seen as well as heard in the film as saloon hall entertainers; they were not actually part of the action, but sang a running narrative which told the story of Cat and her band of outlaw friends.

Ad for *Renegades* (1952), in which Evelyn Keyes plays a lady outlaw. (Author's collection.)

One of the brightest film musical stars of the 1940s and '50s, Betty Grable starred in *The Beautiful Blonde from Bashful Bend* as a gun-toting saloon girl who arrives in a small Western town to hide out from the law and is mistaken for a schoolmarm. This 1949 Technicolor extravaganza was directed by Preston Sturges. Grable's co-stars were Cesar Romero, Rudy Vallee, Olga San Juan, Sterling Holloway and Hugh Herbert, who played a hilarious nearsighted doctor. This film was a major box office disappointment.

In the 1930s and 1940s, several second features had female bandits as their main characters. The star of many "B" films Marie Windsor plays a triple-threat woman of the West who becomes a stagecoach robber when she isn't working as a saloon girl or as an entertainer in a film called *Hellfire* (1949). This film also stars Wild Bill Elliott as a gunfighter-turned-preacher who falls in love with Marie. Forrest Tucker plays a sheriff who is tracking her down but does not know that she is his wife's sister.

Renegades (1952) was another "B" that featured a lady outlaw as its central character. Evelyn Keyes, who played Scarlett O'Hara's sister Careen in *Gone with the Wind* (1939), plays the leading role of a beautiful redhead who rides with the infamous Dembrow brothers, who were, according to the movie's advertisements, "the West's most notorious outlaw mob." Directed by George Sherman, *Renegades* also features Willard Parker as a lawman and Larry Parks as her outlaw boyfriend.

In the 1970 film *Wild Women*, directed by Don Taylor, an army engineer tries to recruit lady criminals from a federal prison. In order to gain their release, the women agree to pose as the wives of construction workers on critical Texas trails which enemy Mexicans hope to sabotage. TV's *Wyatt Earp*, actor Hugh O'Brian, played the engineer and Anne Francis, Marie Windsor, Sherry Jackson and Marilyn Maxwell played a few of the hard-as-nails female convicts.

Chapter Three

Female Entertainers Who
Toured the Western Frontier

During its earliest years of exploration and development, the West was visited by several traveling troupes of actors, singers, acrobats and dancers who offered settlers a few hours of diversion away from the arduous task of taming the frontier. The celebrated English actor Junius Booth toured with a company of professional actors and actresses who mostly performed the works of William Shakespeare. Their audiences, often confused but always appreciative, were composed of miners, cowboys, farmers and other frontier types in various settlements, mining camps, small towns and cities. Booth was a major theatrical attraction in England before he deserted his family there, immigrated to the United States and fathered a second family. The latter group included an actor who became the nineteenth century's most celebrated thespian (Edwin Booth) and another actor (John Wilkes Booth) who became notorious as the assassin of President Abraham Lincoln. Performers who booked tours of the West usually found it financially quite lucrative, sometimes earning them more money in a month than they could make in a year in a large Eastern city. For example, when a pretty young actress named Nola Forrest performed at the famous Bird Cage Theater in Tombstone, she was billed as "the People's Choice" and she proved herself "choice" enough to cause a local bookkeeper to embezzle $800 from his bank to buy jewelry for her. Other performers were just as well compensated, and some became rich because of their Western tours.

ANTOINETTE ADAMS

The first recorded theatrical performance offered by a female entertainer in the Montana silver mining boom town of Virginia City was presented by a middle-aged lady named Antoinette Adams. In spite of the fact that she was a female in an area where few women lived, her performance was not particularly well received by the rough-and-tumble, woman-starved miners. It was reported in a local newspaper that Antoinette was a "faded old blonde who was six foot tall and had a long neck, a large nose, and a singing voice that screeched and often cracked in the middle of a song." Although the men in the audience were disappointed by what they saw and heard, they managed to conceal their feelings and remained stony silent during the early part of Antoinette's recital. By the end of her third song, however, a miner called out, "Let's hear it for Aunty" (a term reserved for elderly, usually unattractive women) and the crowd broke out into loud cheers. Soon a shower of silver coins was covering the stage. The miners hoped that if they threw enough money at her, Antoinette's unpleasant screeching might come to an end. But Antoinette persisted, probably wise enough to realize that the longer she sang, the more money would be thrown her way. Every time she began to sing another song, the miners roared louder than before, and they actually began to beg her to stop singing as they continued to hurl silver coins at the stage. When the singer finally ended her recital, she ordered that the stage curtain be dropped and then hastily began to pick up the coins littering the stage. When she departed Virginia City the next morning, the town newspaper reported that she "left with two sacks filled with silver and wore a big smile on her face."

ANNIE OAKLEY (1860–1926)

The most famous female show-business personality associated with the Old West is the renowned sharpshooting superstar Annie Oakley. Annie was christened Phoebe Ann Moses in Dark County, Ohio, where her parents Jacob and Susan Moses were poor farmers who had eight other children. When her husband died, Susan Moses was unable to feed and clothe her large family by herself, and was forced to ask various friends and relatives to take her children in. Some of the older children were sent to orphanages when homes could not be found, but four-year-old Phoebe Ann was taken in by family friends. Unfortunately, her new "parents" were abusive people and treated the little girl badly. Phoebe stood their abuse as long as she could, then ran away when she was eight to find her mother (who had remarried). Susan Moses was delighted to have her daughter back with her, and the little girl established an instant rapport with her stepfather. When she was 12, Phoebe (who preferred to be called by her middle name Annie) was taught to shoot a rifle by her stepfather, and within a short period of time she became an expert sharpshooter. Annie began shooting quail and selling them to neighbors, and her business eventually became so successful that she was able to help her parents pay off the mortgage.

When she was 15, one of her customers, Charlie Katsenberger, arranged for Annie to compete in a shooting match against Frank Butler, a professional sharpshooter famous throughout the West because of his appearances in various theaters and fairs. The match was held in Cincinnati in 1875, and Annie was declared the winner when she shot one more clay pigeon than Butler did. Impressed by the young woman's expertise, (and by her attractive appearance), Butler asked Annie to join him and tour with his show. Annie jumped at the opportunity to enter the exciting world of show business. At first, she worked as a stage hand, but within a short period of time she joined him on the stage and so impressed audiences with her shooting skills that she became his co-star. This did not seem to bother Butler, who had fallen in love with Annie and asked her to marry him. Annie, who later confessed that she had been in love with Butler "from the first day" she met him, eagerly accepted his proposal. It was decided that Annie would be the star attraction of Butler's show and that her husband would become her manager. Annie changed her last name to "Oakley," feeling she needed a name that was more theatrical-sounding than "Moses." It also gave her an individual identity so that she would not become known as "Mrs. Butler." Annie had seen the name "Oakley" at a train station near Cincinnati, liked the look and sound of it and decided to become "Annie Oakley."

Annie was one of the most successful attractions performing at *The World's Industrial and Cotton Exhibition* in New Orleans in the early 1880s. *Buffalo Bill Cody's Rocky Mountain and Prairie Exhibition* was also appearing at the New Orleans Fair, but Annie attracted larger numbers of people to her show than Cody did. The Buffalo Bill show was near bankruptcy at the time, and when Cody saw Annie shooting cigarettes from between the lips of her husband and a dime from between his fingers, he knew that she might be the salvation of his failing production. He offered her top billing in his show and the Butlers accepted.

Annie and Frank made an impressive financial arrangement with Cody that paid them one-quarter of the show's entire profits, an unheard-of financial arrangement at the time. Cody renamed his show "Buffalo Bill's Wild West" and Annie did indeed become its major attraction. Before Annie joined his show, women in Buffalo Bill's spectacular were relegated to minor appearances in various sketches, dancing in square dance sequences and participating in a popular "Race Between Prairie, Spanish and Indian Girls." Annie, a "top of the bill" performer, gave women their first status in Buffalo Bill's show. By 1887, a dozen other women were also being featured in Buffalo Bill's show, but none could hold a candle to Annie Oakley as far as public popularity was concerned. One pretty equestrienne named Lillian Smith, who had joined the show in 1886, brazenly challenged Annie to a riding contest, knowing that Oakley was not a trained rider. Annie managed to rise to the occasion, however, and won the contest.

Annie Oakley. (Ohio Historical Society.)

Other new female performers in Bill's Wild West show included Mrs. George Duffy, "a rough rider from Wyoming," cowgirl Dell Ferrell, and Emma Lake Hickok, the stepdaughter of Wild Bill Hickok, who square-danced on horseback. But Annie remained unchallenged as the show's top box office draw.

Annie was given the nickname "Little Sure Shot" by no less a personage than Indian Chief Sitting Bull, who also toured with Buffalo Bill's show for a short time. Annie's sharpshooting exhibitions dazzled audiences and she became a legend in her own time, a woman whose reputation preceded her everywhere the show performed. Annie could shoot a card (held up sideways) in half; while touring Europe, she even managed to shoot a cigarette from between the lips of Crown Prince William of Germany, who later became the Kaiser. In time, her fame surpassed that of the Swedish opera singing superstar Jenny Lind, who performed under showman P. T. Barnum's management. Over the 17-year period that she performed with Buffalo Bill's show, Annie Oakley made both herself and Cody extremely rich. Her fame increased when Grand Duke Michael of Russia challenged her to a shooting match in 1897. At first Cody tried to convince her to throw the match, believing that the Russian royal family might be offended if Michael lost and refuse to allow their performances to continue in Russia. But Annie refused, and when she defeated Duke Michael, the incident became front

Barbara Stanwyck played the famous female sharpshooter in the 1935 film *Annie Oakley.* **(Author's collection.)**

page news all over the world and increased the marketability of Buffalo Bill's show ten times over.

In 1901, a train carrying the Buffalo Bill troupe collided with another train outside of Lexington, Kentucky. Annie was seriously injured in the accident and after 17 hours in a coma, she awoke to find that her left side was partially paralyzed. Two years later, after numerous operations and exhausting physical therapy, Annie was able to walk again, and resumed her sharpshooting career. But she was never really the same again. Her youthful charm and graceful appearance had diminished considerably, and even though her sharpshooting skills remained impressive, audiences did not seem to find the obviously crippled, somewhat elderly-looking woman as appealing as they did when she was young and attractive. In 1922, Annie was involved in another accident, this time while she was riding in an automobile. She was so severely injured that she was never able to walk or shoot again. Four years later, Annie died quietly in her sleep.

The 1954 biography *Annie Oakley* by Walter Havinghurst is certainly the most detailed of all of the many accounts of the legendary sharpshooter's life and career. Several of Buffalo Bill Cody's biographies also contain numerous facts about Annie. These biographies are listed in the bibliography at the end of this book.

In 1946, composer Irving Berlin wrote a musical comedy called *Annie Get Your Gun* for the Great White Way. The musical, which starred Broadway legend Ethel Merman as Annie, was an enormous success. It introduced such standards as "Anything You Can Do," "You Can't Get a Man with a Gun," "The Girl That I Marry," and "There's No Business Like Show Business." The play was turned into a film musical in 1950. Judy Garland filled the role until her erratic behavior forced her out in the middle of shooting. She was replaced by Betty Hutton. Howard Keel played Frank Butler in this film, which was directed by George Sidney. Barbara Stanwyck had previously played Oakley in a non-musical film, *Annie Oakley* (1935), which was directed by George Stevens and co-starred Preston Foster as Frank Butler.

Gail Davis, a young woman who really could ride and shoot and had been a rodeo performer before she became an actress, became the star of a weekly, syndicated half-hour television series called "Annie Oakley" in 1953. The show ran until 1956 and can still be seen on occasion in reruns. The "Annie Oakley" series was second in popularity only to "Hopalong Cassidy" (also seen on Saturday mornings) with young TV viewers. Davis had also been featured in over 20 Gene Autry films as well as in over 30 of his television shows before she became Annie Oakley.

MAY LILLIE (1875-?)—ANNIE OAKLEY'S ONLY RIVAL

The only man to equal Wild West showman Buffalo Bill Cody was an enterprising gentleman called "Pawnee Bill" (1860–1942). Pawnee Bill was born in Bloomington, Illinois (his real name was Gordon William Lillie), attended a normal school and trained to be a teacher. After completing his teacher's training, Gordon headed west to teach Native American children living in the Indian Territory of Oklahoma. Lillie mastered the Pawnee language in order to do a more effective job of teaching the children. Major Frank North, who was stationed at the Agency, began calling Lillie "Pawnee Bill" because of his Indian language skill, and the label stuck. At this time, Buffalo Bill Cody was looking for someone to act as an interpreter for the Indians who were touring in his Wild West Show. Lillie applied for the job and was hired.

Pawnee Bill remained with Buffalo Bill's show for several years as an interpreter, then decided to produce a Wild West show of his own. One of his first star attractions was a pretty young woman named May (maiden name unknown), a Smith College graduate whose Quaker parents lived in Pennsylvania. May had taken her degree in Western studies and had become an expert sharpshooter and horsewoman. She won a gold medal in rifle marksmanship in Philadelphia in 1887, and then another medal in Atlanta, Georgia, in 1889. While she was in Georgia, May attracted the attention of Pawnee Bill, who was impressed by her rifle skills and good looks and hired her to star in his new *Historical Wild West Show*. Pawnee Bill's show eventually grew larger and at the height of its popularity featured 300 cowboy ropers and riders as well as numerous female performers in addition to May. Pawnee Bill's lady performers included an Indian princess named Bright Star and a woman named Señorita Rosalie of Mexico, both expert equestriennes. May, however, remained the show's most popular female attraction, and soon became Annie Oakley's only major sharpshooting show business rival. The girls in Pawnee Bill's show were, according to its posters, "the most beauteous, dashing and laughing Western girls who ride and shoot better than any other women in the world." But no matter how popular the ladies in his company became, it was Bill (a colorful showoff) who always managed to receive the most publicity. This did not bother May, who was in love with Pawnee Bill. The two were married, and their union proved a happy one. In 1908, Pawnee Bill and Buffalo Bill decided to join forces and combine their two shows in order to corner the market on Wild West shows. After two years together, however, Pawnee Bill became unhappy playing second fiddle to Buffalo Bill, who also had an enormous ego and was an expert publicity-seeker. Pawnee Bill terminated their partnership and once again formed a Wild West show of his own. In the mid–1920s, Pawnee and May retired and went to live on the 2,000-acre ranch they purchased when their show was at the height of its popularity. The ranch was located near Pawnee, Oklahoma. With May's support, Pawnee opened a trading post and buffalo ranch, hoping "to save the buffalo from eventual extinction." In his declining years, Pawnee Bill became the vice-president of the Fern Oil Company, wrote several books about his Wild West experiences and (once again with May's assistance) established *The Wichita Wildlife Refuge*.

OTHER FEMALE WILD WEST
AND RODEO SHOW PERFORMERS

Many girls of the West had to be expert horsewomen and ranch hands, and several of them naturally drifted into the exciting world of show business. Mary Ann Whittaker was one such ranch-raised girl who enjoyed a successful career as a performer beginning in 1850. Mary Ann became well known throughout the United States as "The First Female Equestrian Artist in America." Whittaker specialized in silent dramatic horse-riding sketches such as "Xanthe Driven Mad By Her Own Infuriated Horse," which she performed in pantomime. A young California-born girl named Polly Lee became the talk of Denver when she performed there in 1871. Polly handled four horses "with grace and ease" and led them through a series of tricks in a stage performance. At the time, Denver newspapers noted that Polly was not only an expert horsewoman, but that she was also "the sole support of her large family of brothers and sisters, since her parents were both dead." Other female horsewomen-entertainers who were elected to the "Rodeo Hall of Fame" included "Prairie Rose" Henderson, "Prairie Lillie" Allen, Lucille Mulhall, Berta Blanchett (a.k.a. Kaepernick) and Tillie Baldwin.

"Prairie Rose" Henderson was the daughter of a Cheyenne, Wyoming, rancher. She protested when rodeo contest managers told her that "a woman could not compete in an all male event." She not only won both the right to compete with men, but became one of the show's star attractions. Rose eventually became famous throughout the United States, billed as "the best female bronco-buster in the world."

Lucille Mulhall's father made the Oklahoma land rush and established a large ranch in Logan County. Her mother, determined to raise her daughter "to be a refined young lady," sent Lucille to a convent school in St. Louis to be educated. But Lucille had her heart set on working on her father's Oklahoma ranch. By the time she was ten years old, Lucille was an expert roper, brander, herder and bronco buster. In 1899, when she was 13, Lucille's father decided to produce a Wild West show with Lucille as his star attraction. Lucille became one of the world's most popular rodeo performers and eventually was called "The Queen of Cowgirls" by the press. Lucille eventually joined *Buffalo Bill's Wild West Exhibition* in the early 1900s and remained active in show business until the 1920s.

Tillie Baldwin was the first female to rope and brand steers in public and, like Lucille Mulhall, was a "champion lady bronco buster." Other popular rodeo cowgirls of the early-to-mid–twentieth century included Dorothy Morrell, Ruth Roach, Vera McGinnis, "Tad" Lucas and Barbara Barnes, all of whom enjoyed long and profitable careers.

LOLA MONTEZ OR MONTES (1818?–1861)

In 1851, no one who lived west of the Mississippi River had ever seen anyone like the beautiful European actress-adventuress Lola Montez. When the legendary Miss Montez decided to grace San Francisco with her presence in 1851 and perform for the numerous women-starved customers settled in that fast-developing community, tales of her sexual reputation and legendary beauty preceded her. The theaters and concert halls of San Francisco were constantly filled to capacity, mostly by men (who outnumbered women in that city five-to-one at the time). These often rowdy but always appreciative spectators roared their approval at Montez's every gesture and word, for to them she was truly a remarkable "star" who surely must have fallen out of heaven, "so breathtaking is her appearance and so elegant her demeanor" (*The San Francisco Examiner*).

From the moment it was announced that the famous Montez would be arriving in San

Francisco on a ship called *The North-erner*, the town "began to work itself up into a frenzy that approached sheer madness," as *The Examiner* reported. "Everybody is in a fever to catch a glimpse of the lioness. Whether she comes as danseuse, authoress, politician, beauty, blue-stocking or noble lady ... she will be seen, admired, sung, courted and gone mad over here as elsewhere."

Who was this woman whose name alone inspired such excitement and adoration? The truth is that in spite of her exotic-sounding Spanish name, Lola Montez was born Marie Gilbert in Ireland. A beautiful child, and then a stunning young woman, Lola was encouraged by her ambitious parents to capitalize on her good looks. With her parents' blessing, the teenage Lola left Ireland and went to England, where she knew she would be more likely to capitalize on

Lola Montez. (Author's collection.)

her physical attributes. A short time after she arrived in London, she married an army officer, but the marriage soon ended in divorce and Marie Gilbert decided that her real destiny was to become a famous dancer.

Although she was not formally trained in dance, and was (as dance critics pointed out) "not a very good dancer," Lola managed to charm her way into a ballet company as a principal performer. Rumor later had it that she became a member of the dance company after she had granted certain "favors" to the company's manager. Her magnetism, charm and beauty onstage soon made her one of London's most popular theatrical attractions. While touring the Continent, Marie changed her name to "Lola Montez" because she thought it sounded "more theatrical." Lola caused quite a stir as a performer in France, Germany and Bavaria and became the mistress of such notable personages as composer-pianist Franz Liszt and novelist Alexander Dumas. While dancing in Munich, Lola attracted the attention of King Louis the First of Bavaria, who was in his 60s at the time, and she subsequently became his mistress. Lola's climb into the upper strata of European society was meteoric; the inexperienced-but-ambitious "guttersnipe" (as many of Bavaria's aristocrats called her) soon began to believe her own publicity and began "acting more like a member of the aristocracy than a mere commoner," according to one society matron. It was said Lola began to order people about and make financial demands that her theatrical producers found impossible to fulfill.

Fortunately for Lola, she no longer needed her stage earnings, since King Louis had fallen madly in love with her and began to lavish money and expensive gifts upon her (as well as providing her with a royal residence). The senile old king even began to seek Lola's advice concerning important matters of state about which she had no knowledge. She told him what she thought he should do about his advisors, about managing his financial affairs and about dealing with his heirs, in spite of her inexperience in these things. Before long,

Lola became convinced that she was someday going to be the Queen of Bavaria, and unwisely began to treat those close to the king "with disdain and distasteful arrogance," according to a leading Bavarian newspaper. Lola gave King Louis one bit of political advice more than she should have, and Bavarian nobles and politicians began to demand that the king send Lola packing. Antagonism toward Lola reached the point that Bavaria was actually thrust into a minor revolution in 1848. Lola was eventually banished by aristocrats who had taken over the King's decision-making, and she returned to England. She soon married, but once again the union proved short-lived. Her wealthy husband soon accused her of infidelity and demanded a divorce, cutting her off without a cent.

When the divorce was finalized, Lola reluctantly decided to return to the stage. Hearing that America was clamoring to get a glimpse of her, she departed for New York City in 1851 to begin her legendary world tours of the United States and the Far East. By the time she arrived in San Francisco, Lola was 33 years old and still a very beautiful woman. Her debut performances in that city attracted record-breaking crowds, as did all of her subsequent appearances in the Western United States. Once again she married—this time a newspaper publisher named P. P. Hull who had been instrumental in orchestrating her triumphant entry into San Francisco. Australia was subsequently conquered, but all of her strenuous touring eventually took its toll on Lola and in 1861 she unexpectedly died in New York City of unknown causes. Lola was 45 at the time and, according to a *New York Times* obituary, still "the most beautiful woman in the world." Among the several biographies of Lola Montez, the best (in this author's opinion) were those written by Amanda Darling and Isabelle Ross (both in 1972) and by Max Ophuls (1986). Ophuls had also directed a legendary French film biography called *Lola Montez* (1955). The movie starred French actress Martine Carol as Lola and featured Peter Ustinov, Anton Walbrook and Oscar Werner in the supporting cast. Ophuls' film is considered a cinema classic in France, but English and American reviewers and audiences did not think that Carol conveyed either "the magnetism nor the great beauty" they thought the real Montez must have possessed.

LILLY LANGTRY (1853–1929)

The beautiful English actress and courtesan Lilly Langtry's well-remembered association with the Wild West is due to the highly publicized performances she gave in Texas during her world-wide tour, and also because of the ardor of one of her most devoted fans, Judge Roy Bean. Bean, who first became famous as a gunfighter, later became the despotic administrator of a town he founded and named "Langtry" in honor of the world-famous actress.

Lilly Langtry was born on Jersey, one of the Channel Islands located off the coast of England. Lilly was one of the very few English women of elevated social rank to appear on the stage; because of this, she became something of a theatrical curiosity in England. Lilly, who became known as "The Jersey Lil," was never considered a particularly good actress by the critics of her time. She was, however, famous as a great society beauty, and then later for her affair with Edward, the Prince of Wales (later King Edward VII of England). In addition to being the mistress of the Prince of Wales, Lilly was also the friend and confidante of many of Britain's most notable writers, performers and socially prominent citizens. One of her greatest admirers and supporters was the eccentric Irish playwright-wit Oscar Wilde, who wrote the play *Lady Windermere's Fan* especially for her. When her first husband died of pneumonia in 1899, Lilly married Sir Hugh Gerald de Bathe and settled down to a more genteel life. In 1925, her memoirs (*The Days I Knew*) were published, but it was not until 1958, when Pierre Sichel's biography *Jersey Lil* was released, that the true story of Lilly's somewhat scandalous life became public.

Long after she became the prince's mistress, Lilly visited the United States on a world tour. It was Lilly Langtry's picture in a magazine that first attracted the attention of Judge Roy Bean. Once he saw that engraving, he obsessively sought out every article he could find about the beautiful young actress. He even had numerous portraits of her painted and hung in his home and above the bars of the many saloons he owned.

Bean (1825–1903) was born in Mason County, Texas, and became a gunfighter when he was a young man. With the money he made in his gunslinging days, Bean began to buy saloons in various Texas towns, and in time constructed the town of Langtry, Texas, which he named after his adored "Jersey Lil." Bean's fame increased when newspapers began to print stories calling him "the only law West of the Pecos" because of the severe punishments he meted out to anyone who did not conform to his ideas of proper conduct while they were visiting or residing in his town. Bean wrote numerous fan letters to Lilly over the years, and he even made sure that a Christmas turkey was delivered to her in England every year for many years. Certainly one of the highlights of Bean's life occurred in 1888 when he attended one of Langtry's performances in San Antonio, Texas. When Bean tried to visit her backstage after the performance, however, he was rudely barred from entering the backstage area; deeply disappointed and embarrassed, he departed without ever having met her. Bean often said that his greatest hope was that Jersey Lil would one day visit the town he had named in her honor. The actress did indeed visit Bean's town in 1903. Unfortunately, her visit occurred ten months after Bean, 78, died of complications from heart and lung ailments. At the time of her visit (a much-publicized event) Lilly was presented with one of Bean's pistols as a memento of his devotion to her.

CHARLOTTE "LOTTA" CRABTREE (1852?–1924)

One of the few nineteenth century actresses who actually grew up in the Western United States and became an internationally known performer was Lotta Crabtree (née Charlotte Crabtree). Lotta's mother Mary Ann was an ambitious woman and a great admirer of the celebrated Lola Montez. When Montez was residing in Grass County, California, where the Crabtrees lived, Mary Ann made a point of getting to know and befriend her. In all probability, it was because of her friendship with Montez that Mary Ann Crabtree began to encourage her pretty little daughter Charlotte to become a performer. "Lotta," as Charlotte was called, first began performing when she was eight years old in Rabbit Creek, California. She sang, recited and danced for customers at a saloon and proved to be a real crowd-pleaser. When Lola Montez decided that she had had enough of California and left for a tour of Australia, she asked Mary Ann Crabtree for per-

Lotta Crabtree. (Bancroft Library, University of California–Berkeley.)

mission to take Lotta with her. Mary Ann refused, realizing that she had a marketable commodity in her talented and beautiful daughter.

Mary Ann Crabtree may have had this mercenary attitude because she lived in rather modest circumstances most of her life. She had married a young man named John Crabtree when she was in her late teens; her young husband had big plans but little sense of responsibility. Before Mary Ann was 20, John Crabtree left her and the newborn Charlotte in New York City and went to California to search for gold. Mary Ann and Lotta eventually joined John there in 1852, but he soon abandoned them; until Mary Ann met Lola Montez several years later, she supported herself as a laundress and maid. Lotta's first major show-business success occurred after she auditioned for Mort Taylor, who owned a variety theater in Grass Valley. Taylor was looking for a child actress to rival the cute young performer-daughter of a competing theater owner. Taylor hired Lotta and taught her to dance an Irish jig, combining it with the song and dance steps she had already learned from Lola Montez. Lotta was an instant success. At the end of her performances, audience members threw gold and silver coins on the stage and Mary Ann rushed on stage before the curtain came down to gather up the money. "The singing and dancing of little Lotta," a Grass Valley newspaper reported, "was admirable and took our hearts by storm."

In 1859, Mary Ann decided that her talented daughter was ready for "the big time" and took her to San Francisco. The pretty young teenager proved a sensation in that city as well; newspaper headlines called her "Miss Lotta, San Francisco's Favorite," "La Petite Lotta, the Celebrated Danseuse and Vocalist" and "Miss Lotta the Unapproachable." The key to Lotta Crabtree's meteoric rise appears to have been her seeming innocence and, of course, her physical beauty. One critic wrote that Lotta was "not a very expert actress," but added, "What she lacks in acting ability, she certainly makes up for in charm and beauty." As she grew into young womanhood, Lotta's fame and celebrity continued to increase. It was reported that Lotta had the power to "titillate miners and cowboys in her audiences, as well as amuse and charm matrons with her uninhibited yet innocent stage performances." As she grew older, Lotta's performances became increasingly more daring. In the days when such things were simply not done, Lotta bared her legs in public and even smoked cigarettes, which shocked many people but delighted the numerous rowdy males who flocked to the theaters. Plays were written to suit her talents and in time she became "a very good light comedienne."

Lotta regularly appeared in a popular farce called "Jenny Leatherlungs" which spoofed the world-famous soprano Jenny Lind. Lotta met with tremendous success wherever she performed this vehicle, whether in a small Western town or in the larger cities of the West and East. Eventually Lotta toured Europe and enjoyed continued success on that continent. Her performances in Europe were always given to standing-room-only audiences. By the time she returned to the United States, Lotta Crabtree was one of the highest-paid actresses in the world. When she died she left an estate which was said to have been in excess of four million dollars, an enormous amount of money for the time.

CAROLINE CHAPMAN (1838?–?)

Another actress making her first major stage appearance in San Francisco was Caroline Chapman. Caroline was the illegitimate daughter of an actor (William Chapman) who had performed on Ohio and Mississippi River showboats. In 1852, Chapman went to California and immediately became popular with Frisco's varied and appreciative theatergoers. Caroline strongly resembled her handsome actor-father and the two often performed together, both when Caroline was a child and later when she was an adult. Most people assumed that the Chapmans were brother and sister, which neither of them ever denied, since the rather vain William preferred people believe he was younger than he actually was. The pretty Caroline soon had more admirers than her father did. Crowds of adoring men followed her to and from the theaters and packed them to capacity. They showered the stage with gold and silver coins when Caroline came out to take her final bow, calling out "Our Caroline!" as they roared their approval and admiration. It was even reported that in the late 1850s, while the Chapmans were acting in the play *She Stoops to Conquer* for an audience of one thousand miners, they received "a small fortune" for their performance. The Chapmans continued to act anywhere, under any circumstances when they were asked, until well after the Civil War, performing with the same gusto and professionalism whether their audience was a group of miners in a rough-and-tumble mining camp or grand patrons in a large city theater. Caroline remained active on the stage long after her father died, but she eventually retired in the late 1880s, a very rich woman.

ADAH ISAACS MENKEN (1835–1868)

Before Lotta Crabtree and Caroline Chapman took San Francisco by storm, an actress named Adah Menken conquered the heart of that city. Adah Isaacs Menken, who was born Dolores Adious Fuertos in New Orleans, Louisiana, made her acting debut in San Francisco in the early 1850s. Adah was not a singer and light comedienne as was Lotta Crabtree, or a classical actress like Caroline Chapman. Menken acted in serious, spectacular melodramas. Her appearance and her performances were often likened to those of Lola Montez, but Adah did not care for that comparison and once snapped at a reporter, "Lola Montez began with a king and ran down the scale through a newspaper man to a miner. I began with a prizefighter, and I will end with a prince!"

Early in her career, Adah recognized the value of publicity, and she granted numerous interviews. She told reporters in San Francisco that she had been an actress in Houston, Texas, and prior to that, a ballet dancer in New Orleans. (The latter claim may be true, since she was apparently born and raised in that city. No evidence exists, however, to support *either* claim.) Menken also said that she had performed in Cuba and Mexico, but again no proof has ever been uncovered. In an interview which appeared in *The New York Police Gazette*, Adah said that she had been kidnapped by Indians when she was a child in Texas and that Texas Rangers had rescued her. This story was probably more fiction than fact, but it made good copy for the pulp magazine writers back East. Whatever the truth concerning her origins were, once Adah Menken stepped into the spotlight on a San Francisco stage, she totally captivated that city with her bizarre, theatrical performances. The public apparently adored her, calling her "The Frisco Frenzy." In her never ending desire for publicity, during the Civil War, Adah placed a large Confederate flag on the wall of her hotel room and made sure that reporters saw it, even though she knew California was a strongly pro–Union territory. Of course, the incident was duly reported in every newspaper in the country.

At one point in her career, Adah decided that she looked particularly fetching in the color yellow and began to appear in public wearing yellow silk gowns and hats. It was said that she even slept on yellow silk sheets. "I doubt," journalist Joaquin Miller wrote, "that any other woman in the world could wear a dress like that in the winds of San Francisco and not look ridiculous."

Adah's most successful stage vehicle was a play called *Mazeppa, or The Wild Horse of Tartary*. The high point of her performance occurred when she rode onstage astride a horse that pranced in front of cardboard cutouts that had been painted to look like mountains. Her costume was delightfully daring, exposing a great deal of her ample flesh, and male theatergoers cheered and clapped enthusiastically every time she made her way across the stage and down a ramp which had been constructed to take her as close to her admiring public as possible.

Adah performed in Virginia City when it was enjoying its boom years as a mining town and she was treated like visiting royalty by the citizenry. Posters publicizing her impending appearance as Mazeppa in Virginia City showed her almost naked riding a horse. A review of her performance was written by a *Virginia City Territorial Enterprise* critic before she actually performed in that town. The critic had decided to give Adah a poor review because he believed she was simply a circus performer. When the first night audience and the newspaper critics saw her performance, they were dazzled by her theatricality and professionalism and the *Territorial Enterprise* critic hastily returned to his office and rewrote his review for the next morning's edition. Author Mark Twain, who was also in the audience, praised her performance and visited her in her hotel room the following day to express his admiration. Only one critic dared to give Adah an unfavorable review. "We hope there were no butchers in the audience," he sniped, "for they must have been lost to the play, and thought of nothing but veal. Such calves! [Adah's legs were quite hefty.] They were never reared on milk. The acting consisted of sneezing, smoking and coughing on the part of [the extras] and some elegant posturing on the part of Menken."

Adah remained in Virginia City for several months enjoying her notoriety and popularity there. The city's miners presented her with a bar of silver bullion worth $2,000 and even named a street and a mine after her. One admirer presented her with 50 shares of mining stock that was reportedly worth at least $1,000 a share. When Adah died, she was performing in California and was only 33 years old. The cause of her death was said to be pneumonia. Undoubtedly the drafty old theaters had been more than Adah's partially clad body could withstand.

HELENA MAJESKA OR MODJESKA (1844–1909)

Helena Majeska was one of Poland's most successful actresses in the mid–1800s. Born in Krakow, Poland, Majeska was the protégé of an aristocrat named Madame Mouchanoff, a friend of the Czar of Russia, whose country was occupying Poland. Fiercely nationalistic, Majeska was an outspoken critic of the Russian occupation; when Madame Mouchanoff died, Majeska fell into disfavor and was denied the roles she wanted to perform on the Warsaw stage. She feigned illness and retired to her countryside villa. Majeska soon left Poland with her husband and immigrated to the United States. The couple settled in California and for a time tried farming. Dissatisfied with her life as a farmer's wife, Majeska decided to return to the stage in spite of the fact that she spoke little or no English and was unknown in the United States. "Call it vanity," she said through an actress friend translator. "I prefer to call it pride of ambition. Some people in Poland know of my intention of appearing on the English-speaking stage, and I hear they already predict my failure. I left Poland as the leading lady of the Warsaw Theater; I will return as an acknowledged star of the foreign stage."

Coached by the same actress friend who had acted as her translator, Helena learned to speak English phonetically and memorized the roles of Juliet, Ophelia and Cleopatra in Shakespeare's *Romeo and Juliet*, *Hamlet*, and *Antony and Cleopatra*. A San Francisco lawyer named Edward Solomon was so impressed with Majeska's stage presence that he got her an audition with John McCullough, owner-manager of the successful and prestigious California Theater. It was reported in the *San Francisco Chronicle* that Majeska's debut performance as Ophelia in *Hamlet* was so "enthralling" that members of the audience did not even notice that she had begun to speak in her native tongue, Polish, in the middle of her mad scene.

Her triumphs in San Francisco and other Western towns and cities led to successful engagements in New York, London and Paris. As she predicted, Majeska returned to her native Poland "an acknowledged internationally known actress," and she once again became Poland's "First Lady of the Theater." Majeka reportedly died of consumption at the age of 65 while she was performing in Paris.

"THE DIVINE SARAH" TOURS THE WILD WEST

Even the nineteenth century's most renowned actress, Sarah Bernhardt ("The Divine Sarah") performed in the wild and woolly West, or at least as far west as Missouri, when she was on one of her many world-wide tours. Miss Bernhardt who was French and spoke no English, performed all of her roles in her native tongue, sometimes while the other actors in the play spoke English. This did not deter the multitudes from vying for tickets to see the woman critics called "The World's Greatest Actress" in one of her legendary performances.

Newspaper reporter Ed Howe wrote a review of Bernhardt's performance in *Camille* for the *Atchinson* (Kansas) *Globe* when she was appearing in St. Louis. Howe's review was not only highly critical of Bernhardt's acting, but also mentioned the rowdy antics of the rather unsophisticated audiences of the American West. (An actress named Miss Leslie, when writing to a friend in 1877, also referred to "the rip roaring lustiness of the men who attended the play.") If Howe's review of Bernhardt's acting was less than enthusiastic, he was brutally cruel about her physical appearance. His review read in part, "The only thing Bernhardt does extraordinarily well is to put her arms around a man, and look into his eyes. If her face [which he previously described as being "extraordinarily ugly"] could be hidden at these moments, she would be sublime." Howe further reported that he attended a reception following the show: "Bernhardt consented to come down and watch the mob *if* nobody spoke to her. She stood around for an hour, and all St. Joe walked in front of her, stared her in the face, jostled her, eyed her dress through glasses, and had a good time. At one o'clock, she retired, and at nine this morning her maid shook the sheets to find her, as time had arrived to depart for Leavenworth."

ENTERTAINERS OF THE WEST IN FILMS

In 1936, singer Jeanette MacDonald appeared with Clark Gable in *San Francisco*, which took place at the turn of the century in that city. MacDonald played a young singer hired by saloon and theater owner Gable, who subsequently falls in love with her. She becomes the bright and shining rage of Frisco; even the San Francisco earthquake, which is the film's climax, fails to diminish her luster. The film was directed by W. S. Van Dyke and also starred Spencer Tracy, Jessie Ralph and Shirley Ross.

One of the most interesting films about entertainers out West in the nineteenth century was *Salome, Where She Danced* (1945). Not very well received by either the critics or the public, this Technicolor film was about an exotic dancer who somehow becomes involved in spying. Yvonne DeCarlo played the dancer and her co-stars were Rod Cameron, David Bruce, Walter Slezak and Marjorie Rambeau. The film was directed by Charles Lamont.

"The Jersey Lil," Lilly Langtry, appeared briefly as a character in a film called *The Life and Times of Judge Roy Bean*, which starred Paul Newman. Actress Ava Gardner played Langtry in this 1972 film which was directed by John Huston and also starred Jacqueline Bisset, Victoria Principal, Anthony Perkins, Tab Hunter and Roddy McDowall.

Chapter Four

Prostitutes, Madams and Gaming Ladies of the Wild West

Filmmakers usually portray the saloon girls of the Wild West as quick-witted, tough ladies who for the most part had tender hearts. Popular films of the '30s, '40s and '50s convinced moviegoers that these girls were usually just "wronged" women, led astray by black-hearted men who profited in some way from their work in the various "watering holes" (saloons) of the West. Residual prudish Victorian morality of the time could not admit that the opposite might have been true and that these girls had willingly sought the easy, "carefree" life of a saloon entertainer or waitress. There was usually only the slightest suggestion that these women were actually prostitutes. From the 1960s until the present, of course, it has been an entirely different story, as witnessed by many recent films and TV mini-series. Current films make no attempt to portray the West's saloon girls as anything other than the prostitutes that they were.

Movie saloon girls such as Marlene Dietrich in *Destry Rides Again*, Marie Windsor and Ann Dvorak in countless second-feature Westerns and even the very young Angela Lansbury in the musical *The Harvey Girls* never "sold sexual favors" to anyone. They were, we were led to believe, merely hostesses and entertainers in the West's drinking establishments.

Actual saloon girls of the Wild West were usually hard-, not soft-boiled eggs. They not only prostituted themselves, but drank and smoked (an unheard of thing for women to do in those more "proper" times) and were not averse to "rolling" a drunken customer and relieving him of his cash. These women were also the owners and madams of many of the brothels and saloons, and did whatever they had to in order to survive. The names of many of the prostitutes and madams catering to the sexual appetites of outlaws, cowboys, miners, soldiers, muleskinners *et al.*, went unrecorded. Many of the prostitutes who worked the mining camps and cattle towns were known only by catchy nicknames such as "Contrary Mary," "Spanish Queen," "Little Gold Dollar," "Em Straight Edge," and "Peg Leg Annie." One such woman, "Molly b'Damned," was an Idaho prostitute who was described by one of her customers as having "an uncommonly ravishing personality. Her face gave no evidence of dissipation, her clothes no hint of her profession. About her, at times, was an atmosphere of refinement and culture." Molly b'Damned was also somewhat of a scholar and often quoted Shakespeare, Milton and Dante for her patrons.

Brief newspaper items occasionally appeared about popular prostitutes, but only rarely was the full legal name of any of these notorious *dames de la soir* published. Most of these women quite understandably did not want their friends and relatives back home to know that they had resorted to selling their bodies in order to make a living. There were, of course,

A western saloon in the 1860s. (Author's collection.)

a few exceptions. Colorado's celebrated madam, "Diamond Lil" Powers, and the professional gambler "Poker Alice" Tubbs, for example, were proud of their professions, and welcomed any and all publicity. They felt that it was "good for business" to be mentioned as often as possible by the press.

Prostitution was a fact of life throughout the West and these ladies of ill repute prospered. But Western towns, determined to exercise a certain degree of supervision over these ladies of the evening, made sure that they remained relatively segregated from respectable citizens and heavily regulated and taxed them in order to control their activities. The tax money taken in from these women often became a major source of their communities' incomes and paid for schools and other public facilities, lessening the tax burden on the "good" people of the town. Little, therefore, was done to actually remove members of the world's oldest profession from their midst.

An after-hours break. (Author's collection.)

JANE BARNES (DATES UNKNOWN)

In 1813, Donald McTavish was waiting for a ship to take him from Portsmouth, England, to the West Coast of North America where he had been assigned to work for the Crown as an inspector of properties England had acquired after the War of 1812. Great Britain had confiscated businesses owned by American businessman John Jacob Astor's Northwest Lumber Company, which had its headquarters at Fort George on Oregon's Pacific coast.

Governor McTavish was "a real womanizer" who had a distinct preference for young blonde girls. While waiting for the ship in Portsmouth, he met a beautiful, fair-headed barmaid named Jane Barnes who immediately took his fancy. McTavish asked Jane to accompany him on his voyage, promising her "an unlimited wardrobe of dresses and hats" and, when they returned to England, "a large annuity in cash." Of course, Jane would have to supply McTavish with sexual favors in return. The barmaid did not consider McTavish's proposition long. She promptly accepted his invitation to accompany him to the "New World."

McTavish's ship the *Isaac Todd* laid anchor in the mouth of the Columbia River at Fort George, Oregon Territory, on April 24, 1814. McTavish's reception committee included a very proper, apparently prudish young man named Alexander Henry, who was managing the Northwest Company for the English Crown. "He met me on deck," Henry wrote in his journal (later published in Elliott Coues' book *New Light on the Early History of the Greater*

Northeast [1987]), "and we went into the cabin where I was introduced to Jane Barnes." Henry was "astonished that a young white woman, and a courtesan at that," was in the new Governor's cabin. News of Jane's presence in the community was warmly received, but McTavish, not wishing to share his prize female possession with the rest of the settlers, made Jane remain in the cabin of the *Isaac Todd*, where he could spend his nights with her. "A vile discourse took place one night," Henry wrote in his journal, "when the subject of venereal disease among the Chinook Indian ladies who serviced the white men of Fort George came up." Jane apparently became outraged at the talk of the Indian women's looseness and immorality, and this impressed the puritanical Henry, who immediately began to change his mind about her. Henry offered Jane the use of his rooms at Fort Henry and Jane, bored with living the life of a recluse on the ship, eagerly accepted his invitation. On May 8, Jane left the ship with all of her baggage, leaving McTavish to sleep on the *Isaac Todd* by himself.

As soon as she was settled in Fort Henry, Jane began her reign as the virtual "queen" of the settlement. Henry admiringly wrote that Jane soon became "the greatest curiosity that ever gratified the wondering eyes of the Native Americans. The Indians daily thronged in numbers to our fort for the mere purpose of gazing on, and admiring her fair beauty." According to Henry, Cassakas, the young son of the Chinook chief, became so enamored of Jane that one day he appeared before her with his face painted blue and his half-naked body smeared with whale oil (which was what Chinooks did when courting a young woman). He told Jane he would send her relatives 100 sea otters and make her the mistress over his four other wives if she agreed to marry him. The insensitive Jane firmly replied that she had "no use for a husband with a flat head, a half-naked body and copper-colored skin besmirched with whale oil." Cassakas was deeply insulted and vowed never to return until she had left Fort George. It was rumored, according to Henry, that Cassakas plotted to kidnap Jane while she was walking on the beach, "which was her custom every evening." Jane was warned about this possibility and discontinued her evening strolls.

While she was in residence at the fort, Jane held daily receptions and recited literary quotations that she had memorized in an obvious attempt to gain a certain amount of respectability among the settlers. In his book *Adventures on the Columbian River*, Ross Cox related that Jane alienated the affections of a handsome Fort George clerk when she once again attacked the morality of Chinook women. The young clerk answered that they "were certainly no worse than many white women he had known," and then, after a long and glaring look at Jane, departed.

When McTavish completed his inspection and tax collecting duties at Fort George, he decided it was time to depart for Montreal, from where he would sail home for England, inspecting other English Crown properties along the way. McTavish thought Jane would return on the *Isaac Todd* with the furs he had collected. But Jane had other ideas and decided that she enjoyed being the center of attention at Fort George and did not wish to leave. In Henry's journal he wrote, "Conferred with Mr. McTavish regarding Jane; his three stipulations were: first her person: second, the table [?]: and third, to cause no misunderstanding with the young gentlemen, etc. This was the sum total... My part is mainly to protect her from ill usage. Affection is out of the question; our acquaintance is too short, and she has placed her affections elsewhere. I shall, therefore, make it my duty to render her situation as comfortable as possible, not as a lover, but through humanity. I know the ground on which she stands, and the pros and cons of the whole situation." McTavish had apparently agreed to leave Jane behind at Fort George.

Two days later, while McTavish and Henry were crossing the Columbia River from Fort George to inspect a fur trapper's camp one last time before McTavish departed for England, their rowboat capsized and both men drowned. Jane did not grieve at their loss because by then she had become the mistress of the fort's physician, Dr. Swan. With him she had planned to leave on the *Isaac Todd*, which would sail to Canton, China, before heading back to England. Shortly after arriving in China, Jane deserted the doctor and almost immediately became the mistress of a wealthy English gentleman employed by the East India Company. Nothing is known of Jane's activities between the time she settled in Canton and resurfaced in Montreal several years later to claim the annuity she had been promised by McTavish. Documentation proving that Jane received the promised money has never been uncovered. Nothing is known about Jane after she filed her application for her annuity.

ELEANORA "MADAME MUSTACHE" DUMONT (1829-1879)

Among the West's prostitute-madam-gamblers, one name stands out prominently above all the rest: Eleanora "Madame Mustache" Dumont. According to Duncan Aiken's book *Calamity Jane and the Lady Wildcats*, Dumont was born in New Orleans, Louisiana, in 1829, the daughter of Creole parents. (Dumont always claimed that she was born in Paris, France, which she apparently thought made her seem more exotic.) A dusky, frizzle-haired woman of short stature, "La Mustache," as she was called later in her life, first burst onto the Western scene in Nevada City, California. It is probable that before she arrived in that town, she spent some time in Sacramento and San Francisco, since that was where the stagecoach she arrived on in Nevada City had come from. Dumont told people in Nevada City that she was French, and her pronounced Gallic accent seemed to support her claim. Her name, she said, was "Madame" Eleanora Dumont, but as far as anyone could determine, there had never actually been a Monsieur Dumont. Madame Dumont was 25 years old when she arrived in Nevada City and her vivaciousness and charm, as well as her attractive complexion and flirtatious ways, totally captivated the male citizens of that town. But no one in the raw little mining town could figure out why such a worldly, exotic lady had decided to grace them with her unique presence.

The answer came less than two weeks after Dumont arrived in Nevada City, when she rented a small store on Broad Street and opened a gambling parlor where *vingt-et-un* (blackjack or 21) was to be played. Her gambling establishment, which she hastily decorated in whatever Victorian finery she could find in Nevada City, was an instant success. Well-staked miners rushed to be among the first patrons at the establishment, which to their unsophisticated eyes was a really "first class hall." Madame Dumont always insisted that her customers wear jackets, ties and stove-pipe hats, or at least some sort of a hat, when they came to her place. She called all her customers "Zee bhoyss" and her "fr-r-r-reens" and did everything in her power to make them feel comfortable, including supplying them with "good time" girls who arrived in town a week after the madam did. Madame Dumont also insisted that there could be "no rough conduct, knife fights, eye-gougings or gunplay" while they were under her roof. Between games of chance, she circulated around the room, pausing at each of her guests' tables, greeting each man with a familiar word or two and flirting outrageously with all of them. Miners were soon telling visitors and friends from neighboring towns that they "would rather lose their money at the Madame's place than win from any male tinhorn in northern California."

A year after her arrival in Nevada City, Madame Dumont was making enough money to hire a male assistant to help her keep her patrons in order. He was a charming young gambler named David Tobin. Good-looking and polished, the sophisticated Tobin added a refined masculine presence to the establishment.

Dumont's Nevada City prosperity continued until 1855, when there was a slight falling

off in the mining activities in that area. At this time, Tobin and Madame Dumont decided to part company. It was rumored that the couple had had a lovers' quarrel, but it was also said that Tobin had become dissatisfied with his lesser share of the profits. Ten years later, when Madam Dumont heard that Tobin had died, she was said to have been genuinely distressed.

In 1865, Dumont decided to leave Nevada City, claiming that she had "grown tired of northern California." She did not surface again until four years later, when she was seen working as a gambler and madam (with her stable of girls in tow) in mining camps throughout Arizona, Colorado and Nevada. The gold and silver rushes of the period had apparently taken Madame Dumont from one rough mining camp to another, and from all reports she was physically paying the price for her wanderings. A miner who knew her in her Nevada City heyday wrote to a friend that he had seen Dumont in Colorado and that she was "beginning to look rather worn-out and bedraggled." The miner also wrote that

Eleanora "Madame Mustache" Dumont. (Author's collection.)

she "had grown a thin line of hair on her upper lip" and that the miners were beginning to call her "Madame Mustache." Few of them, however, dared say it to her face, "lest they bring down her wrath upon them," the miner stated.

In 1864 Madame Dumont was known to have been in Bancock, where she met and befriended 15-year-old Martha "Calamity Jane" Canary and introduced her to the "fine art" of prostitution. After leaving Bancock, the madam and her girls apparently spent a hectic summer following the construction camps of the Union Pacific railroad, and then turned up in Cheyenne, Wyoming, where miners were seeking their share of Black Hills gold. Madame Dumont was in Deadwood with the "seventy-sixers" when silver was discovered there. After spending time in Eureka, Nevada, she finally ended up in Bodie with the surviving forty-niners who had panned for gold at Sutter's Mill in California and had gathered in Bodie for a reunion.

One cold September morning in 1879, Madame Mustache's body was found lying in a ditch at the side of the road two miles from Bodie. A bottle of poison lay next to her. There was no suicide note and no sign of a struggle. Nor was there any ceremony at the time of her death. A brief item published in the *Sacramento Union* in September 1879 stated that "a woman named Eleanora Dumont was found dead about one mile out of town, having committed suicide." It seems a worse-for-wear Madame Dumont had simply decided, perhaps after seeing herself in the eyes of the tired old miners who gathered in Bodie for the gold rush reunion, that it was time to cash in her chips and call it a day. "Calamity Jane had shrugged at the fact that she had grown older with boisterous acceptance, and Belle Starr had grown dowdy in half-savage contentment," Duncan Aiken wrote in *Calamity Jane and the Lady Wildcats,* but Madame Mustache Dumont was a very vain woman and apparently could not accept the fact that she was no longer the pretty young coquette who burst upon the Western scene in Nevada City many years before. Death was undoubtedly preferable to old age and obscurity.

BLONDE MARIE DUBONNET, DUBARRY, OR DURRANT (C. 1860-1935)

More practical and certainly more fortunate than Madame Mustache was a beautiful woman who was known as "Blonde Marie." Marie, whose real name remains in question, was born in Paris, France, to working-class parents. In order to obtain the things she felt she richly deserved, the lovely, fair-haired young Marie took to the streets when she was barely in her teens and sold her body to anyone who could meet the high price she placed on her sexual services. By the time she was 15, Marie was a beautiful, full-figured woman and one of the Left Bank's most popular streetwalking tarts.

In the Paris of the 1870s, many ladies of the evening talked about "the fortunes" that could be made by a good whore in the woman-hungry, gold-rich Western United States. Excited by visions of riches, Marie saved until she had enough cash to buy a one-way ticket to the United States, vowing to return to France a rich woman.

Marie arrived in New York City penniless but eager to succeed. After convincing immigration officials that she had been a seamstress in France, she immediately headed to New York's notorious Tenderloin District, where selling sex was commonplace. Sailors, urban playboys and hen-pecked husbands proved eager patrons, and within a year Marie had once again saved enough money to buy a ticket—this time on a train heading west. Marie arrived in St. Louis and remained just long enough to save enough money to buy yet another ticket—this time on a stagecoach headed for San Francisco.

When she arrived in Frisco, Marie immediately took up residence in one of that city's most fashionable whorehouses. She soon proved to be the house's most popular girl, even surpassing the popularity of ample "Big Minnie" Bignon, the establishment's major attraction. In two years' time, Marie had put aside enough cash to buy the place from its debt-ridden owner. The brothel became one of San Francisco's most frequented whorehouses under Blonde Marie's efficient management, and the sensible young woman did not squander her money. She carefully put away almost everything she made, and over a 15-year period accumulated the fortune that she had dreamed about having when she was walking the streets of Paris as a teenager. When she reached her fortieth

"Blonde Marie." (Author's collection.)

birthday, Marie felt that she had finally saved enough money to retire and return to her native France. A wealthy woman by anyone's standards, Marie bought a country villa in a suburb of Paris, moved into it with her parents and a newly acquired banker husband who managed her affairs. She apparently lived happily ever after, dying when she was 78 years old in 1935.

"BIG MINNIE" BIGNON (C. 1855-C. 1920)

"Big Minnie" Bignon received her greatest notoriety as the owner of "The Old Bird Cage Theater and House of Pleasure" in Deadwood. When Minnie arrived in Deadwood, it was already one of the West's fastest-growing boom towns. The nearby gold and silver mines were in full operation in the Black Hills, and the town had become a mecca for all sorts of fortune-seeking opportunists and adventurers. Minnie's "Old Bird Cage Theater and Saloon" was frequented by many of the West's most publicized personalities, both famous and infamous; her friends and acquaintances included such Western notables as Wild Bill Hickok, Calamity Jane, Bat Masterson, the Earp and Dalton brothers *et al.* It was said that Big Minnie was the daughter of middle-class parents who lived "somewhere east of the Mississippi River." The details of Minnie's early life remain clouded in mystery since, like most prostitutes, she preferred relative anonymity. It is known that before she acquired "The Old Bird Cage," she worked as a faro dealer and prostitute in San Francisco and El Paso where she met and eventually became the mistress and long-time companion

"Big Minnie" Bignon. (Author's collection.)

of "Colorado Charlie" Utter. Utter was a gambler and confidence man as well as a show-business entrepreneur; it was Charlie who engineered Wild Bill Hickok and Calamity Jane's colorful entry into Deadwood. (Wild Bill and Calamity hooted and hollered like wild Indians, fired their six-shooters into the air and then proceeded to drink themselves into stupors—all for the benefit of representatives of the Eastern press who had been summoned to Deadwood by Charlie Utter to record the event for posterity.) Wild Bill, Calamity and other members of their party granted numerous interviews, exaggerated their previous adventures, and received world-wide recognition (as well as handsome fees) for their stories. Minnie, of course, was a participant in this event and undoubtedly added color and excitement to the proceedings. In spite of her *avoir du pois,* the fat, four-foot-ten-inch Minnie was always handsomely attired in the height of fashion.

After remaining in Deadwood for a few years, Minnie and Charlie returned to El Paso, where they opened a gambling parlor. The couple remained in El Paso for 20 years until 1904, when an anti-gambling law forced them out of business. They then migrated to Mexico, where they ran a medicine show and performed card tricks for the dazzled but ignorant natives who eagerly purchased Utter's bogus cure-all tonics. Minnie and Utter traveled throughout Mexico and Central America until Charlie died of yellow fever in Panama in the early 1920s. When Charlie died, Minnie returned to the United States and settled in Los Angeles, where she reportedly lived a life of comfort on the profits she and Charlie had accumulated south of the border. She died in the 1920s.

"POKER ALICE" TUBBS (1851-1930)

The most celebrated lady gambler of the Old West was an Englishwoman who became famous as "Poker Alice" of Deadwood. She was born Alice Ivers in Sudbury, England, to middle-class parents who moved to the United States in 1865, when Alice was in her early teens. The Ivers settled in New York City. Alice's father was an avid card player and taught his daughter to play poker when she was a child. In New York expert card player Alice discovered that easy money could be made playing poker with the less-skilled out-of-towners who frequented the city's numerous gaming parlors. When Alice made a killing in a three-day poker game in 1872, she and her family left New York and headed West to continue to practice their trade in the gold-rich mining towns of Arizona. Like many other fortune-seekers, the Iverses settled in Deadwood, where Alice's formidable talents as a poker player earned her a good living. Alice made numerous tours of the West, gambling in most of that vast area's most famous towns, but she consistently returned to Deadwood, which she had come to think of as "home." Although the story has never been confirmed, Alice claims she was in Deadwood on the day Wild Bill Hickok was shot to death during a card game; Alice spent hours comforting a grieving Calamity Jane, who she said was "genuinely heartbroken" at the loss of her friend and partner.

Poker Alice Ivers continued her card-playing activities until she was well into her 60s. She granted interviews to newspaper reporters who remained fascinated by her proper English manners and speech which contrasted sharply with her hard-boiled gambling skills and craggy looks. Over the years, Alice acquired several husbands. One was a mining engineer named Duffield who left her a widow after a few short years of marriage. In 1890, she married a fellow gambler named Tubbs, whose name she retained until she died even

Poker Alice Tubbs in later life. (Author's collection.)

though she had one more husband (George Huckert) after Tubbs' demise. In 1908, Alice and Huckert bought a chicken farm where she lived for two years. But Alice soon became bored with life as a chicken farmer's wife and returned to the gambling tables. The Huckerts eventually opened a gambling casino between Fort Meade and Sturgis, South Dakota.

Alice spent the last ten years of her life residing at an Old Folks residence near her "home town" of Deadwood, and died at the age of 79.

In 1987, a made-for-television movie called *Poker Alice* gave a totally fictitious account of the celebrated lady gambler's life. The movie starred a glamorously gowned and coiffed Elizabeth Taylor as Alice. It began with Alice heading to New Orleans with her playboy cousin (George Hamilton). During a poker game on a train, Alice wins cash and a whorehouse from a fellow traveler and goes to a wild Western town to look over her newly won property, hoping to sell it. During the journey, she meets a bounty hunter (Tom Skerritt), falls in love with him and, as the last scene fades, rides off into the sunset to be married. Also appearing with Taylor were Liz Torres and Susan Tyrrell as prostitutes and Richard Mulligan as a competitor. Of course, none of these events ever actually happened; Poker Alice's real story, which was certainly more interesting than this bit of nonsense, has yet to be filmed.

KITTY LE ROY A.K.A. "KITTY THE SCHEMER"

Only one gambling lady in Deadwood rivaled Madame Mustache and Poker Alice Ivers as a card player and madam. That lady was Kitty Le Roy, who was known to citizens of Deadwood as "Kitty the Schemer." In the 1870s, several years before Alice descended upon Deadwood, Kitty (a beautiful faro dealer who was not above selling her body) reigned supreme among the town's gambling ladies. Unfortunately, Kitty did not enjoy Poker Alice's long life and, like many Westerners, died in her prime at the tender age of 28. A real Western lady wildcat, Kitty also enjoyed dressing up in men's clothing on occasion and shooting it out with prospective bridegrooms and husbands. Kitty was described as "a starry beauty" who had thick brown hair, "always adorned herself in colorful, gypsy-like dresses" and wore "numerous precious gems on her neck, wrists and fingers." During her brief life, she acquired no fewer than five husbands, several of whom lost their lives in shooting matches with her.

Little is known of Kitty's parentage or background. She first attracted the attention of the public when she was discovered dancing jigs in Dallas, Texas, for whatever money people would toss her way. Her jig-dancing was apparently good enough to be mentioned in a Dallas newspaper. By the time she was in her early teens, Kitty was dealing faro in the Dakotas and eventually in the Black Hills, deciding upon Deadwood as the site to build her own gambling parlor.

Kitty, whose gunslinging talents became famous throughout the area, met her end in a gunfight with her fifth husband, whom she challenged to a duel after a bitter argument. Her husband beat her to the draw, killed her and then shot himself in the head, "deeply distressed by his wife's death," according to the *Deadwood Dispatch*.

Kitty the Schemer, to her Deadwood rivals, she claimed that she was the highly respectable "Daughter of the Confederacy" and said that she had been "the queen" of the Barbary Coast gambling ladies in San Francisco before she came to Deadwood. When business in San Francisco waned, Kitty told people that she set sail for Hong Kong and then Yokohama, where she operated popular gambling halls. After her Orient adventures, Kitty said she went straight to Deadwood, which she heard was a promising place to practice her trade. Her reason for leaving the Orient, Kitty coyly admitted, was that she was running away from an Oriental gentleman who had "fallen madly in love" with her and wanted to make her his "white slave." When Madame Mustache heard Kitty's tale, she merely shrugged her shoulders and haughtily announced, "I have never had the honor to hear of Kitty the Schemer in California." She then openly accused Kitty of being "an obvious liar."

When author Duncan Aiken did research for his book *Calamity Jane and the Lady Wildcats*, he hoped to include information about Kitty and her San Francisco and Orient adventures, but he could find no mention of Kitty in any Frisco newspaper. No one in that city had ever heard of Kitty the Schemer. Madame Mustache was probably right in her evaluation of Ms. Le Roy.

TWO PROSTITUTES WITH HEARTS OF GOLD: ROSA (MOLLY) MAY (1867–1891) AND JULIA C. BULLETTE (1860?–1887)

Rosa (Molly) May and Julia C. Bullette were two "ladies on the line," as prostitutes who worked the West's mining camps were called. Both were admired and loved by local residents due to their many kindnesses to miners and their families who lived in the miserable mining camps and towns of Montana, Wyoming and Colorado.

Little is known about the early lives of these women. Rosa (Molly) May was reportedly born in "some Midwestern state" and arrived in Leadville, Colorado, at the height of the silver boom. She immediately pitched her tent and went to work at a mining camp, becoming very popular with the men. Rosa was well known for her patience and comforting ways. She would listen sympathetically to miners' tales of woe and showed great interest in the loved ones they had left at home. During the many epidemics that swept through the mining camps, Rosa May was always there to lend a helping hand, nursing the sick and comforting the dying. Her efforts on behalf of the miners and their families was greatly appreciated by the camp's inhabitants. When she became infected during a smallpox epidemic in 1870 and died, the miners and their wives openly displayed distress at her passing. Her gentle kindness and sweet nature inspired an anonymous poem which was published in *The Leadville Chronicle*:

Rosa "Molly" May. (Author's collection.)

> Talk if you will of her
> But speak no ill of her.
> The sins of the living are not of the dead.
> Remember her charity,
> Forget all disparity;
> Let her judge be they whom she
> sheltered and fed.

The other prostitute whose generosity became legendary among the miners in the camps of Montana was the beautiful mulatto who called herself Julia C. Bullette. Julia arrived in Virginia City, Montana,

Julia C. Bullette. (Author's collection.)

soon after the fabulous Comstock Lode was discovered in 1859. For a while, Julia was one of the few women selling her sexual services to miners in the booming gold and silver camps where hundreds of womenless men paid handsomely for female company. In three years, the pretty young woman had accumulated a small fortune, and it was said that one night she was paid as much as $1,000 for her company by a lonely miner who had struck it rich. Although rumor had it she was born in France, some of the miners who availed themselves of her services believed that Julia was from New Orleans and was a mulatto Creole. Whatever the truth concerning her origins was, one miner wrote to a friend, "Her skin may be dark, but her heart is white." At the time of her death, a local Virginia City newspaper reported that she had in truth been born in Liverpool, England, and that her birth name was "Julia Smith." None of these reported "facts" concerning Julia's origins have ever been definitely documented.

Julia's financial success in Virginia City enabled her to build a magnificent house with all the latest conveniences, including indoor plumbing. Located on "D" Street, the house was a rococo mansion which contrasted sharply with the other whores' shacks that surrounded it. Called "Julia's Place," her house became one of the most popular brothels in town. Like Madame Mustache, Julia would not tolerate raucous behavior at her establishment. She served only the finest French wines and the best of French cuisine. Julia and her girls wore beautiful clothes imported from Paris. Not one Virginia City resident ever resented her prosperity, however, because Julia was a generous-spirited and good-natured woman who stood by the miners and their families and helped them when they were in need. Julia's boom year was 1863, when Virginia City's population reached 30,000 and it became the largest city west of Chicago. Its red light district was larger than any other in the West.

One cold winter night, three men (their faces hidden from view) were seen knocking on Julia's door. About a half-hour later, they were seen leaving Julia's Place. Unknown to onlookers, however, was the fact that their pockets were filled with jewelry and money that they had stolen from Julia's house after they killed her. The next morning, Julia's girls (who had been given the evening off) found her body in her bedroom. The kindly madam had been brutally strangled.

Virginia City went into deep mourning for Julia C. Bullette. The mines, mills, saloons and other businesses shut down on the day she was buried, and thousands of people attended her funeral. It wasn't until one year later that one of her murderers was apprehended. After an anonymous tip to the local sheriff, a man named John Millain was arrested and many of Julia's jewels were found in his room. Millain admitted that he was involved in the robbery, but claimed that he did not participate in Julia's murder. Millain was placed on trial, found guilty of robbery and murder and hung on April 24, 1868. On the day of Millain's hanging,

Virginia City businesses again closed down as hundreds of people attended the public hanging, cheering wildly as the death door trap was sprung. City residents placed a white picket fence around Julia's grave because their gentle friend had always said that all she ever wanted in life was a small cottage with a flower garden and a pretty white picket fence around it. Her wish, or at least the fence part of it, had been granted.

There were many other Western prostitutes whose names are merely footnotes in the history books. Most of what is known about these women is anecdotal, but these anecdotes certainly give us insights into the West and its colorful shady ladies:

"CRAZY HORSE LIL"

An enterprising, full-blooded Indian woman, "Crazy Horse Lil" was the widow of a prospector who struck it rich in Colorado but had the misfortune to die shortly after he married Lil. His widow bought a saloon and house of pleasure in Tombstone, Arizona, which was said to have been one of the town's most popular drinking establishments. Lil attracted the attention of the press when her outlaw-boyfriend Con O'Shea was tracked down by a posse and killed by a lawman during a gunfight. (O'Shea had committed a series of brutal murders during a bank robbery which went wrong.) Instead of allowing her lover to be buried in the dismal Boot Hill cemetery on the outskirts of Tombstone, Lil insisted on giving him the biggest and best funeral the town had ever experienced.

Even the impressive funerals of the Clanton and McLaury boys (killed in Tombstone by the Earp brothers and Doc Holliday at the O. K. Corral) were nothing compared to Con O'Shea's elaborate funeral. The event was described in detail in most of the nation's newspapers, giving Crazy Horse Lil the 15 minutes of fame Andy Warhol said most people enjoy at least once in their lifetimes.

Crazy Horse Lil. (Author's collection.)

DORA HAND

One prostitute who worked in many of the West's celebrated towns was a beautiful faro dealer named Dora Hand. None of the numerous amateur portrait artists who painted the lovely Miss Hand seem to have captured the real beauty that contemporary reports claimed she possessed. But one can still see in these somewhat crude efforts traces of her physical appeal. Portraits of Dora hung over many bars in towns throughout the West, but no written information remains to confirm the fact there had ever actually been a gambling lady named Dora Hand. Unfortunately, Dora was killed by a jealous suitor in Dodge City when

Dora Hand. (Author's collection.)

she was still in her 20s. The young cowboy who shot her became upset when she chose to be the town sheriff's girlfriend. Lawman Bat Masterson tracked the young killer down and he was arrested, but because he was the son of well-to-do parents, he went unpunished.

AH TAY

Many artists traveled around the West and made meager livings by painting likeness of anyone who would pay them a few dollars or provide them with a meal or a bed for the night. One was a young man named William Arista. While he was visiting San Francisco in 1852, Arista availed himself of the services of a beautiful young Chinese prostitute named Ah Tay. The young artist fell madly in love with the delicate Oriental girl, who told him that she had been sold to a madam by her parents when they arrived in San Francisco to work on the railroad lines. They felt that they "would have one less mouth to feed," Ah Tay sadly told Arista. The artist painted Ah Tay's portrait and later claimed that when he returned to San Francisco a year

William Arista's portrait of Ah Tay. (Author's collection.)

or so later hoping to marry the girl, she was nowhere to be found. Arista kept her picture with him until he died in 1926, when it was sold to a junk dealer who found the story of Ah Tay handwritten and pasted on the back of the picture.

FANNY PORTER

Fanny Porter was an enterprising prostitute and madam who had a long and prosperous career in the Old West. At her peak, Fanny had a stable of over 20 girls working for her and serviced cowboys, farmers and outlaws throughout the West. After working in just about every well-known Western town, Fanny settled in San Antonio, Texas, where she owned and oper-

Fanny Porter. (Author's collection.)

ated a popular whorehouse for many years. Among Fanny's customers was the infamous Wild Bunch gang and its leader Butch Cassidy, who was said to be her lover at one time. Unlike the unfortunate Madame Mustache, Rosa May and Julia C. Bullette, who died in their primes, Fanny had the good fortune to lead a long life. When she died in the early 1930s, years after she retired from the whoring trade, none of her San Antonio neighbors knew anything about her sordid past. She was eulogized in local newspapers as "a pillar of society" and praised for her "many generous acts" on behalf of the community.

SEVERAL SUCCESSFUL COLORADO MADAMS

The most prosperous and longest-lasting of the West's celebrated whorehouse madams were the enterprising ladies of Denver, Colorado, many of whom continued to supply rest and relaxation (and sexual favors) to male citizens of that city as late as the 1930s. There was the elegant Mattie Silks, who wore only the finest of Parisian fashions and lived to be an old lady. Mattie spent all her hard-earned money on fine furnishings for her house of pleasure and on lovely gowns and lingerie for her girls and herself to wear, and had little left over to support herself in her old age.

Madam Jennie Rogers, whose real name was Leah J. Wood, operated what was reportedly "one of the finest, most lucrative brothels in Denver" during Colorado's gold and silver

Miss Mattie Silks. (Author's collection.)

boom days. Unlike Mattie Silks, Jennie saved her money while she was active in the business and died in the early 1940s, comfortably well off. When she died, she received considerable attention in the press when her husband A. T. Fitzgerald contested her will (which left him nothing of her considerable estate). The will stood, and Fitzgerald died several years later, an unhappy and poor man.

Colorado's two most successful madams were Laura Evans and "Diamond Lil" Powers. In spite of being in competition,

Portrait of Jennie Rogers. (Author's collection.)

these two women remained good friends until the late 1940s, when Evans died. Not much is known about Evans' background, but Lillian Powers (well known in Denver as "Diamond Lil") craved publicity and willingly granted interviews with newspapermen during her lifetime. She received an impressive two-column obituary in the *Rocky Mountain News* when she died in 1960 at the age of 87. Delighted whenever she was the center of attention, Diamond Lil eagerly discussed her life as a Colorado madam. Lil was born in 1871 and her real name is thought to have been Evelyn Hildergard. She operated pleasure palaces in half a dozen cities and mining camps in Colorado and Wyoming, but her most successful operation was in the city of Denver. During the glory days of Leadville and Salida, Lil had as many as a dozen girls who worked for her, shared their earnings with her and "helped brighten the night life of the towns they inhabited." Lil had arrived in Colorado when she was in her late teens "from some Midwestern farm state" seeking

"Diamond Lil" Powers. (Author's collection.)

excitement and the easy money that was to be had in the numerous mining camps. Her chosen profession took her to such places as Silver Cliff, Aspen, Fairplay, Crede and Cripple Creek, where she steadily increased her fortunes. Diamond Lil operated a whorehouse on Denver's Market Street, and it was from there that she established successful branch brothels in Leadville and Salida. Lil always boasted that she had "a kindly spot in [her] heart for all of [her] girls," and many a former worker who was past her prime and in need of help found it at Lil's place. "After all," Lil said in an interview, "this was a business where you had to make it in a few years."

In 1920, Lil moved to Florence, where she ran a successful brothel until 1950, when Fremont County's District Attorney John Stump Witcher closed down her establishment and put her out of business once and for all. The remaining ten years of Lil's life were spent in comfortable retirement. Few people in her Denver neighborhood knew anything about her past. Most of them believed the attractive, well-dressed old lady who lived in their midst was "some sort of a society lady" who "knew all sorts of famous people"—which indeed she had.

Ladies of Questionable Reputation as Depicted in Films and on TV

Few actresses portrayed ladies of easy virtue on the silver screen or on the stage better than the indomitable Mae West (1892–1980). Mae's tough-talking, hip-swaying characterizations became the prototype for numerous film saloon girls of the 1930s and '40s. Her censor-upsetting dialogue included such lines as, "Is that a gun in your pocket, or are you just glad to see me?" and "It's not the men in my life that counts, it's the life in my men." When a woman character remarked, "Goodness, what lovely diamonds you are wearing," Mae replied, "Goodness has nothin' to do with them!" This sort of dialogue helped bring about the infamous

Saloon scene from *Bella Union* (1912), an early Western silent. (Author's collection.)

Hays Office, censors who practically drove Mae out of the motion-picture business.

Mae fashioned her screen portrayals on the numerous actual Eastern and Western prostitutes she had befriended. Mae first appeared on the stage in 1912, when many of the West's most notorious ladies of the evening were still around. In the 1930s, West brought her inimitable persona to the silver screen and appeared in such Westerns as *She Done Him Wrong* (1933), *Belle of the Nineties* (1934), *Klondike Annie* (1936), *Go West, Young Man* (1935) and *My Little Chickadee* (1940).

One of the biggest box-office attractions that featured a saloon girl as a major character was *Destry Rides Again* (1939), which starred James Stewart as a gentle sheriff who tames a rowdy Western town and Marlene Dietrich as a tough saloon-owner. The film, directed by George Marshall, also featured Jack Carson, Charles Winninger and Irene Hervey and Una Merkel as two of the town's more respectable women. Dietrich's singing of "See

Mae West. (Author's collection.)

Marie Windsor. (Photofest.)

What the Boys in the Back Room Will Have" and her rough-and-tumble fight with Merkel, have become a part of filmdom's folklore.

Two actresses who probably played more saloon girl roles than anyone else in films were Marie Windsor and Ann Dvorak. Marie was featured in such Western films as *Romance of Rosy Ridge* (1947), *The Fighting Kentuckian* (1949), *Hellfire* (1949), *Dakota Lil* (1950), *Frenchie* (1950), *Outlaw Women* (1952), *Silver Star* (1954), *Two Gun Lady* (1955) and others. Dvorak appeared in *Way Out West* (1930), *Flame of the Barbary Coast* (1945), *Abilene Town* (1946), *The Return of Jesse James* (1950) and more.

Top: Ann Dvorak and John Wayne in *Flame of the Barbary Coast* (1945). (Photofest.) *Bottom:* One of the "girls on the line" in *McCabe and Mrs. Miller* (1971). (Author's collection.)

Probably the best-known fictional saloon girl, however, is Miss Kitty, Sheriff Matt Dillon's closest friend in Dodge City on the long-running radio (1952–1961) and television (1955–1975) series "Gunsmoke." On radio the role was played by Georgia Ellis and on television by Amanda Blake. Miss Kitty certainly typified the image most people have of the hard-as-nails tough girl with a heart of gold (which was usually worn on her sleeve).

In 1971, Robert Altman directed what is surely the most realistically gritty film ever made about prostitution in the Old West, *McCabe and Mrs. Miller*. The film, which centered around a small-time confidence man who goes into partnership with an experienced madam and sets up a bordello in a mining town, starred Warren Beatty and Julie Christie as the title characters. Featured in the supporting cast were Shelley Duvall, Michael Murphy, Keith Carradine, John Schuck and an unusual assortment of odd-shaped, down-to-earth-looking girls who played the "girls on the line."

Chapter Five

Remarkable Respectable Women
of the Western Frontier

Not all of the West's remarkable women were tomboys, criminals, performers or prostitutes. Most of the women on the western frontier were law-abiding, respectable citizens who tirelessly toiled as wives and mothers on the numerous farms and ranches or in the many shops and restaurants as clerks and waitresses, or as schoolteachers, cooks, laundresses, seamstresses, or maids. A few managed to become successful businesswomen and several owned large ranches and mines, but in the United States of that time, women still did not have the right to vote and in some areas were not even allowed to own property. This certainly limited their opportunities to be independent. Persevering and inventive women braved countless hardships during their long and arduous trips west, often fighting off bandits, Native Americans who considered them intruders, famine and disease. When they finally arrived at their destinations, they cleared the land on which they built their farms and ranches. It is these remarkable Western women whose lives will be chronicled in this chapter. The adventures that these women experienced were as varied as the areas which they chose to inhabit.

The Reed family consisted of an elderly woman, her daughter Margaret and her husband James, and their 13-year-old daughter Virginia and two young sons. The family decided to head west and establish a homestead, but tragedy struck during their journey and for a while the women were left entirely on their own. They not only eventually reached their destination, but established a successful cattle ranch. Flora Pearson Engle, who joined an expedition of prospective brides headed for the Washington Territory to wed bachelors in need of wives, married well and became one of Colorado's grand dames. Josephine Meeker, a 20-year-old graduate of Oberlin College, was captured by Ute Indians. Susan Shelby Magoffin, who was said to be the first white to travel the Santa Fe trail, did so in style, with silk sheets on her sleeping cot, a dressing bureau and a maid. Ann Eliza Young, a Mormon, married and then divorced Brigham Young and began a crusade for women's rights that lasted until she died. Also helping to settle the West were schoolteachers and missionaries such as Eliza Hart and Narcissa Whitman, who rode sidesaddle all the way from Independence, Missouri, to the Oregon Territory on their mission to serve God and save Indian souls. Soldiers' wives went to desolate outposts on the Western frontier with their husbands; one was Martha Summerhayes, who joined her husband when he was assigned to the hostile lands inhabited by the Apache Indians in Arizona. Martha managed to survive many ordeals traveling west, as well as the hardships of living in a remote and primitive corner of the earth. There were individualists like Annie Sokalski, who wore wolfskin riding clothes, traveled with 13 hunting dogs and went to support her soldier-husband when he was court-martialed at Fort Kearney.

Frances Grummond was a young Tennessee girl who married an army officer and only learned to cook after she joined her husband at an outpost in Wyoming. Her heart was broken when her young husband was killed by Indians during the famous Fetterman massacre. And there was Elizabeth, the loving wife of the celebrated General George Armstrong Custer. Elizabeth traveled all around the West with her beloved husband to whatever post his Army career took him, was close at hand in a nearby fort when Custer was killed at Little Big Horn and wrote detailed accounts about her life as an Army wife.

Women were in short supply in the Western United States of the nineteenth century. One very proper young lady from New England named Caroline Leighton toured the Pacific Northwest in the early 1860s and wrote home that she "had received such honors" from the miners in the region that she was afraid she might get "a very mistaken view of [her] importance" if she lived in such an area. "At every stopping place," she wrote, "the miners made little fires in their frying-pans, and set them around me to keep off the mosquitoes while I took my meal. As the column of smoke rose about me, I felt like a heathen goddess, to whom incense was being offered."

In addition to the wives of miners, ranchers, farmers and townsmen, there were several independent-minded single women who decided to leave the comforts of their Eastern environs for what homesteader Edith Ammons Kohl called "the wild adventure and enchantment of the West." One such woman was Abbie Bright. Abbie later wrote that she wanted to go west ever since she was a little girl because she "always had a desire to cross the Mississippi River and loved traveling." In a letter she wrote to family members back home, another independent woman homesteader, Martha Stoecker of Wyoming, said she originally went west after she received an invitation from her brother to visit him at his homestead in the Dakotas. When she arrived and saw the beauty and openness of the land, she decided that it would "be a thrill" to own some land of her own and staked out a claim for herself in Wyoming.

Once they established their claims, many single women found that homesteading involved a great deal of hard work, and most displayed remarkable strength and endurance as they maintained their properties and established homes for themselves. They learned how to use rifles, how to be enterprising and original in their search for food and how to become carpenters, wallpaperers and furniture makers while constructing their own homes.

In spite of the numerous difficulties these women pioneers faced, W. H. D. Koener, a prominent nineteenth century artist, painted what became the definitive portrait of the "ideal" pioneer woman. In their book *The Women's West*, Susan Armitage and Elizabeth Jameson described Koener's painting as follows:

> In this work a beautiful young woman with clear eyes and rouged cheeks, seated on a covered wagon, stares past the viewer into the land beyond. The canvas of the wagon forms a halo around her head... She holds the heavy black reins in delicate hands.

Lovely as it is, this was a highly romanticized portrait of a pioneer woman. But people back East did not want to see the raw-boned, often dirt-covered, weary women who made the trek west. The everyday lives of pioneer women left them little time to "gaze fondly" at the pastoral splendor of their habitats, though there is no question that these women loved their new homes or they would have headed straight back East. Their "rouged" faces, however, were reddened from the cold, biting wind and blinding sun. Their "delicate hands" were callused from hours of toil and struggle and the "hope" in their eyes had in all probability turned into the apprehensive look of a person who does not know what the future held.

One need only read about the horrific events endured by members of the Donner Party to appreciate the hardships and horrors many women headed west often faced. The experiences of the Donner Party (a group of pioneers traveling to California in 1847) included spending a seemingly endless winter stranded in the snow-covered foothills of the Sierra Mountains without food—some resorting to cannibalism in order to survive. This was well publicized when word reached civilization about their trials and made the Donner Party survivors subjects of suspicion and curiosity.

One survivor of the Donner tragedy, Virginia Reed, was a 13-year-old girl who not only managed to live through the ordeal, but wrote about it to warn people about the perils and hardships faced by travelers going West. Virginia's father James Frazier Reed, his wife Margaret, his mother-in-law "Granny" Keyes and his four children set off from Springfield, Illinois, in April 1846 on their journey to California, where the family hoped to resettle. A prominent family in Springfield, the Reeds were given a big send-off by citizens of the town; guests at their *bon voyage* party included Mary Todd Lincoln (whose husband was a prominent Springfield attorney at the time) and her son Robert, who was one of Virginia's classmates at school. The Reeds traveled in an elaborate, two-story wagon filled with luxuries like a four-poster bed for Granny Keyes, porcelain toilets and wash basins, James Reed's extensive library of books, various pieces of expensive furniture and trunks filled with clothing. The Reeds crossed the Missouri territory and were on the Kansas plains when tragedy first struck. Granny Keyes died and was buried under a large tree on the Kansas prairie.

While stocking up on supplies at Fort Laramie, James Reed decided to join a California-bound wagon train led by a man named George Donner. Unfortunately, Donner proved to be an inept guide and, on their way to the Great Salt Lake, the group became lost in the desert. The party's oxen began to die for lack of water, and their food supply diminished after a month of wandering about the desert. By the time the group reached the foothills of the Sierra Mountains, it was late September and the winter snows had already begun to fall, making it too late for the travelers to attempt to cross the mountains. Tempers began to surface, and James Reed killed a man named John Snyder in self-defense during an argument. Reed was ordered to leave but was encouraged to let his family remain with the party to give them a better chance of survival, which he decided was the proper thing to do. Reed said good-bye to his family, promised them that they would soon be reunited and left.

Donner ultimately decided that the group would try to cross the Sierras, even though winter was upon them. The group soon found it impossible to go on because of deep snow. They found small abandoned shacks scattered about the foothills and decided to split up, the Reeds living in one shack and the Donner family and others settling a considerable distance away on the shores of the lake.

By November, the entire group was facing starvation. Virginia recalled eating field mice and their slaughtered oxen, and eventually boiling the oxen hides for nourishment. The Donners and the travelers living near them were apparently less resourceful than the Reeds and resorted to eating the frozen bodies of their dead comrades when their food supply ran out.

James Reed eventually reached the safety of Sutter's Fort and immediately organized a search party. In February 1847, the search party found Margaret Reed and her children. They also found the few survivors of Donner's camp and learned of the horrors that had taken place there (one of the Donner women was murdered to provide meat for a survivor who had begun to prefer human flesh as food). One month after her ordeal ended, Virginia Reed wrote a letter to her cousin in Springfield from her new home in California. In her letter she wrote, "There were three died and the rest eat them, they were ten without anything to eat but the Dead" [*sic*].

The remainder of Virginia Reed's life was spent in relative comfort. An attractive, lively girl and an expert equestrienne, Virginia married an Army officer named John Murphy who

Survivors of a massacre by a Native American tribe at Lake Shetak, Minnesota. (Library of Congress.)

later became a successful real estate developer. When Murphy lost his eyesight in an accident, Virginia took over his business, and the Murphys continued to prosper because of her determination to survive.

NATIVE AMERICAN WOMEN

Unlike the legendary warrior women of European folklore and history, Native American women were not known to have been participants in battle. The Indian way of life was more closely allied to that of the Far East (Asia), where women were mainly responsible for the domestic affairs of their communities. Unlike Asian women, however, Indian women were considered equal in importance to males and could freely speak their minds. Only Sacajawea and perhaps Pocahontas, the daughter of the Indian chief Powhatan, distinguished themselves as leaders of a kind. A Native American woman who lived in Minnesota and was known only as "Old Bet" did gain a certain fame when she saved several settlers from being massacred by hostile Indians at Lake Shetak, Minnesota, in the late 1800s.

Sacajawea (1786?–1812), also called "Bird Woman," led the American explorers Meriwether Lewis (1774–1809) and William Clark (1770–1838) into uncharted regions of the Northwestern United States and guided them through her native Shoshoni country, which few white men had ever seen. She proved herself invaluable to the Lewis and Clark Expedition not only as a guide, but also as a translator.

When she was a girl of 12, Sacajawea was abducted by members of the rival Hidatsa tribe and sold into slavery to a French fur trader. She was subsequently won during a card game by a fur-trapper named Toussaint Charbonneau. Charbonneau fell in love with his lovely young Indian "possession" and married her in a proper Indian ceremony. It was Charbonneau who was originally hired by Lewis and Clark to guide and interpret for them during their exploration, but Sacajawea ultimately proved more helpful. While the party was visiting the Mandan Indian village in the autumn of 1805, Sacajawea gave birth to a son, so the group decided to remain with the Mandans until spring arrived and the child would be strong enough to travel. Charbonneau did not feel that he was physically able to continue to act as the expedition's guide since he had been ill most of that winter. Sacajawea decided to fulfill her husband's commitment to Lewis and Clark and take over his duties. She led the group through her native Shoshoni country, an area which included the vast Rocky Mountain chain. Quite by accident, she was reunited with her brother Cameahwait, whom she had not seen since her abduction as a child. The expedition was badly in need of new horses and other supplies which Sacajawea managed to obtain for them with her brother's help. Rather than desert Lewis and Clark and stay with her own people, Sacajawea decided to remain with the expedition. Led by this stalwart woman, the party crossed the Continental Divide through the Lemki Pass, went north following the Salmon River and then down the Bitterroot Valley until they reached the mouth of Lola Creek, near what is now Missoula, Montana. They then followed the Clearwater, Snake and Columbia Rivers until they eventually reached the Pacific coast. The expedition then headed back east, reaching the Mandan village where Sacajawea rejoined her husband. One report claims that the Bird Woman died while giving birth to a second child when she was 22 years old, but according to another account she died at the age of 94 on an Indian reservation in Wyoming in 1884. Neither report has ever been confirmed, but Sacajawea's contribution to the early exploration and the subsequent development of the untamed West is unquestionable and she remains a great American legend.

A detailed account of Sacajawea's early life and of the time she spent with the Lewis and Clark Expedition can be found in the book *Sacajawea*, which was written by Harold P. Howard and published in 1971.

Unlike Sacajawea, who was immortalized because a Euro-American recorded her adventures with the Lewis and Clark Expedition, most Native American women's lives were rarely written about. Only occasionally did an anthropologically minded historian come upon a Native American woman who was willing to talk about her life, and subsequently wrote down what they were told. One such writer-historian, Ruth Underhill, met an Indian woman named Maria Chona, who had lived in Arizona throughout the latter half of the nineteenth century and died at the age of 90. Maria told Underhill about her amazing life, which was typical of the lives led by numerous Native American women throughout the North American continent.

Maria Chona began her oral account by simply saying, "I was born there, on the land." To her biographer, who recorded her exact words, this was the essence of how most Native Americans seemed to view their place in the world in general. Human beings, Native Americans believed, were simply one part of the much-larger earth and the even bigger universe in which they lived. The land and the people, therefore, were one.

Maria Chona told her memories to Underhill, who later had them published in a book which credited Chona as author and herself as "editor." In this autobiography, Maria gave numerous descriptions of the ceremonies, songs and "curing" rituals she remembered, as well as the everyday events she experienced as a Native American woman living in the West.

When she was a young woman, Maria married a young medicine man who took her with him from tribe to tribe to perform various ceremonies as he practiced his faith healing and herb dispensing. In addition to the "happy times" she remembered as the wife of a respected tribal medicine man, there were also many sorrows. Several of her children died in infancy and hunger was a constant threat, especially as the white man began to encroach upon the Indian's hunting grounds. But Maria accepted both the happy times and the hardships of life as part of what had been dealt to her by the forces of nature. She told Underhill that her first child arrived at a totally unexpected time that she had to deliver the baby herself. Her sister-in-law later asked her why she had not warned her family that she was about to give birth and allowed them to assist. "We didn't know you were suffering in there," her sister-in-law said. "We heard you laughing." Maria answered, "Well, it wasn't my mouth that hurt. It was my middle."

Maria was also a very creative woman whose talents as a storyteller and singer of songs did not go unnoticed or unappreciated by members of her tribe. "I did not go into the desert [where Indian braves proved their manhood while in young adolescence] as my brother and husband did, because I was a woman," she told Underhill. "Besides, I had no time. I had to work! But in those days I used to see things around me that no one else saw. Once a song came to me. I cannot tell you when it came, but I think it was when I was very little. You see, I came from a singing family. It is natural for us to see strange things and to make a song."

When her medicine man-husband decided to take a second wife, the independent Maria admitted that she was heartbroken and decided, in the Indian manner, to divorce him by placing his belongings outside their dwelling.

> Most men did not take two wives with us then but medicine men always did. In fact they sometimes took as many as four. But I had never thought my husband would do it. You see, we married so young, even before I had really become a maiden. It was as if we had been children in the same house. I had grown fond of him. We had starved so much together.

For many years Maria endured being moved from one reservation to another by the United States government and constantly faced starvation. She lost several of her children, family members and friends because of the miserable conditions and diseases they were forced to endure. These trials, however, apparently never turned Maria into a bitter woman. She simply accepted everything that happened to her, both the good and the bad, with quiet and dignified reserve. This, however, did not mean that she did not occasionally become discouraged with her life.

> Once I was digging roots to eat and I got very tired. I made a pile of earth with my digging stick, put my head on it and lay down to sleep for good. In front of me was a hole in the ground made by the rains, and there hung a gray spider, going up and down, up and down, on its long thread. I began to go to sleep and I said to it, "Won't you fall?" Then the spider sang to me, and when it finished its song, I got up.

When asked by Underhill if she had ever become angry because she was a woman in a male-dominated society, Maria indignantly replied, "We *have* power! Men have to dream to get power from the spirits and they think of everything they can—song and speeches and marching around, hoping that the spirits will notice them and give them some power. But we *have* power! Children! Can any warrior make a child, no matter how brave and wonderful he is?"

ENTERPRISING WOMEN OF THE WEST

One woman who went west to fulfill her American dream lived a life that reads more like the scenario for a movie than anyone's actual life. The woman's name was Loreta Velasquez. Loreta masqueraded as a man during the Civil War, taking her soldier-husband's place in the Army when he was killed in battle. She gained national attention when her secret was discovered and she was discharged from military service. Velasquez then headed west hoping to find a new husband and a new life for herself. She resumed wearing feminine attire and arrived in Omaha, Nebraska, without a dollar to her name in 1865. Loreta managed, however, to charm an affluent Omaha businessman named Colonel W. S. Harney, who was intrigued with her past life. Harney gave Loreta a buffalo robe, blankets and a gun so that she could continue her journey westward to the mining regions of Nevada, where she hoped to either find employment or a rich prospector-husband.

In an interview, Loreta later said that while she was en route to Nevada, she stopped at the Cheyenne House hotel. She described the place as being "the worst hotel I had ever met in the course of my rather extensive travels." She went on to describe it as "a crudely constructed wooden frame building... The bedrooms were separated by sheets of canvas that did not allow for any privacy. Double mattressed bunk beds with pillows and mattresses made out of old flour bags and stuffed with straw, were all that was supplied by the management, and if a guest at the hotel did not have a blanket of his own when he arrived, he would have to make due [*sic*] with one of the thin army issue coverings that were on the beds, which were hardly sufficient to keep off the cold. One small pot-bellied stove heated the entire sleeping area of the hotel and the customers were mostly blaspheming, tobacco-smoking and chewing males who spat on the floor."

The worst thing about her stay at the Cheyenne hotel, Loreta said, was that she had to share her bed with a stranger "who happily happened to be another woman, albeit a drunkard who thankfully slept soundly the entire night," unlike Loreta. "The woman," Loreta said, "seemed totally unaware of the crawling vermin that covered the bed." Two days later, Loreta arrived in Austin, Nevada, and the very next day, she received her first proposal of marriage from an old, woman-starved cattleman. Mrs. Velasquez declined his proposal, believing that since he had been quick to offer his hand in marriage, a younger, more attractive suitor would soon be found. A few days later she met a younger, better-looking gentleman, married him and moved into his newly constructed ranch house.

Another ambitious woman who made her fortune out West was Bridget Grant, who selected one of the most remote areas of the post–Civil War Western frontier—the Oregon territory on the Pacific coast—as the place to seek her slice of the American pie. Bridget, an Irish immigrant, did not make her mark in any of the usual Western ways, or even in an area that is usually associated with the Western frontier. Her contribution to Western commerce was as a boarding house owner in Astoria, Oregon on the Pacific Ocean.

Bridget was born in Ireland in 1831. When she was barely out of her teens, she met Peter Grant, a handsome young fishing-ship skipper from Prince Edward Island in Canada. The two were married and returned to Canada, but decided to sell his fishing boat and move to Gloucester, Massachusetts, where they bought a boarding house for sailors. This venture proved to be far more lucrative than fishing, and the Grants prospered. When the Civil War ended in 1865, Peter and Bridget decided to migrate west to the Pacific coast, where they heard fishing and shipping was a fast-growing industry.

The Grants opened another boarding house for sailors in San Francisco and operated it for one year, then headed north to open another in Astoria, Oregon. The area was known for its impressive catches of salmon and as an important shipping port for the lumber business and the many mines in the territory. Bridget thought that Astoria was a perfect place to establish their new boarding house for sailors, since it was a place where many sailors who jumped ship hid from the shipowners they had contracted to serve. As the shrewd Grants had anticipated, these men soon found themselves without money and Peter and Bridget acted as their agents, finding them employment with other shipowners. For their agenting services, the Grants earned handsome fees for each sailor they delivered into the hands of shipowners.

Just when things were beginning to look up financially for the Grants (whose union produced nine children) Peter was drowned when he became entangled in fishing gear and fell off the dock near his boarding house. Bridget, 40 years old at the time, suddenly found herself a widow with a house full of children to support all by herself. In spite of her grief, Bridget did not mourn for long, firmly taking charge of the family business, determined to survive and prosper. An illiterate, Bridget made sure that her children were well educated and she even encouraged her three daughters to become schoolteachers (which they did). Her six sons, Bridget decided, would go into the family's boarding house business; they (like her daughters) dutifully adhered to her wishes. The family business continued to prosper under Bridget's careful and determined guidance. In addition to providing her children with training and experience that would enable them to make their way in the world, Bridget also encouraged them to "shun liquor and all rowdy pleasures" and "to always be true to [their] promises."

Portland was a long way from home for sailors from foreign and Eastern United States ports, and it must be remembered that there was no Panama Canal to shorten sea voyages. Sailors encountered unregulated discipline and unrestrained brutality while at sea, prompting many of them to jump ship.

This fact obviously offered certain advantages to the Grants and other boarding house owners as far as the sailor-recruiting business was concerned. Boarding house owners would attempt to convince deserters that it was in their best interest to return to sea once their money began to run out. When sailors were reluctant, boarding house owners often enlisted the aid of a strong-arm boarder or two to "convince" the sailors to ship out as soon as possible. As Bridget's well-muscled young sons Jack, Peter and Ulysses grew into manhood, they took over the strong-arm end of the family business. They were later joined by Bridget's three younger sons Alexander, Ignatius and William, all fine specimens of sturdy manhood.

Bridget was eventually able to expand her business and bought other boarding houses in Astoria. She also purchased a large dwelling in Portland and placed her eldest son Jack in charge of the boarding house operation in that town.

Bridget and her sons operated their successful businesses throughout the 1890s and well into the early 1900s. When she was 74 in 1905, Bridget was forced into retirement when the U.S. government decided it could exert "a better guardianship" over the "welfare of the sailors of Oregon," which by then had become a state. The U.S. government placed the whole sailor-employment problem into the hands of an agency.

Bridget left Astoria and retired to her farm on Young's River, living out the remaining years of her life in comfort. While in retirement, she took in many down-on-their-luck sailors and fed and housed them until they could get on their feet again. Her ever-increasing family frequently congregated at the farm, and Bridget cooked and cleaned up after her large brood of children, grandchildren, great-grandchildren, and even great-great grandchildren, until she died in her ninety-second year in 1923.

Newspapers had little good to say about Bridget Grant's passing, believing that her fortune had been questionably established on what was commonly called "shanghaiing sailors for profit." One Portland newspaper reported that she "received as much as $175 a man for delivering each sailor into servitude when her business was at its peak." An old waterfront friend said, however, "She was a great lady and a friend whom I honor. I would not be a party to anything that would make people who do not know the sea or the people of the sea, hold any thought that would belittle her." This was apparently said in response to the growing criticism of Bridget's activities. Whatever her business practices were, there is no question but that Bridget Grant was a remarkable woman at a time when to merely exist, much less make a success of one's life, was a challenge.

Another of the West's legendary innkeepers was Katrina Murat, who claimed that she was "the first white woman to settle in Denver, Colorado." Katrina was born in 1830 in Germany, where her father was a well-to-do winemaker. She immigrated to the United States in 1848 with her young husband, who died shortly after the couple arrived. In 1859, Katrina, her second husband Henri Murat with a man named David Smoke opened a hotel and restaurant called "The Elderado" in Aurania, Colorado, a mining camp near Denver. The hotel was less than luxurious: It was a roughly constructed, drafty and poorly furnished place, but Katrina's food was said to be "very fine indeed." In addition to cooking for the hotel's restaurant, Katrina also served as chambermaid and laundress. Henri took care of the bartending chores and both he and Smoke (who also worked as the hotel's janitor and handyman) served meals to the customers. The Elderado's main claim to fame, besides Katrina's wonderful cooking, seems to be that newspaperman Horace Greeley (who had urged his readers to "go west, young man") was once a guest at the hotel.

Unfortunately, the Murats did not make a go of it in Aurania and decided to cut their losses and move into Denver where they bought a combination restaurant-barber shop. Once again it was Katrina's good cooking that attracted the most attention, not Henri's haircuts. Before long, everyone in Denver was talking about Katrina's fantastic homemade noodles, coffee cake, wiener schnitzel, German pot roast and herring salad. Eventually the Murats saved enough money to sell their business and take a trip to California, and then to Germany. When they ran out of money in Europe, they returned to the United States and opened a first-class Virginia City, Montana, restaurant which they called "The Continental." Their restaurant became famous for serving French champagne and homemade ice cream as well as Continental gourmet treats such as caviar and mushroom soup. Again, their restaurant became very popular and they were rewarded with an ever-growing bank account. Katrina's pies were "the finest in all the West," according to a local newspaper article. People would travel to Virginia City from hundreds of miles away just to sample Katrina's baked goods and ice cream specialties. After saving $10,000, Katrina and Henri sold the business and moved back to Denver, planning to retire. Unfortunately, the couple lived well beyond their means, and by 1870, they once again found themselves out of money. The Murats died destitute (Henri in 1885 and Katrina in 1910) at the Pioneer Old Folk's Home, but memories of their legendary restaurants lived on in the minds of people fortunate enough to have enjoyed Katrina's fine cooking.

Women like Bridget Grant and Katrina Murat made their fortunes in pursuits then considered "feminine": cooking and keeping house. Renowned Westerner Nellie Cashman dabbled (and succeeded) in those arts as well, but she amassed her fortune—which was considerable—through less traditional means.

Born in Ireland in 1854, Nellie easily rivaled Calamity Jane for sheer individualism and independence, but with far less destructive results. According to her sister, Nellie had always been a nonconformist. She never married and over a 50-year period traveled all around the

Nellie Cashman. (Author's collection.)

West, from Mexico to Alaska, as well as abroad. Nellie prospected for precious metals and worked at various jobs that were not usually performed by women. Unlike Calamity Jane, however, Nellie made a fortune for her labors and was a living legend because of her financial success. Her philanthropic deeds earned her the nicknames "Frontier Angel," "The Angel of Tombstone," "The Miner's Angel" and "The Saint of the Sourdoughs." Nellie made several rich strikes while mining for gold and silver and operating various mining businesses. Most of the money she accumulated she gave away to those she felt were less capable of taking care of themselves. She contributed large sums to various hospitals and church missions, and she personally nursed, fed, clothed and cared for hundreds of less-fortunate miners, earning the reputation of "the best woman in the West."

Nellie and her sister Frances immigrated to the United States from Ireland in 1860 when Nellie was in her late teens. The sisters first settled in Boston, where Nellie found employment in a hotel as a bellhop and messenger, a job she was able to obtain because the Civil War "was using up most of the country's young men." In 1869, the transcontinental railroad was completed and the Cashman sisters bought one-way tickets to San Francisco. Shortly after they arrived, Frances met and married a Mr. Cunningham and began to raise a large family.

In 1872, Nellie left San Francisco and went to Virginia City, Montana, where she became a cook in a short order restaurant. In 1874, when she 20 years old, Nellie joined the large number of people heading north to British Columbia, Canada, where gold had been discovered, and became a prospector. She found gold and made her first fortune, subsequently using her profits to open a boarding house for other prospectors. In 1880 Nellie went to Arizona's rip-roaring town of Tombstone, where she operated the Russ House hotel and served what residents called the best meals in town. According to one long-time Tombstone resident Nellie's place became as much a Tombstone landmark as the Old Birdcage Saloon and Theater and the O.K. Corral. Nellie was friendly with the Earps in Tombstone and was in residence during the famous corral gunfight. She was very fond of Virgil Earp, his wife Allie, and Wyatt's mistress-wife Mattie, but not particularly fond of Wyatt or Josie Earp, who she regarded as "arrogant and stuck-up." Even though her Tombstone hotel was prospering, the ever-restless Nellie decided to sell it and in 1883, with 20 other prospectors, traveled to Mulage, a town on Mexico's Baja, California, peninsula, to pan for gold. Again she "found a few nuggets," according to Nellie.

In the late 1880s, Nellie traveled east and crossed the Atlantic Ocean on a cargo ship, eventually arriving in South Africa where she began searching for diamonds. Her usual luck held and she did manage to find a few gems. But by 1895, Nellie had grown homesick and returned to the United States and her "beloved West." Nellie Cashman's adventures made her a national celebrity and the *Arizona Star* proudly announced, "Yesterday Tucson was visited by one of the most extraordinary women in America, Nellie Cashman, whose name and face have been familiar in every important mining camp or district on the coast for more than 20 years. She rode into Tucson from Casa Grande on horseback, a jaunt that would have nearly prostrated an average man with fatigue. Nellie showed no sign of weariness, however, after the journey, and went about town in her usual calm, businesslike manner that belongs particularly to her." Nellie was in her mid–40s at this time.

In 1898, Nellie packed her suitcases and once again took to the road, traveling north to the Klondike to pan for gold. Her reputation preceded her: When she entered a hotel upon her arrival, every man in the place stood up in her honor. Once again, Nellie struck it rich, staking a claim that eventually brought her more than $10,000. She spent the money buying other miners' claims and continued to prosper. As she approached the end of her life, Nellie said in an interview with an Eastern newspaper, "You never quite know what's going to happen next, or when your time will come to cash in your checks. It all adds interest and variety to life." Nellie Cashman had certainly lived a life that was both "interesting" and "varied" by the time she died shortly after World War One began. She accomplished more in any single year of her life than most people do in their entire lifetimes.

The West provided unusual business opportunities. One enterprising, independent-minded New York woman went West and became a successful businesswoman supplying wives for miners in California. Her name was Elizabeth Farnham. Elizabeth was a prison matron in New York City before she headed for San Francisco where her husband Thomas had previously gone to establish a dry goods business. Unfortunately, Thomas died before Elizabeth could join him. When she finally arrived in Frisco to settle her husband's estate, she found his affairs in a deplorable state and decided to remain to attempt to salvage what she could of her husband's business. While there, Elizabeth became aware of the severe shortage of women in the area and decided to do something about it. She went back to New York and published a circular that stated:

> "Wanted: Women to Go West! It is proposed that this company shall consist of persons not under twenty-five years of age, who shall bring from their clergymen, or some authority of the town where they reside, satisfactory testimonials of education, character, capacity, etc., and who can contribute the sum of two hundred and fifty dollars, to defray the expenses of the voyage, make suitable provisions for their accommodation after reaching San Francisco, until they shall be able to enter upon some occupation for their support, and create a fund to be held in reserve for the relief of any who may be ill, or otherwise need aid before they are able to provide for themselves [by getting married]. It is believed that such arrangement, with one hundred or one hundred and thirty persons, would enable the company to purchase a vessel, and fit it up with everything necessary for comfort on the voyage, and that the combination of all for the support of each, would give such security, both as to health, person, and character, as would remove all reasonable hesitation from the minds of those who may be disposed and able to join such a mission. It is intended that the party shall include six or eight respectable married men and their families...
>
> The New York built packet ship Angelique has been engaged to take out this Association... She will be ready to sail from New York about the 12th or 15th of April.

Elizabeth managed to obtain the endorsement of such notable New Yorkers as news-paperman Horace Greeley, lawyer William Cullen Bryant and educator-writer Henry Ward Beecher for her venture. Two hundred women answered her circular, but Elizabeth became ill and could not answer their replies. Only three women joined her on her first trip back to San Francisco. Her project, however, became widely talked about throughout the West; an entry in a journal written by one California miner stated, "Went to church three times today. A few ladies present. It does my eyes good to see women once more. Hope Mrs. Farnham will bring 10,000." That is indeed what she eventually did. Mrs. Farnham's second recruitment trip was more successful; each subsequent trip brought increasing numbers of women to the West and increased Elizabeth's fortunes in the process.

REAL LIFE "MEDICINE WOMEN"

In the latter half of the nineteenth century, many well-educated women wanted to become physicians. The male-dominated Eastern medical establishment, however, discouraged women from entering this profession and refused to admit them into their closed fraternal orders. Many of the ladies who earned medical degrees migrated West, where they felt the citizenry would be less inclined to reject their services due to the lack of medical practitioners on the frontier. In 1870, Dr. Sarah Hall began practicing medicine at Fort Scott, Kansas, where she specialized in women's and children's diseases with little resistance from the public. A few years later, Dr. Charlotte Brown founded the Pacific Dispensary for Women and Children in California.

One of the most remarkable lady doctors of the Western frontier was Bethenia Owens (1849–1910?). Dr. Owens certainly rivaled television's fictional "Dr. Quinn, Medicine Woman" in determination and resolve. Born in Roseberg, Oregon, Dr. Owens was one of nine children born to well-off middle-class parents. In 1859, Bethenia married a man named Leonard Hall, but she soon became disillusioned with his male chauvinism. After giving birth to a son, she asked him to give her a divorce. Hall was no more satisfied with Bethenia's "unwomanly" behavior and desire to "make something" of herself than she was with his narrow-mindedness, and he unhesitatingly agreed to the divorce. Bethenia went to work as a laundress in order to support herself and her son without any help from Hall, but soon became a nurse for a Roseberg doctor. By 1861 she had saved enough money to buy a small cottage in Astoria, Oregon, where she began a millinery business. By the time her son had grown into young adulthood, Bethenia had managed to put enough money aside to send him to medical school, a goal she always had for herself and instilled in her son as well. With her son well on his way to becoming a physician, Bethenia decided it was time to do something about her own medical ambitions. She sold her house and went to work as a nurse for an elderly doctor. When the old physician physically hurt a child he was treating, Bethenia brashly took over the child's treatment and brought him instant relief. It was at that moment that she decided it was time to begin her studies and become a doctor. She enrolled at the Philadelphia Eclectic School of Medicine, which was not one of the country's best medical schools, but readily admitted women. After she graduated, Bethenia stopped in Roseberg on her way to Portland, where she hoped to open a practice of her own. Roseberg's medical professionals, disturbed at the idea of a female physician in their midst, decided to invite her to attend an autopsy, hoping that she would either turn their invitation down or be dissuaded from pursuing her practice after witnessing the dissection. To their surprise, Bethenia accepted their invitation. When Dr. Palmer, a young medical student, said that he thought it was "improper" for a lady to attend the autopsy of a male cadaver, Dr. Owens replied, "I came here by written invitation, and I will leave it to a vote whether I stay or not. But I would like to ask Dr. Palmer what is the difference between the attendance of a woman at a male autopsy, and the attendance of a man at a female autopsy?" The young doctor departed in a huff, and the other doctors voted to allow Dr. Owens to remain.

Instead of going on to Portland, Dr. Owens remained in Roseberg and set up her practice in her hometown. One of her reasons was that her brother was a Roseberg resident and she felt that he would be able to run interference for her if townspeople resisted her presence in their town. Dr. Owens' practice did not exactly flourish in Roseberg, and after a year she moved to Portland, a far less conservative community, and set up practice there. Before long, the number of patients who sought her treatment increased and she began to prosper. In 1879, Bethenia decided that she wanted to further her medical education and enrolled at the University of Michigan. When she completed her studies, Dr. Owens went on a tour of European medical training centers, and then returned to Portland in 1881. Bethenia was then 40 years old and at the height of her career, earning $7000 a year (a great deal of money for a woman of the 1880s). Bethenia eventually remarried and slowly but surely established herself as one of the most respected physicians in the Northwestern United States. Bethenia retired at 65 and began to enjoy the hard-won fruits of her labors. She had fought a long battle against prejudice and injustice and had triumphed.

THE HARVEY GIRLS: RESPECTABLE WAITRESSES FOR THE WEST'S RESTAURANTS

One way for an unmarried young woman to support herself in the West was to become a waitress. There were two kinds of waitresses out West in the years following the Civil War: the so-called "pretty girls" who served drinks (and often themselves) to men and the "good girls" who worked in respectable restaurants. The best known of the West's "good girl" waitresses were the celebrated Harvey Girls who worked for the Fred Harvey restaurant chain. Harvey's restaurants were located at or near train stations along the Atchison, Topeka and Santa Fe Railroad lines and the girls who worked for him came from good families and had high morals. The Harvey restaurants (founded by Harvey in 1876) were known throughout the West for serving good, wholesome food and beverages and for providing a clean and decent atmosphere. At the height of their popularity, there were over 40 restaurants in Harvey's chain, as well as 54 lunchrooms and 50 dining cars in localities that stretched from the Great Lakes to the Pacific Ocean. Because he recruited decent young women for his restaurants, Harvey was also providing many men with good, hard-working wives in the process.

Harvey required that his girls be strong, healthy, independent, hard-working and morally beyond reproach. He recruited young women from such places as New York City, Chicago and even from several Pacific coast cities and towns. The girls were required to reside near their places of employment in company-owned dormitories. One Harvey waitress, Joan Thompson, remembered getting up at five A.M. on the morning of her wedding day in order to serve passengers who were arriving on a westbound train. Laura White, who worked in Harvey's Gallop, New Mexico, restaurant, recalled a day when she served three companies of soldiers, the regular train passengers and the residents of the town. "By ten o'clock at night all of us were walking in a daze," Laura reported. "We would climb the stairs and throw ourselves across the bed, clothes and all—Oblivion—never longer than a minute, it seemed—then we heard the dreaded callboy marching down the hall. 'Four o'clock,' he'd cry. 'Five hundred marines for breakfast this morning!' Wearily, we would pull ourselves together off the beds, put on clean aprons, brush our hair, and start all over again."

Fred Harvey preferred hiring inexperienced girls. The girls began their training with a week or two serving food and beverages in Harvey's smaller units. They were then transferred to the more important restaurants in the chain. A waitress was contracted to work for a maximum of six months, and was given transportation to and from work (if required), a place to sleep and all of her meals. Every six months each waitress was entitled to a month's vacation.

The Harvey girls were uniformed in crisp, clean black dresses, bright white aprons and a white cap to keep their hair away from their faces and their customers' food. Their appearance was in sharp contrast to the "pretty girl" waitresses who usually wore gaudy gowns with feathers and beads and had rouged lips and cheeks. They sometimes served their customers topless and, in some of the more lurid establishments, wore nothing beneath their waist.

The Harvey girls' pay was quite adequate for the time. During its earliest days, the girls earned $17.50 a month plus room and board. The pay increased, of course, the longer the girls stayed with the chain. By the time the Harvey restaurants served their last meals in the early 1960s, waitresses were earning $150 plus tips.

WOMEN ARTISTS AND WRITERS

Visitors to the United States Centennial Exhibition of 1876 (held in Philadelphia) saw a breathtaking display that was labeled "Woman's Work." Hundreds of animals that had been shot and mounted in lifelike positions by naturalist/hunter/taxidermist/artist Martha Maxwell were displayed in front of a painted Western landscape. Maxwell, who became known as "The Colorado Huntress," was an expert markswoman and obviously possessed hunting skills that were extraordinary for a woman.

Martha was ten years old and living in Wisconsin when she first picked up a gun and killed a rattlesnake that was preparing to strike at her four-year-old sister. Martha practiced her sharpshooting until her reputation spread all across Wisconsin. In 1860, when she was 20, Martha married James Maxwell and moved to Colorado, where her young husband had bought a lumber mill. Martha was dazzled by the area's abundant wildlife, and after seeing the work of a local taxidermist she decided she wanted to learn his art so that she could preserve some of the animals she had shot. She accompanied her husband and his friends on various hunting trips to the Rocky Mountains, carefully observing the movements and living environments of animals and birds. The earliest examples of her work were displayed in her Boulder, Colorado, home, but as her reputation grew and demand to see her work increased, she moved and converted her house into the Rocky Mountain Museum in 1873. Two years later, she moved her museum to Denver, where it came to the attention of state legislators who asked her to display her work at the Centennial Exhibition. Martha was acclaimed as the nation's most successful female naturalist and thus earned herself a place in the history of the American West.

Several women gained international reputations as fine artists by painting and photographing Western landscapes and personalities. One of the most prominent was Helen Brodt, who painted a much-publicized portrait of the beautiful English actress Lilly Langtry for Judge Roy Bean of Texas. Helen was born in New York City and was living in Texas when she met Bean, who asked her to paint the Jersey Lil's portrait for him. Later, while moving to California, Helen was totally captivated by the beauty and grandeur of the West and began to paint everything and everyone that she believed represented the true Western experience. Brodt remained active as an artist until shortly before her death in 1906. By the time she died, she was acknowledged as one of America's finest female artists.

Another artist whose work earned her a fine reputation was landscape painter Emma Green. Emma painted the state seal of Idaho after completing her art studies in New York City and continued to paint panoramic landscapes which can still be viewed in many of the nation's most prestigious museums.

Eliza Barchus was yet another Western landscape artist whose work became very popular with critics and the public during her lifetime. Eliza was a widow with young children to support when she first put brush to canvas. Her work attracted the attention of many successful local politicians and socialites in her native Oregon and soon she was being called "The Oregon Artist" by the nation's press. Her work earned her a decent living as she sold her paintings to various museums and art collectors throughout the United States and abroad.

Several women of the West became successful photographers, taking pictures of the scenic wonders and colorful characters of the frontier. Evelyn Jephson Cameron, who was born in England and immigrated to the United States with her husband as a young woman, first laid eyes on the beauty of the West when she spent her honeymoon in Montana. She was so taken by the magnificent scenery that she took hundreds of photographs. Her photographs were displayed at a London art gallery after she returned home from her honeymoon. When Evelyn's husband was offered a job as a naturalist in Montana, the couple eagerly accepted the offer and returned to that state, where they spent the remainder of their lives. Evelyn's work was soon being exhibited in photographic galleries throughout the United States and Europe. Evelyn was called "Lady Cameron" by her Montana neighbors (who were impressed with her refined British accent and proper demeanor) and could be seen carrying her bulky camera from place to place, photographing the people and places she wished to record for posterity. Mrs. Cameron's photographs of everyday Western life (a cluster of wagons sitting on a vast plain; a typical pioneer family sitting in front of their crudely constructed log cabin; a young couple sitting in front of a pot-bellied stove in their one room house) were honest, simple and artistic. Mrs. Cameron became one of the nation's most famous photographer-artists and she soon rivaled the celebrated Mathew Brady. An expert horsewoman, Mrs. Cameron was proud of the fact that she was reportedly the first woman in Montana to ride a horse astride (like a man) rather than sitting sidesaddle. This did not seem to conform to the ladylike image Evelyn's Montana neighbors had of her, but many greatly admired her individuality and unconventionality.

Writing was another way for educated, literate Western women to support themselves. Writing was an occupation respectable ladies could pursue without making public spectacles of themselves. One of the most successful female authors of the West was Sharlot Hall of Arizona. Sharlot became well known as a historian and fiction writer and drew much of her inspiration from her Arizona homeland. Sharlot was born in 1870 in Lincoln County, Kansas. One of Sharlot's earliest recollections was of watching her mother wash the bleeding heads of men who had been scalped by hostile Indians. In 1879, the Hall family left Kansas and settled in the Indian Territory of Oklahoma. They moved once again in 1881, traveling the Santa Fe Trail as they herded their horses to Prescott, Arizona, where her father had bought another ranch. In addition to his ranching chores, Sharlot's father also tried his hand at mining for a while, but eventually returned to full time ranching. The same year the Hall family moved to Arizona, Sharlot's spine was badly injured when she was thrown from a horse. Sharlot was bedridden for many years, and it was during this time that she began to write and have her work published. The stories she wrote for Eastern periodicals about her life out West earned her enough money to purchase 160 acres to add to her family's ranchland.

When Sharlot's article "Land of Sunshine" was published in 1897, it met with great success. The article attracted the attention of publisher Charles F. Lummis, who decided to republish the article under a new title ("Out West") in one of his highly successful magazines. It was praised by critics and Lummis became Sharlot's mentor, guiding her writing career for many years thereafter. In 1909, Sharlot was elected "territorial historian" of Arizona and became the first woman to hold public office in that state. In 1912, she returned to her family's "Orchard Ranch" when her father became an invalid and could no longer manage the place by himself. Sharlot's spinal problems, however, resurfaced and reluctantly she decided she could no longer hold onto the ranch. The people who bought the place, however, failed to meet the mortgage payments and Sharlot returned to the ranch once again and began to run it by herself. She continued her writing as well, and had hundreds of articles published in many popular periodicals. Her father could never understand why Sharlot spent her time "dabbling with words," as he put it, and he never really appreciated his daughter's literary accomplishments. Sharlot's final years were spent arranging and displaying items for a museum that contained her large collection of Indian and pioneer artifacts. After Sharlot Hall died in 1949, a collection of her poems about her life as a rancher were published posthumously and met with great success.

No less an authority than poet Ralph Waldo Emerson called Helen Hunt Jackson "America's greatest female poet." Jackson's book *Century of Dishonor* demanded better treatment for Native Americans, who she felt were being unfairly treated by Euro-American settlers and the U.S. government. She also wrote a novel, *Ramona*, which became a best-seller and helped to advance the cause of Native Americans. Published in 1881, *Ramona* was a sad tale about a half-breed Indian girl's doomed love affair with an Indian youth and their mistreatment by whites. Jackson sent copies of her books to every member of Congress, hoping to win their sympathy for the Indians' cause, but this failed to effect the reforms she hoped for. *Ramona* did, however, persuade Congress to enact the Dawes Act (1887), which granted every Indian family 160 acres of farmland (in selected Western territories).

WOMEN REFORMERS

The ratio of males to females in the nineteenth-century West was approximately ten to one. Since they were so few in number, and therefore highly prized, Western women could make demands that women in other parts of the world could only dream about. Two rebellious ladies, Fanny Stenhouse and Ann Eliza Young, were among the first to speak up for equality and justice in the treatment of women. Members of the Church of Jesus Christ of Latter-Day Saints (or Mormons), Fanny and Ann Eliza became effective spokeswomen for members of their sex.

Eliza Young was born Ann Eliza Webb in Nauvoo, Illinois, where her Mormon father had multiple wives, which was condoned by his religion. "Mormon women did not like polygamous life," Eliza later wrote, "and only endured it because they thought they must. They were not happy women…no women in polygamy are happy, however loudly they may claim to be. Neither did they quarrel with each other or complain of one another to their husbands."

When Eliza was 18, she attracted the attention of Brigham Young, leader of the Mormon Church, who was visiting her family in Nauvoo. Young asked Eliza's parents to allow her to return with him to the Mormon community in Utah and become an actress in his Salt Lake City theatrical company. Eliza was eager to accept, intrigued with the idea of a life in the theater, and the Webbs reluctantly agreed. While she was training to be an actress, Eliza met and fell in love with a handsome English Mormon named James L. Dee, an actor in Young's theatrical company. Eliza and Dee married in 1863, but Dee turned out to be much less of a husband than Eliza expected: He mercilessly beat his young wife in an attempt to "break her independent spirit." When he beat her in her last month of pregnancy and she lost the child, Eliza asked Brigham Young to help her get a divorce. Young, outraged at Lee's brutality, granted Eliza a divorce and she returned to her parents' home in Illinois. When Young later revisited the Halls, he proposed marriage to Eliza and she refused him. Young persisted until Eliza's father convinced her to accept. Eliza was unhappy with life as one of

Brigham Young's 19 wives, feeling she was being treated as if she were merely someone's property. Totally ignored by Young's other wives and living in a small cottage near the Young mansion, Eliza began to take in boarders in order to obtain a degree of financial independence for herself.

In 1873, Eliza sold her furniture and moved into the Salt Lake City Hotel. When news spread that one of Brigham Young's wives had deserted him and the Mormon Church, "reporters called on me, seeking interviews for the California, Chicago and New York newspapers. I had gone to bed a poor, defenseless, outraged woman... I arose to find that my name had gone the length and breadth of the country and that I was everywhere known as Brigham Young's rebellious wife." Eliza sued Young for divorce, charging that he had neglected her and did not offer her proper support. Young offered Eliza $15,000 and a divorce if she would drop her suit. Rather than accept his offer, Eliza demanded $200,000 in damages. In court, Young claimed that he had never actually been legally married to Eliza since he was never divorced from his *first* wife and therefore owed her nothing. The divorce was eventually granted and Young was ordered to pay Eliza's court costs, but he did not have to pay her any damages or alimony.

After the divorce, Eliza toured the country lecturing about the evils of polygamy and about the rights women should expect and demand in a supposedly democratic society. After successful speaking engagements in Boston, New York, and Washington, she returned to Salt Lake City to speak in 1874. According to her book *Life in Mormon Bondage* (1908), Brigham Young did not attend her lecture, but he did send his wives and daughters. While she was delivering her lecture, the Young women (sitting in the front rows of the auditorium) made funny faces at Eliza, trying to distract her. But nothing they did could make Ann Eliza Webb turn her back on her crusade for women's rights. She continued to speak out for her gender until shortly before she died.

Fanny Stenhouse was another Mormon woman who became an avid spokeswoman for equal rights. Fanny immigrated to the United States with her husband Thomas from England, where they both became interested in the Mormon faith and became Latter Day Saints. Invited to make the westward journey to Salt Lake City (which Mormons called "The Promised Land"), the Stenhouses endured many hardships while on the trail. Salt Lake City, situated in the middle of a barren-looking area, did appear to be a "paradise" to Fanny, she later wrote, but it soon turned out to be a living hell for the sensitive young woman. Shortly after they settled in Salt Lake City, Thomas Stenhouse decided that he was going to take a second wife, as was the Mormon custom. "The idea that some day another wife would be added to our household was ever present in my mind," Fanny wrote in her memoirs, "but somehow, when the fact was placed before me in so many unmistakable words, my heart sank within me, and I shrank from the realization that our home was at last to be desecrated by the foul presence of polygamy." When her husband's soon-to-be second wife suddenly fell ill and died, Fanny admitted that she was greatly relieved. When her husband began to court yet another young woman, Fanny fell into a deep depression. "I would kneel, and pray, and weep with passionate emotion; and again I would pace the floor, my heart overflowing with anger and indignation... I longed to die."

Fanny was forced to attend the wedding, which was performed by Brigham Young himself, but she had already decided that she no longer wished to be a member of the Mormon church. She continued to live with her husband and his new wife, however, for about a year, "suffering constantly," until Stenhouse decided to build a second house for his new wife. When Thomas announced that he had decided to take a *third* wife, an outraged Fanny left her husband and Salt Lake City once and for all. She divorced him and went on an anti-Mormon lecture tour that made Eliza Young's seem mild by comparison. As the years wore on, Fanny Stenhouse, like Eliza Young, became one of the nation's most eloquent and best-known spokeswomen for female equality.

Another social reform movement that attracted many women prior to the outbreak of the Civil War was the struggle to abolish slavery. Although the idea of freeing African-Americans from bondage was advanced as early as the beginning of the nineteenth century, it was not until the early 1860s that abolition became a national *cause célèbre*. By that time, the developing Western United States was beginning to choose sides in the debate; migrants from the Northeast had strong anti-slavery sentiments while settlers from Southern states sided with the pro-slavery forces.

A woman named Joanne Harris Haines recalled the violent reaction she caused when she was a child and sang an anti-slavery song while headed for Iowa by train with her parents in 1852. Joanne also vividly recalled the "sense of loneliness" she experienced while living with her parents in the mainly pro-slavery town of Grinnel. Because of her parents' avid anti-slavery sentiments, her home became one of the stops on the Underground Railroad, the route runaway slaves used on their way to Canada and freedom. Many prairie women who came West from Northern states formed active abolitionist societies in their communities as early as the 1830s and they organized fund-raising activities and lectures about the evils of slavery.

Another movement actively supported by Western women involved guaranteeing sanitary conditions for soldiers stationed on the frontier during the Civil War and Indian wars. One of the best-known female advocates of sanitary conditions for soldiers was Annie Turner Wittenmeyer of Iowa. While the Civil War was raging, Annie joined the legion of women who rolled bandages, sewed clothing and packed food for the Union troops. Annie discovered that more groups of this sort were desperately needed throughout her state and organized "The Soldier's Aid Society of Iowa." She traveled to the front and sent back first-hand reports of what was needed by the Union soldiers. After visiting her soldier-brother at the front and seeing his breakfast (bacon swimming in grease and a single slice of bread), she also became an activist for establishing sanitary kitchens and providing nutritious food for the troops.

In 1863, Wittenmeyer took on another cause: finding homes for the orphaned children of veterans. Wittenmeyer founded several institutions to house these children and, according to her assistant Mary E. Shelton, she wrote hundreds of letters each year to government officials seeking support for her causes. She eventually succeeded in getting backing from the U. S. government for her orphanages. Wittenmeyer continued her work on behalf of various soldiers and veterans' causes for many years after the Civil War ended.

Kansas was a state that nurtured several female reformers and crusaders. Clarina Irene Nichols, for example, went on extensive lecture tours in the late 1850s and throughout the 1860s and '70s, urging women not to get married unless they were given the right to vote. Mary E. Lease was one of the major forces behind *The People's Party*, a political organization that encouraged farmers to stand up to the powerful Western cattlemen. In 1890 alone, Mary delivered 160 speeches all around the country and was partly responsible for her party becoming a formidable rival of the established Democratic and Republican parties. The crusades led by these Kansas women eventually brought about many of the reforms that they advocated, though most of them took place well after they were active.

RANCH AND FARM WOMEN

Pioneer women who went west by the thousands after the end of Civil War encountered rough terrain, extreme weather conditions, starvation, attacks by hostile Native

Americans and other difficulties. In 1849, young Janette Riker, for example, survived an extremely severe winter in Montana while totally on her own. The Riker family was heading west via covered wagon when they decided to make camp for a few days in order to graze their oxen and replenish their food supplies. Janette's father and brothers went on a hunting expedition; when night came and they failed to return, Janette (whose mother died several months before) crawled into the wagon where she spent a restless night with a rifle cradled in her arms as wolves howled all around her. The next morning, she set out to look for her father and brothers but failed to find any sign of them. At dusk, she returned to the wagon. She waited for them to return for six days. Since she did not feel that she had the strength or skill to drive the team of oxen by herself, and since heavy snows had already begun to fall, Janette decided she needed a better shelter. She took an ax and a spade and built a crude shelter out of small trees and logs, stuffing the cracks with dried grass. She then used the canvas wagon cover as a roof for her one-room hut and placed the small wood-burning stove, blankets and the remaining food supplies into the hut. She killed the fattest oxen and, after salting it in order to preserve the meat, packed it away under the snow. She then chopped as much wood as she could for fuel for the stove. Before long, snow covered her hut and the temperature fell to well below zero. A blizzard raged for several days in January and practically buried her shelter, but Janette managed to keep the stove hole in the roof of her hut open. In the spring the weather became milder and her hut was flooded, so she returned to living in her wagon. Late in April, when she had only enough food to last her a few days, an Indian hunting party came upon her. They were amazed that the teenage girl had survived such a severe winter on her own, and led her to the safety of an army post located near Walla Walla. Janette never learned what had become of her father and brothers. She eventually married a rancher, well prepared for any difficulty she might encounter, and lived a long life.

Berta Josephson was a Danish woman who worked as a dairy maid in Denmark and married a young farmer who decided he wanted to immigrate to the United States. Berta's young husband heard there was ample land and numerous opportunities in the great American West for ambitious and hard-working young farmers. Berta's brother had previously settled in Montana and so the couple left Denmark in 1889 and headed for Montana, to join her sibling on his farm. With money that they saved while living in Denmark, the Josephsons bought several milk cows and, utilizing Berta's skill as a milkmaid, began to produce milk, butter and cheese which they sold to neighboring farmers and residents of the nearby towns. Since they spoke little English, Berta conducted her business transactions by using hand signals and facial expressions. Berta also worked long and difficult hours alongside her husband clearing and haying fields and maintaining her house. In 1895, the Josephsons (who had several children by then) applied for U. S. citizenship. In addition to her own brood of seven children, Berta raised the children of relatives who died in young adulthood after immigrating to the New World. In her old age, Berta wrote an account of the years she spent as a pioneer farmer. In the 1940 book, Berta concluded, "We were happy and gratified to be part of the lives of our new country, but there were also regrets when those wonderful pioneer days were over, as difficult as they often were."

Abbie Bright was a free spirit who farmed her own land, planted corn and beans and built her house all by herself. Abbie occasionally hired a male helper or two if she needed assistance with her farm chores and construction, but those times were indeed rare. She could do almost anything any member of the opposite sex could do, and often do it better, as many of her neighbors readily admitted. In a letter to her sister in Ohio, Abbie described her first home as "split limbs covered with dirt"; on the roof she planted sunflowers. "A fireplace and chimney are dug out and built up on one end, plastered with mud it answered well [*sic*]...

My bed is in the center and has one leg… Then comes my hay filled tick [mattress], and my bed is also a couch for comfort. In the corner, at the foot of the bed, are boxes and various things including the tub, which is often pushed under the bed. Boxes are nailed to the wall, in which the table furniture [dishes and eating utensils] are kept, also some groceries. Chairs are pieces of logs." These were the type of accommodations familiar to many farm women out West.

Most of the West's cowpokes who rode the ranges, roping and rounding up cattle and then branding and taking them on cattle drives to east-bound stockyards, were men. There were, however, expert cowgirls who could rope and ride with the best of the West's cowboys. Rancher Fritz Becker, who had no sons, taught his three daughters to rope and brand cattle on his large ranch in the San Luis Valley of Colorado when they were little girls. Becker wanted his daughters to take over his ranch after he died, which they did. The Becker girls' ranch became one of the most prosperous spreads in the West.

Another cowgirl, Sadie Austin, was the daughter of a well-to-do rancher and worked as a hand on her father's Nebraska ranch at the turn of the century. A photograph from the early 1900s shows her standing next to a horse in the middle of her father's range. The photo was widely circulated throughout the United States and was later reproduced in one of the Time/Life *Old West* volumes.

The everyday lives of ranch women consisted of backbreaking work. For the most part, they were mainly responsible for cleaning the ranch and bunkhouses and feeding family members and the ranch hands. When a husband died, a ranch woman sometimes took over the operation of the family business and quite often did as good a job as her husband. Agnes Freeman, who went West with her husband in 1860, took over the management of their ranch after his death and raised seven children by herself in the bargain. She even managed to become a physician later in life.

In Time/Life's *Old West* volume *Cowboys*, author William M. Forbis profiles the lives of six ranch women who he calls "Baronesses of the Prairie." These women did more than just cook and clean up after their families and the ranch hands and were more than actively involved in the running of their families' successful ranches. Awbonnie Stuart was one of the women profiled in Forbis' book. Awbonnie was a full-blooded Shoshone Indian. She and her husband had nine children and when her husband's brother and sister-in-law died, Awbonnie also raised *their* children. Awbonnie not only took excellent care of her house, she also assisted her husband and his ranch hands as they rounded up and herded their cattle to market.

Another of the six "baronesses" profiled in *The Old West* was Eula Kendrick, who was described as "one of the most stylish and elegant women who ever lived on the Western frontier." In addition to being a snappy dresser, Eula was also a first-rate bookkeeper, and she helped manage her husband's large and successful ranch, "The R Trail End," near Sheridan, Wyoming.

Elizabeth Ileff was a clerk in a Singer sewing machine store when she met and then married John, owner of a large and prosperous Texas ranch. When John died at the age of 48, Elizabeth took over the operation of the ranch. It was reported that on the day John died, Elizabeth remained calm enough to telegraph the ranch's foreman and tell him to "double the guard on the herds before rustlers move in."

Nellie Wilbaux, whose first home out West was a crude log cabin with a sod roof, worked long hours at her husband's side until their ranch became one of the most successful cattle operations in the West.

Augusta Kohrs preferred managing the domestic affairs of her husband's ranch, which was prosperous enough for Augusta to hire a staff to cook and clean. Augusta, who acted as if she were indeed an actual baroness, enjoyed traveling and made frequent trips to Europe and New York where she bought beautiful clothes and fine furnishings for her home. She especially enjoyed attending the opera when she was in the East or abroad. Augusta was 93 years old when she took her last trip to New York in 1942.

The most endearing of Forbis' six cattle baronesses was Mary Anne "Molly" Dwyer, who became known as "the darling of the open range" and "the mother of the Panhandle." Molly was 14 years old in 1854 when her parents migrated to Texas from somewhere in the Deep South. The family settled in Waxahachie and when her mother died, Molly took over the family's household chores, raised her younger brothers and took care of her father. In 1870, Molly married Colonel Charles Goodnight and settled down on a ranch in Pueblo, Colorado. The Goodnights' ranch prospered and after several years in Colorado they decided that they needed a larger spread to accommodate their ever-increasing herd of cattle; they moved back to Texas where they bought a larger ranch. Molly worked alongside her husband on the range and managed her household chores as well. In time her kindness and generosity towards others became legendary throughout the Texas Panhandle. She would cook for, doctor and mother numerous down-and-out cowboys, drifters and even Native Americans (Molly was "very frightened of Indians" when she first moved to the Panhandle). Molly became well known for the wonderful parties she threw for the entire county's residents at holiday times. The Fourth of July was Molly's particular favorite holiday and she entertained as many as 175 people at her ranch each year on that day. One of Molly's parties was described by a guest who wrote home about his Christmas visit to the Goodnights' ranch: "The long tables in the form of a cross were loaded with food: roast beef, wild turkey, antelope, cakes, pies and other delicacies. At the point where the long tables met, was a Star Navy tomato box decorated and covered with a spotless glass and pretty pebbles and covered with a spotless white cloth. Upon this central table stood a Christmas tree, ornamented with bunches of frosted raisins and strings of popcorn and cranberries. Each guest received at least one present." Molly's biographer Phoebe Kerrick Warner recalled that Molly was also an expert with a rifle and an impressive horsewoman. Long after Molly Goodnight died, she was remembered fondly by her neighbors, and stories about her are still legends around the Palo Dura Panhandle of Texas.

Stories of other independent, wealthy ranch women abound. For example, Lizzie Johnson Williams' life was chronicled in an article by Emily Jones Skelton that appeared in *The Southwestern Historical Quarterly* in 1946. She was a woman well ahead of her time as far as being "liberated" was concerned. Lizzie managed her own cattle empire, taught school and was an expert bookkeeper who not only kept her own accounts, but also those of several other St. Louis cattle barons. Lizzie was also an author and teacher (her father founded "Johnson's Institute," the first institution of higher learning in Texas). A strong-willed young woman who used various *noms de plume* when writing for *Frank Leslie's Magazine*, Lizzie did not tell many people about her ventures into writing, but made enough money to invest in the cattle market. At one time she bought $2500 of stock in a Chicago cattle company; this eventually earned her $20,000 on her original investment. Lizzie registered her own brand of cattle in 1871, but she also continued to write and to teach at her father's college. The Civil War gave Lizzie the opportunity to expand her cattle enterprises since large numbers of unbranded cattle wandered the ranges of Texas. (Many of the former owners had either been killed in the war or had abandoned their ranches for the large Eastern cities once the war ended.) Cattle barons who gathered herds of wandering steers from the brush ("brushpopping") made fortunes for their efforts.

When Lizzie was 36, she married a widower named Hezekiah Williams who was a cattleman. Hezekiah, an alcoholic and a poor businessman, was also handsome, intelligent and charming, and Lizzie fell madly in love with him. Nevertheless, Lizzie decided that Hezekiah would tend to his business concerns and she would attend to hers. Of course, Lizzie was always there to bail her husband out of any business trouble he found himself in. Until Lizzie married Hezekiah, she had not been involved in the actual rounding-up of cattle (she always hired others to do her brushpopping). But when she married Hezekiah, she began to take a more active interest in her business and thought nothing of asking the men who gathered the strays to give her the choice of the cattle they found. Lizzie also made many trips with her ranch hands along the famous Chisholm Trail, a series of cattle trails that went from south Texas into Kansas, from where the cattle was sent east by rail. Lizzie often cheated her own husband because she knew she was much better at business than he was and that ultimately she would be saving them both money. Lizzie once bailed Hezekiah out of a particularly bad business deal and wrote a check to his debtors for $50,000. When Hezekiah died in El Paso, Lizzie had his body sent home to Austin for burial, paying the unheard-of sum of $600 for his funeral. Across the bank draft she made out to the funeral director, she scrawled, "I loved that old buzzard this much!"

When it came to business, Lizzie had no sentiment and she became well known in the El Paso area for her blunt, often rude manner of speaking to people. If her acerbic personality made people dislike her, they never let her know it. Lizzie wanted people to believe that she was a generous and philanthropic woman, but her actions were not without motive. Biographer Emily Jones Skelton wrote, "Lizzie kept churches, schools, and even the University of Texas ever hopeful of donations, which she gave them to understand she was considering. In this way, she made people act nice to her, as they anticipated the money which, from the beginning, she had no intention of giving them."

Even though she actively rode the range with her cowhands, Lizzie never gave up dressing in a very feminine and stylish manner. She was fond of silks, satins and lace, and everywhere she went she always wore fine riding clothes and fancy bonnets. Although she was not a particularly beautiful woman, Lizzie was described as being "tall and stately" and "striking" in appearance. When Lizzie died in 1923, she was known as one of the richest and most eccentric women in Texas. Lizzie spent the last few years of her life alone in her large mansion. She spent her money on only the barest of necessities and seldom saw anyone. After she died, her surviving relatives found all sorts of unusual things at her mansion. Her jewelry was found in an unlocked box in the basement while a locked box found in her bedroom contained parrot feathers and some dried flowers from her husband's funeral wreath. The family also found $2,000 in five and one dollar bills hidden all around the bedroom.

Another remarkable and unconventional cattle queen, Alice Stillwell Henderson, did her cattle raising on the wide open expanses of Big Bend country of Texas, along the Rio Grande river. Alice became famous throughout Texas for being a tough and aggressive businesswoman. When a band of Mexican bandits rustled some of her cows, she rode across the border, took the law into her own hands and reclaimed them.

Alice Stillwell's family originally settled in the Big Bend area in the late 1880s when Alice was in her teens. She married a man named Henderson (first name unknown) in 1890, and the couple began to build a large cattle empire. The Hendersons were known for dealing harshly with anyone who dared steal any of their cattle and (according to a cowboy who knew them) "they would shoot anyone on sight who was found with an animal bearing their brand in their possession." The cowboy described Alice as "an enduring and splendid woman. Every man and woman who knew her, though women were mighty scarce over her range, respected her." Her cousin Hallie Stillwell, who became a Justice of the Peace in Alpine, Texas, wrote, "Alice rode astride and often wore men's trousers and a hat. But when she went into town, she always wore a skirt over her trousers and acted like a lady at all times.

Alice made many trips alone from Mexico leading a pack horse, and had no fear of making camp alone." In addition to her cattle activities, Alice also found time to establish a school in Marathon, Texas, and (unlike Lizzie Williams) was an extremely philanthropic woman.

E. E. Townsend's book *Boatright Files* gives an account of one of Alice's typical danger-filled cattle drives. On one occasion when Alice and her cowhands were herding cattle they had picked up across the border, they were surrounded by Mexican bandits who tried to prevent them from crossing the river back into the United States. Alice pulled out her rifle and held them at gunpoint for over three hours until her entire herd was driven safely across the river by her men. Townsend also reported that Alice was once shot at by a similar group of thieves until she reached the safety of Texas.

Alice was also known to be a great admirer of the infamous cattle rustler Sally Skull and even wrote a book (never published) about Sally's life. Alice's manuscript was lost and, along with it, a wealth of information about Sally Skull. It is hard to believe that Alice thought Skull's life was any more exciting and adventure-filled than her own. Alice's life ended quietly in self-imposed isolation on the Texas ranch she and her husband had made one of the biggest and best in the West.

Ann Bassett Willis was a cattle queen of an entirely different kind. She was born in a small cabin at Brown's Park, Colorado, in 1878, while Narcisco, a renegade Ute Indian, and a group of his followers were camped a few hundred yards from her family's home. Ann was wet-nursed by a Ute squaw named Wee-a-baka when her mother proved unable to nurse the child herself. Brown's Park (or "Brown's Hole," as it was called by most of its residents) was a primitive community, but it was in an area of Colorado that abounded with wild game and good grazing lands. Although its citizens were hardworking and honest, they also believed that what others did was no business of theirs and so their settlement became a refuge for outlaws on the run. One of Ann's close outlaw-friends was Elzy Lay, a member of the notorious Wild Bunch.

Early in her life, Ann and her family were involved in the Range Wars between the cattle barons of the Middlesex Cattle Company and the small-time cattle ranchers. One of her father's calves, a pet of Ann's, was rounded up by the Middlesex Company's cowboys. Ann, who was eight years old at the time, located her pet with the help of a friend and, after spitting at the cowboys, she managed to separate her calf from the Middlesex group's herd. In 1879, when Ann was in her teens, she and several friends came upon a small herd of cattle which did not appear to belong to anyone in the area. The group gathered the cows and began to herd them across the Green River. Several of the group were drowned. Ann's appropriation of cows that other cattlemen considered their property did not endear her to them.

In 1910, Ann married H. H. Bernard and together they amassed a large herd of cattle. Although she often used salty language and preferred dressing in men's clothing, Ann apparently did know how to act like a lady when she had to. (She had been educated at a Salt Lake City convent school.) For the most part, however, Ann's demeanor was usually more masculine than feminine. Her womanly charms managed to surface when she was arrested for stealing a heifer belonging to Ora Haley, the owner of the prosperous Two Bar ranch. Ann showed up for her trial dressed to the nines in feminine attire and acting as delicate and ladylike as the ingenue in a play. Newspapers of the time recorded every detail of her trial, and by the time it was over, it was cattle baron Haley who might as well have been on trial. In his book *When the Old West Stayed Young*, John Rolfe Burroughs wrote that Ann "was as guilty as sin," but that it "was besides the point." In her own autobiography, written many years after the trial, Ann wrote, "I did everything they ever accused me of, and a whole lot more. Everyone knew it." Ann became a national celebrity during her trial and she played the part of a wronged heroine with the skill of an accomplished stage actress. Burroughs wrote, "A lone woman, a smallish woman, a woman still young and exceedingly attractive had fought the mighty Haley to a standstill. Holding him up to public obloquy, Ann Bassett had whipped the daylights out of him."

In 1920, Ann (now a widow) married a man named Frank Willis and the newlyweds moved to Arizona, where they bought ranches. One of Ann's ambitions was to become a member of the U.S. Forest Service and she applied for a position with that organization. She was deeply disappointed when her application was returned because she was a woman. Ann's last years were spent in retirement in Leeds, Utah, where she died at the age of 78. None of her neighbors was aware that one of the West's legendary cattle women had been living among them.

One cattleman's widow, Mabel Doss Day, began her successful cattle operation by rounding up stray cows in New Mexico, Colorado and Mexico. She owned a large tract of land in Coleman County, Texas. Mrs. Day became involved in the much-publicized fence-cutting war of 1883 and was one of the major cattle owners who put wire fences around their property to keep other independent cattlemen from grazing their cows on her range. The free rangers cut the wire fences Mrs. Day put up and said that she was denying them grazing land for their herds. Mrs. Day, however, proved a formidable foe and she fiercely defended her property.

Before she became a cattle queen, Mabel, the daughter of well-to-do parents, had been a music teacher. She married William Day in 1879 and went to live on his ranch in Coleman County, Texas, where she learned to rope, ride a horse and herd cattle. Widowed shortly after she gave birth to a baby boy, Mabel was determined to run her family's ranch by herself and she went to the state capital and asked to borrow money to expand her business. She tried to convince the politicians that her business would pay high dividends to the state, but they refused her request for a loan. Several Kentucky backers, impressed with her presentation, offered to loan her $200,000 and she formed her own company, the Day Cattle Ranch, which prospered. In time, a law forbidding the cutting of wire fences was passed and fence cutters who continued the practice were arrested and given from one to five years in prison. In 1889, Mabel married Captain Joseph C. Lea and moved to New Mexico where she helped found the New Mexico Military Academy which her husband ran. She is said to have lived the rest of her life quietly and comfortably.

Though these women were well known in their time, only one well-to-do Westerner had her life transformed into a Broadway musical. When composer Meredith Willson's musical comedy *The Unsinkable Molly Brown* became a success on Broadway and the silver screen, few people realized that the leading character was an actual person who lived a life very similar to the one Willson romanticized in his musical. On Broadway, actress Tammy Grimes played Molly Brown and on the screen, the role was played by Debbie Reynolds.

Born Maggie Tobin in Hannibal, Missouri, in 1867, Maggie—or Molly as she preferred to be called—was the daughter of an illiterate ditch-digger and his wife. Molly married a mining engineer named James Brown when she was 19 and the couple settled in Leadville, Colorado, where Brown decided that he wanted to mine gold for himself. For a while, Molly lived a comfortable, ordinary life and eventually gave birth to two children. But in 1894, everything changed for the Browns when Jim struck a vein of gold and overnight became one of the richest men in Colorado. He built an 18-room Denver mansion for Molly and their children and the couple filled it with expensive furniture and works of fine art. Molly hoped she would be able to make a place for herself in Denver society, but because she was "common," the city's social elite snubbed her. Determined to improve herself and gain social acceptance, Molly hired a private tutor and began to read every book she could get her hands on. She toured the United States and Europe in order to "obtain class," as she later put it, and learned to speak several languages fluently. During her travels she became friendly with such prominent socialites as the Astors, the Whitneys and the Vanderbilts, who admired her down-to-earth and refreshingly honest personality. Molly obtained the "unsinkable" label while she was returning from one of her European tours on the ocean liner *Titanic* in 1912. She received a great deal of publicity throughout the world due to her heroism and many kindnesses to fellow survivors after the ship struck an iceberg and sank, killing over 100 passengers. By the time Molly returned to Denver, she was world-famous and the city's leading citizens suddenly began to court her favor. In a typically gracious manner, Molly never held a grudge against those who treated her so badly before the "unsinkable" *Titanic* went to the bottom of the Atlantic and Molly fulfilled her desire to become one of Denver's most celebrated citizens.

Although accounts of ranch baronesses and ambitious Western women are numerous and impressive, these womens' stories were certainly the exception rather than the rule. The majority of frontier farmers and ranchers lived and worked on relatively small tracts of land and barely managed to eke out meager existences. Little documentation remains about the lives of their wives, but the bits and pieces that have surfaced reveal them to have been mainly decent, hard-working women who managed to raise families under the most difficult of conditions. One ranch owner's wife, Mrs. Charlie Hart of New Mexico, roped and herded her family's cattle with her husband. She carried her children strapped to her back as she rode alongside him and went on long cattle drives. Her children knew how to ride by the time they were four years old and joined their parents on cattle drives as cowhands as soon as they were old enough. Another ranch owner's wife, Mrs. Viola Slaughter, was born in Missouri in 1860 and settled in Montana with her family when she was five years old. While in her teens, Viola met and fell in love with a 19-year-old widower with two small children. She married him and the couple moved with Viola's parents to Sulpher Springs, Arizona, where they bought a ranch and began to raise beef which they sold to the U.S. Army. Viola often rode with her husband when he bought cattle in Mexico and herded them back to the family's Arizona ranch. In 1883, John and Viola sold their share of the ranch to her parents and the couple and their children traveled to Ogden, Utah, where they bought another ranch and began to supply beef to military installations in the area. Viola thrived on excitement, and when her husband accepted the job of sheriff of Cochise County, Viola joined the posse that hunted down a murderer named Juan Lopez. In addition to her husband's children by his first wife, Viola and John had several children of their own and Viola even adopted an Apache baby girl she found abandoned after an Indian camp was raided by Arizona ranchers and the village's population massacred. Viola was heartbroken when the little girl died of burns she suffered in a fire when she was six years old.

During the Pleasant Plains War of 1892, one of the first casualties was a young farmer named Tom Graham who was shot by a hired gunslinger. While the gunman was being brought into court to be charged with murder, Tom's distraught wife Anne pulled out a gun and shot him. Because the court was in sympathy with Anne, no charges were brought against her for the attempted murder.

One of the most touching accounts of the life of a rancher's wife was written by rancher Frank Alkire. His book *The Little Lady of the Triangle Bar*, which was about his beloved wife Asenath, was never published, but the manuscript was presented to the Pioneer Historical Society of Tucson, Arizona. Alkire owned a hardware store in Phoenix, Arizona, until it failed in 1889 when he bought a small ranch north of Phoenix which he called the Triangle Bar. His wife Asenath, the daughter of a well-to-do cotton broker, was hardly ready to face the hardships of ranch life when she first moved to the Triangle Bar with her husband. In his manuscript, Alkire described in detail the difficulties Asenath faced as she attempted to adjust to her new life. Although Mrs. Alkire's house was apparently better furnished than most other modest ranch houses, it was hardly what she was used to in her hometown of New Orleans. Since Asenath's grandfather was a physician, she had learned quite a bit about medicine, bone setting and such as a child. Her knowledge was extremely useful to the couple and their neighbors whenever there was a sick animal that needed treatment.

When her first baby was about to be born, Asenath (a small, frail woman) went to California to stay with relatives in order to be near a doctor. After the baby was born and she returned to Arizona, Frank announced that he was going to Mexico to buy horses. Asenath told him that she and the baby would be going with him. Frank protested, but Asenath would not take "no" for an answer. She packed up a few belongings, placed the baby in a tomato box that she tied to the saddle in front of her and set off with Frank for Mexico. The couple and a hired hand encountered a violent snowstorm and an avalanche, suffered from severe sunburn and endured many other difficulties on their horse-buying expedition. When they finally returned home, Frank decided that was the last time Asenath would accompany him on a horse-buying trip.

In his book, Frank wrote that as his son grew older, the boy always seemed to be getting into trouble. One day Asenath found him playing with a rattlesnake in their front yard. Asenath used a stick to push the snake away from the child just as it was about to strike.

Asenath died several years before Frank wrote her biography; he lived on until the 1940s. Shortly before his death he donated his loving account of his life with Asenath to the historical society.

Another small ranch owner who depended upon her own resources to run her farm was a woman called "Granny" Jeffers. Granny was born and raised in New Mexico. When she was a young woman, she married a rancher and the couple herded cattle in Mexico and Texas until his untimely death when he was in his mid–20s. Thereafter, Granny took care of their small herd and raised the couple's four children. When Granny was an old woman, her daughter-in-law wrote an article for the Arizona Historical Society newsletter that stated, "Granny drove cattle, flanked calves, ran horse races, repaired windmills, pierced dozens of quilts, raised four children and was never too tired to dance all night to fiddle music." When Granny was 81, "she was still able to leap into the saddle and, even though she only had one arm at the time, went after two unbranded calves that had run off during a roundup."

SCHOOLTEACHERS

Schoolteaching was one career that respectable women could pursue without leaving themselves open to criticism. Intelligent, relatively well-educated young women flocked to the "normal" (technical education) schools and the normal school departments of colleges and universities to receive their training as teachers. At a normal school in Cedar Falls, Iowa, the number of women enrolled in the teacher-education program outnumbered men for the first time in 1876. Many of the women who graduated from these schools went West to teach as soon as they received their diplomas.

Schoolteacher Angie Brown, who was educated in Massachusetts and then Kansas normal schools, went to Arizona in 1875 to teach. She wrote many letters to friends and family members back home in Kansas in which she chronicled the difficulties she experienced as a young teacher in the wide open West. In one letter, Angie wrote that she had to teach her class in a well one day in order to escape the fierce winds that blew down her regular classroom (little more than a converted chicken coop). On another occasion, Angie and her students were in the middle of their studies when they discovered that their schoolhouse was surrounded by a band of hostile Apache Indians. Cowboys who were working nearby managed to chase the Indians away before any harm came to Angie or her students. Believing that she could make a greater contribution to the West's development, Angie applied to take an examination for certification from the U.S. Indian Service to teach Indian children on the reservation. She passed the examination with an unprecedented 100 percent score and spent the remainder of her career teaching Apache children.

Lucia Darling arrived in Bancock, Montana, in 1863 to teach the miner's children their ABCs and arithmetic. For a woman who had grown up in an orderly, conventional Ohio town, Bancock's muddy streets, shack-like buildings and rough-talking inhabitants seemed like something from another world. Lucia wrote home that Bancock was a place where "lawlessness and misrule [appear] to be the prevailing spirit. I believe there are more desperadoes and lawless characters in Bancock than ever infested any other mining camp of its size. Murders, robberies and shooting scrapes are an everyday occurrence in the daylight as well as at night." In spite of the hostile environment, Lucia began teaching with great hopes for the futures of her students. She took over a small room in her uncle's log cabin and began teaching a class of 20 children. "The school was not pretentious," Lucia wrote home, "but it was in response to the yearning for education and it was the first."

FEMALE CAPTIVES AND CHAMPIONS OF THE NATIVE AMERICANS

One of 1956's most successful films was *The Searchers* with John Wayne, Jeffrey Hunter, Vera Miles and Natalie Wood. The film, directed by John Ford, concerned a subject seldom explored on the silver screen: the abduction and confinement of Caucasian women by Native American tribesmen. Natalie Wood played a young woman who was abducted as a child and is eventually found and rescued from captivity. This subject was depicted once again in *Little Big Man* (1970) with Dustin Hoffman. In this film, Hoffman plays a white man who grew up with the Indians who abducted him when he was a child; he eventually returns to live among whites. His sister, kidnapped by a different group of Indians, chooses to remain with the tribe, having totally accepted the way of life of the Indians. European settlers faced similar situations from the time they first landed on the Atlantic shores of North America. The Viking sagas tell of a Viking explorer coming upon a woman he thought was an Indian and discovering that she spoke the Viking tongue and had bright blue eyes. This indicated that his people must have visited those shores before he had gotten there.

Many women who were abducted by Indians in the eighteenth and nineteenth centuries later wrote about their experiences, and books by such former captives as Mary Rowlandson, Fanny Kelly and Abbie Gardner were read by millions of people.

Olive Oatman was one of the Native Americans' most famous female Euro-American captives. Olive was 13 years old in 1851 when the covered wagon in which she was traveling west with her family was attacked by Yavapai Indians in the Gila River valley. While Olive and her seven-year-old sister Mary Ann were carried off by the Indians, her mother and father were killed by the Indians. After one year in captivity, the girls were sold to Mojave Indians who took them north to their Colorado River village. Although their life was slightly better with the Mohaves, in 1853 Mary Ann died of starvation during a long, hard winter. Olive's brother Lorenzo, who had been left for dead by the Yavapais, had survived, and as soon as he was able he began to search for his sisters. His search continued for five years, when finally a Yuma Indian informed him that a white woman who fit Olive's description was living among the Mojaves. Lorenzo found Olive and paid the Indians a ransom for her release. Olive had the sun-dark complexion of her Native American captors and wore Indian garments which made her unrecognizable to her brother. He took her to Fort Yuma. At first, Olive refused to speak and merely sat with her face buried in her hands. In time, she readjusted to life among her own people, and later went on an extensive lecture tour to tell the world about her captivity. She admitted that it was difficult to endure "being stared at and questioned about her life among the savages." Eventually, Olive married and settled down to a relatively normal life, but for the remainder of that life, she bore the mark of her captivity by the Indians: Her face had been heavily tattooed in the manner of Mojave women.

Fanny Wiggins Kelly survived a similar experience and wrote about it in her book *Narrative of My Captivity Among the Sioux Indians*, a nineteenth-century bestseller. Fanny was a 19-year-old bride in 1854 when she, her husband, his five-year-old daughter from a previous marriage and several other settlers headed west from Fort Laramie. About 80 miles later, the wagon train was attacked by a war party of 250 Oglala Sioux Indians. Fanny's husband was chopping wood some distance from the wagon train when it was attacked, and he managed to hide from the raiding party while the other men in the group were slaughtered. Fanny, her little stepdaughter Mary, a woman named Sarah Larimer and her eight-year-old son were taken captive by the Indians. As they were being transported to the Sioux encampment, Fanny cleverly dropped pieces of paper to let any rescuers know the direction they were being taken. Later, unseen by her captors, she told little Mary to follow the pieces of paper back to her father. She also told the child that she would join them later as soon as she could. But Mary's absence was almost immediately noticed by the Indians, who followed her trail and then killed and scalped the child. Fanny was badly beaten by her Indian captors and told that if she attempted an escape herself, she would be put to death.

Ignoring the warning, Fanny began to leave another trail behind her, this time pieces of an Ottawa pipe that she had given her husband. When this trail was discovered, the Indians tied her arms to two horses which were to pull her body apart. The ever-resourceful Fanny had pulled $120 from her purse and handed it to her captors. When they asked what the money would buy, she greatly exaggerated the value of the currency. The Indians took the money and untied her. While Fanny was negotiating with the Indians, Sarah Larimer and her son slipped away unnoticed and eventually reached safety.

Fanny Kelly. (Special Collections and Archives of the Colorado College Library.)

Fanny's life among the Sioux seemed to last an eternity. After she was finally liberated, Fanny wrote of being badly mistreated by the Sioux women and compromised by the Indian males. She wrote that she realized the only way she would survive her ordeal was to behave obediently and be as servile as she could. She proved right, and before long she won the approval of Indians who began to call her "Real Woman" (which was considered quite an honor). Although the Oglala Sioux heard that the Army was offering money for Fanny's safe return, they refused to take her to Fort Sully and claim the reward. It was a Blackfoot Sioux who eventually convinced the Oglalas that it would be in their best interests to release Fanny. Fanny realized that the Blackfoot tribe had ulterior motives; they hoped to gain entrance into the fort and then overcome the fort's occupants. When the Indians and Fanny arrived at the fort, the soldiers opened the gates and admitted Fanny and a few of the braves. Fanny whispered what she thought the Blackfoots' intentions were, and the gates were immediately closed and secured, preventing any hostilities. Fanny was exchanged for three horses and a wagon load of food supplies. Her ordeal was finally over. She was later awarded $15,000 in damages when she filed a lawsuit against the Oglala Sioux. She also made a great deal of money from the sale of her book.

The outrages the Indians committed against Euro-American women were usually exaggerated in the press. They also encouraged (and even justified) in the minds of most Americans the taking-over of vast Western lands from Native American inhabitants. Little, however, was ever said about the atrocities committed against the Indians by white settlers in the developing West.

Because of the press coverage that abductions received, it is little wonder that the one thing female settlers feared most was the possibility that they might be taken captive by Native American "savages." These incidents were made to seem commonplace, which they certainly weren't.

When Matilda Lockhart was taken captive by Comanches in 1849 and finally rescued, her face and body were said to have been horribly bruised and covered with untreated sores inflicted by her Indian captors. All of the flesh was reported to have been burned off the tip of her nose as punishment for an infraction of Native American social behavior, and she told horrible tales of consistent beatings and rapes. Again, this sort of behavior on the part of Native Americans was the exception rather than the rule.

No account of captivity among the Indians was more publicized than the ordeal of Josephine Meeker, who was kidnapped in 1878. Josephine was a

Josephine Meeker. (Denver Public Library.)

graduate of Oberlin College who arrived at the White River Indian Agency where her father (an Indian Agent) and her mother Arvella were living. Josephine, a tall, thin, intelligent girl with a quick wit, immediately began teaching Ute children at the agency's school. Meeker dealt rather harshly with errant Indians at the agency and proved very unpopular with the Native Americans under his jurisdiction. The Indians, who had a long history of being hunters and nomads, deeply resented Meeker's attempts to turn them into farmers. They protested to government officials but their complaints were ignored. One day several braves entered the agency office and attacked Meeker, throwing him to the floor and beating him. Agency employees witnessed the incident and saved him.

On a September morning in 1878, Nathan Meeker entered his house and told his wife and daughter that he thought they were "in for trouble." He asked Arvella for the key to the government room where the agency's guns were kept and then went outside. His family never saw him again.

Gunfire soon began to shatter the quiet of the morning and Mrs. Price, the wife of an agency employee, rushed into the Meekers' house breathlessly sobbing that the Indians were attacking and killing their menfolk. The three women hid under the bed in Josephine's room for a while as the gunfire continued, but then decided it might be safer to hide in the milk-house. In the darkened milkhouse, the women soon smelled smoke and realized that the building had been set on fire. They tried to make a dash towards the woods and safety, but Arvella had a bad leg and could not run very fast. The Indians fired at the fleeing women and Mrs. Meeker fell wounded to the ground. A young Indian brave named Persune reached Josephine and Mrs. Price as they were trying to help Mrs. Meeker to her feet and demanded that they surrender. Josephine asked Persune if he intended to kill them and he assured her he did not. Persune then led her away from the others (who had been surrounded by other Indians) and took her to the river bank. He ordered her to sit on a pile of stolen army blankets while he packed other things stolen from the agency on a mule. He then ordered Josephine to mount a stolen horse and led her away to the Indian settlement.

Josephine was rescued from her captivity on October 21, 1878, when Charles Adams, a general with the Colorado militia, negotiated with the Indians for her return. Two weeks later, the full story of Josephine Meeker's treatment at the hands of her Indian captors was made public. Josephine testified at the hearing that the entire time she was held captive, she was considered to be Persune's exclusive property. Asked how Persune had treated her, Josephine stated that she had been "insulted" (raped) many times. She then explained that Persune's abuse had been a regular thing, and that she was considered his "squaw" (wife). Of course, the other Utes did not interfere with her, since Persune was the chief's son. Josephine was not the only survivor of the Indian attack who had been assaulted. Her mother Arvella, who had also been rescued, was raped numerous times by an Indian who called himself "Douglas."

A short time after she testified at the hearing, Josephine left Colorado. For a while she worked as a transcriber in the Office of Indian Affairs in Washington, D.C. She later became a secretary for Colorado Senator Henry Moore Teller and also frequently lectured about her life among the Native Americans. When still quite a young woman, Josephine died from a pulmonary infection. When Persune heard about her untimely death, he reportedly painted his face—a sign of deep mourning among the Utes.

In spite of the numerous violent acts against Euro-Americans by Native Americans, many women of the frontier believed that Indians had been badly treated by both white settlers and government officials. These crusaders believed the Indians deserved more consideration and even financial compensation. After all, these women argued, Indians were merely defending what they considered to be their homeland. One crusader for Indian rights, Miriam

Colt, published a well-distributed report which described in detail the cheating of Indians by greedy Euro-American opportunists. "Is it right," Mrs. Colt asked in her pamphlet, "that Indians are given three dollars for a buffalo robe, worth 12 at home?"

Frances Roe, the wife of an Army officer, was openly hostile toward Native Americans when she first arrived out West, but later became one of their staunchest supporters. "If the Indians should attempt to protect their rights, it would be called an uprising at once, so they have to lie around on sand hills and watch their beloved buffalo gradually disappear, and all the time they know only too well that with them will go the skins that give them teepees and clothing, and the meat that furnishes almost all of their sustenance." Another army wife, Frances Carrington, wrote in a *New York Times* editorial, "At the time of my arrival at Fort Laramie, it became apparent to any sensible observer that the Indians of that country would fight to the death for home and native land, with spirit akin to that of the American soldier of our early history, and who could say that their spirit was not commendable and to be respected?" Many other women of the West criticized the government's policies concerning Native Americans, especially the practice of trying to place Indians on reservations. These protests were too few in number to effect much change in the government's policies. But their point, that depriving Indians of their land and forcing them to depend upon handouts and was the cause of the problems between white settlers and Indians, was certainly well taken.

Even the widow of General George Armstrong Custer proclaimed, "It confuses my sense of justice," when she heard about retributive assaults against Indians after the soldiers at a fort had been massacred. "Doubtless the white men were right, but were the Indians entirely wrong? After all, these broad prairies had belonged to them."

Many frontier women who felt a sense of responsibility for the plight of the Native Americans taught in Indian schools and did missionary and charity work among Indians, often nursing the sick and attempting to control the spread of diseases. If they could afford to, women would often hire Indians (as handymen, ranch hands, cooks, laundresses and even as nurses for their children) in order to provide them with an income.

One crusader for Native Americans' rights, a woman from South Dakota, traveled to Washington D.C. at the turn of the century to complain about the Indians "displayed as side-show freaks" in Buffalo Bill's Wild West show. Her protests fell on deaf ears and her name was not even recorded in the *Congressional Record*, in which she was identified simply as "a woman."

Temperance and religious reformer groups (which were mainly supported and led by women) were successful in forcing Kansas to establish a "Quaranteen Line" which confined wild and woolly cattle towns to the western half of the state. These groups' main purpose was to eliminate the rowdy cowtowns from their midst. Famous cowtowns like Wichita and Dodge City were "breeding grounds for sin," these reformers argued, since the cowboys spent their time and money frequenting the hundreds of brothels, saloons and gambling parlors located in those towns. The reformers claimed that these towns had been "built by Satan himself" and were determined to close them down. Eventually these groups succeeded in drawing up their "quaranteen line," which legislated that Wichita and other towns east of the line cease all shipping. In time the entire state of Kansas was declared "off-limits" to the cattlemen. This actually made little difference at the time the law was enacted, because the railroad's octopus-like tentacles had already extended southward to Texas, and the need for long cattle drives to Midwestern cattle shipping centers had been eliminated.

ARMY WIVES

Unlike women who settled on Western farms or ranches or in towns, army wives were nomads who followed their spouses from one military establishment to another. They had to adhere to the strict code of behavior the Army demanded. This included a well-defined and often cruel class system. There was a distinct pecking order among military wives. The higher a soldier's rank, the more privileges his wife enjoyed. Not that any of the Army accommodations could be considered luxurious. The best housing available was, however, assigned to the highest-ranking officer and his family. Enlisted men's wives and families were usually assigned to the most primitive housing at the forts and military installations. But whether they were the wives of officers or enlisted men, these women faced difficult conditions and constant danger.

Besides having to accept the fact that they would never have a permanent home, enlisted men's wives were expected to work as cooks, housekeepers and laundresses. Officer's wives worked as teachers and nurses and served as hostesses at formal social functions. They were also expected to perform all sorts of charity work, such as preaching Christianity to the "heathen" Indian scouts who lived at the fort, and taking up collections for Army widows and their children. The living conditions at the forts were often quite deplorable. Their quarters usually consisted of minimally equipped kitchens, the sparsest of furniture and what little decoration they could manage to bring along with them. In spite of the austerity of their dwellings, all Army wives were expected to keep their quarters tidy and neat, in typical Army "spit-and-polish" tradition.

In 1874, Martha Summerhayes traveled in a covered wagon to be with her husband at a remote Western military outpost. As she crossed the Mojave desert, Mrs. Summerhayes recorded the details of her journey in a journal. "The wagon in which I am riding," she wrote, "is sometimes called an ambulance." She described it as a good-sized vehicle with two seats facing each other under a canvas roof, and a seat outside for the driver. The inside could be closed by drawing the canvas sides and the ends could also be covered by canvas to give the riders in the wagons some degree of privacy. "The massive blue Army wagons are heavily loaded and carried the laundresses and enlisted men's wives and children in them." The wagons traveled with marching troops out front, followed by the ambulances carrying the officers' wives and single officers, the blue Studebaker wagons, the baggage wagons and a small group of soldiers guarding the rear. Mrs. Summerhayes' journal was also filled with complaints about the conditions under which she traveled. "A hot wind blew constantly," Mrs. Summerhayes wrote "Everything was filled with dust. Because of the heat, I discarded my hat and my head became a mass of fine white dust." When she said she needed a bath, an "Army girl" (camp follower) told her she should not complain about such minor things. Mrs. Summerhayes also complained about the salty language used by the muleskinners. (Her husband later explained that it was necessary for the men to use foul language because that was how they vented their frustrations.) When Mrs. Summerhayes finally arrived at Fort Russell, Wyoming, she was distressed to find that she had to share her quarters with the family of a soldier of lower rank than her husband. When she complained to the post's commanding officer, he told her to tell the family they had to leave. "They will hate you for it," he advised her, "but if you do not, they will not respect you." During one five-year period, the Summerhayeses were transferred no less than 50 times, as officers of higher and lower rank came and went in the various forts in which they were serving.

Frances Grummond's experiences included everything an Army wife could expect. Mrs. Grummond's husband, George, a lieutenant in the Army, was awaiting assignment orders in Tennessee when he asked her to marry him. She accepted his proposal, and George was eventually assigned to the 18th Infantry, which was under the command of Colonel Henry B. C. Carrington. The Grummonds, after a short honeymoon, left Tennessee to take up their new post. They arrived at Fort Laramie, Wyoming, where 700 soldiers were stationed, after a difficult journey west. "The soldiers traveling with us," Mrs. Grummond wrote home, "had been most courteous and obliging during our uncomfortable trip west." She also told her family back home that she was the only woman traveling with the large group of men. In September 1866, George and Frances left Fort Laramie with a second detachment for his permanent assignment at Fort Phil Kearney, where Colonel Carrington had been busy supervising the construction of the new fort. The Grummonds' temporary accommodation at the uncompleted Fort Phil Kearney in Wyoming was a tent. This alarmed Mrs. Grummond because it was winter and she was pregnant with the couple's first

Army wife Frances Grummond. (American Heritage Center, University of Wyoming.)

child. During their first night at the fort, a heavy snow fell, and when Frances awoke in the morning, she was surprised to find her face was covered with melting snow that had found its way into the tent. By December, the fort was completed, but Sioux Indians led by Chief Red Cloud began to gather around it in ever-increasing numbers. When the Sioux began to prepare for a major assault, Colonel Henry B. C. Carrington ordered two companies consisting of 75 men (including Frances' husband George) to "run the Indians off." Frances was standing in front of her quarters "filled with dread" as the columns of soldiers exited the fort. A young Sioux warrior named Crazy Horse lured the troops away from what appeared to be the main body of Indians and into a trap. In a matter of minutes, the soldiers were surrounded by hundreds of Indian warriors and massacred. When Colonel Carrington heard the shots, he sent out a second force of soldiers to investigate. The Indians had already departed and the troops found the bodies of their comrades scattered about the snow-covered countryside. There were no survivors. "Mrs. Carrington took me in her arms," Frances later wrote in her memoirs, "and into her home, where we sat in silence. Henceforth my home was Mrs. Carrington." (Ironically, five years later Frances became "Mrs. Carrington" when she married Colonel Carrington after his wife's death.) After the massacre, Frances wrote home, "The horrors of the following days ... the making of coffins and digging in the hard, frozen earth for a burial place, when the cold was so intense that the men worked in 15-minute reliefs, and a guard was constantly on the alert lest Indians should interrupt... One half of the headquarters building, which was my temporary home, was unfinished, and this was utilized by carpenters for making pine cases for the dead. I knew that my husband's coffin was being made, and the sound of hammers and the grating of saws was torture." In March 1867,

Frances Grummond arrived home in Tennessee with her dead husband's body. A few weeks later, their son George was born.

While Frances Grummond was making her journey back to Tennessee, she had an overnight stopover at Fort Sedgewick. Accommodations were scarce and Frances had to share a room with an Army widow named Annie Sokalski, who was traveling with her dogs, Romeo and Juliet. When Mrs. Sokalski unbuckled her belt, Frances noticed that she had two revolvers strapped to her waist. Annie Blanche Sokalski was an unconventional and bizarre woman who seemed to attract attention wherever she went because of her unusual appearance and behavior. Annie always wore a wolfskin riding habit, with wolf tails on the bottom of her skirt that swept the ground. Her head was topped by a fur hat from which she had draped another string of wolf's tails. Annie was an expert sharpshooter and challenged others to compete with her whenever the opportunity arose. When the celebrated Civil War general Philip Henry Sherman first saw Annie at an army outpost, he asked in astonishment, "What the devil kind of a creature is that? Wild woman, Pawnee, Sioux or what?"

When Frances Grummond met Annie Sokalski, Annie was also heading home after the death of her husband. Her spouse was an Army captain who had been court-martialed and discharged for disobeying the orders of a superior officer. His commission was later reinstated mainly due to Annie's persistent lobbying on his behalf. Unfortunately, Captain George Sokalski died shortly after he returned to active military duty. When Annie arrived back East, she failed to attract the attention to which she had become accustomed and she simply faded into obscurity, just one unconventional woman among the thousands of odd souls who inhabited New York City.

No woman typified the loyal, loving and stalwart "Army wife" more perfectly than Elizabeth Custer, the marriage partner of one of the nineteenth century's most famous soldiers, George Armstrong Custer, whose place in history was assured when he was killed at the infamous Battle of Little Big Horn.

When Custer was a young man, he attended a normal school and became a teacher. Custer taught school in a one-room schoolhouse in Ohio for a short while, but he was an ambitious man who wanted more adventure and excitement out of life. When he heard that Army officers were being paid $28 a month (much more money than he was earning as a teacher), and that he could receive a free college education, he applied for admission to West Point Military Academy and was accepted. Although Custer did not distinguish himself there as a student (he graduated last in his class), he obtained his officer's commission just one month before the Civil War erupted. Custer proved to be an exceptionally daring and brave soldier and became one of the heroes of the Battle of Gettysburg, when he led 500 men on horseback in a fearless charge.

Because of his bravery, Custer received a great deal of publicity in the Northern press, and in 1863 he was appointed to the staff of General of the Army McClelland. Twenty-two years old at the time, he was promoted to the rank of Brigadier General. When McClelland was dismissed by President Lincoln, who had become dissatisfied with his performance as the head of the Union Army, Custer was given leave and went home to await reassignment. While on leave, he attended a dance and met a beautiful young woman named Elizabeth Bacon, whom he began to court. In 1864, Custer gathered up enough courage to ask her to become his wife and Elizabeth readily accepted his proposal. When Custer helped lead the forces that defeated General Robert E. Lee at Appomattox, he became one of the Civil War's most decorated Union heroes. After the war, Custer attempted to repeat his Civil War successes as the commander of army units which fought hostile Native American tribesmen in the West. The country's newspapers reported on his every skirmish and he soon became a legendary Western character as well as a Civil War hero.

Elizabeth and George Armstrong Custer. (Library of Congress.)

Because of his love for his wife, Custer arranged for her to accompany him whenever possible to the various posts to which he was assigned, both during the Civil War and afterwards, when he was out West. The Custers' first Western post was at Fort Riley, Kansas. The couple often had to sleep in the wagons that carried them from one fort to another, sometimes for days and even months on end, and Elizabeth (like other Army wives) had to adjust to the living quarters they were assigned. These quarters ranged from barely acceptable to downright primitive. While she and her husband were stationed at Fort Leavenworth, Mrs.

Custer wrote home that she was living "in a place whose walls were hung with old canvas and had a sheet-iron stove in the middle of the only room." The furniture consisted of a few campstools and unpainted chairs and a rough-hewn table (three wooden planks stretched across two wooden horses). Her dressing table was an old packing box and on it she had a tin pitcher and a crude mirror. An animal skin and old army blankets covered the wooden floors; the curtains on the windows were old sheets dyed red with beet juice to give them color. At night a single kerosene lamp furnished the only light. These accommodations were actually quite luxurious compared to what most army wives were used to.

"Sometimes we had no eggs all summer long," Elizabeth wrote in her memoirs. "The cooking was maddening to us. The recipes always called for eggs, butter and cream, all unobtainable most of the time, and I pray for some Army women to prepare a little manual for the use of housekeepers stranded on the frontier."

Elizabeth and George Custer remained devoted to each other, even though there is evidence that George had somewhat of "a roving eye." Women found him exceptionally handsome and dashing and he flirted outrageously with them, often in the presence of Elizabeth, who always appeared amused by his actions. George had long, flowing golden hair and clear blue eyes. Elizabeth was a beautiful, slim and girlish-looking woman with intelligent eyes and a reserved demeanor. The Custers never called each other by their given names: Elizabeth called George "Armstrong," (his middle name) or by his nickname, "Autie," and he always called her "Libbie." (Custer also called Elizabeth "Old Lady" from time to time, but this was always said with the deepest of affection.)

The only record of any infidelity on the part of Custer occurred after a long winter campaign against the Cheyennes in Indian Territory, when he was parted from Elizabeth for almost six months. After his troops attacked a Black Hills Indian village on the Washita River and defeated a band of hostile braves, Custer gave orders that the captured Indian women be "matched up" with the men under his command. Custer himself took Monahseetah, the 20-year-old daughter of the chief. Custer even wrote about his affection for Monahseetah in his book *Life on the Plains,* but Elizabeth never publicly commented on this relationship and remained fiercely loyal to her husband. Elizabeth later met Monahseetah and reportedly became very fond of the lovely young Native American.

One of the only problems that seemed to surface in the Custers' relationship involved George's fondness for dogs. He had numerous canines which he took with him wherever the couple was stationed. At one point Custer had over 30 hounds, but Elizabeth apparently endured the animals' constant presence with the patience of a saint. George was also known to be somewhat of a practical joker, but Elizabeth (often the butt of his jokes) accepted his pranks with a tolerance most wives might not have exhibited.

While the Custers were stationed at their final post, Fort Lincoln, Elizabeth claims that she actually had a premonition as her husband rode off to meet Sitting Bull and his braves at Little Big Horn that it was going to be the last time she would ever see him alive. Later, Elizabeth wrote that when she heard the news that her husband had been killed in battle, "I wanted to die." She went into a deep depression that lasted almost a year. Left with only a few hundred dollars upon her husband's death, Elizabeth decided after a year of mourning that it was time to do something for herself if she wanted to survive. (George had speculated in the stock market and lost the couple's meager $13,000 savings.) In 1877 she went to New York City and became a secretary at the Decorative Arts Society, a ladies' organization that made and sold various homemade objects. She also began to write articles for a New York newspaper about her experiences as George Armstrong Custer's wife and her life out West. When President U. S. Grant stated that he felt Custer was responsible for the Little Big Horn massacre, Elizabeth came to her husband's defense. Over the next 57 years, she went on lecture tours, wrote three books about her Army years and became one of America's most celebrated and beloved females as she traveled across the country staunchly defending her husband. She eventually succeeded in turning Custer's death into the very symbol of American patriotism. By the time Elizabeth Custer died at the age of 91 in 1933, she had become a very wealthy woman mainly due to her lectures and was living on New York's swank Park Avenue. She never remarried, remaining true to the end to the memory of her beloved husband.

The Army wives and sweethearts were quite accurately portrayed in many Western films. Especially realistic were two films directed by John Ford, *Fort Apache* (1948) and *She Wore a Yellow Ribbon* (1949). The climax of both films involved Indian attacks on Army outposts. *Fort Apache* starred John Wayne as an army scout and Henry Fonda, John Agar, Victor McLaglen and Ward Bond as soldiers at the fort and Shirley Temple and Anna Lee as devoted Army women. Fonda's performance as an officer with a pompous, by-the-book attitude was particularly effective. *Fort Apache* is also remembered by movie buffs as the film in which former child star Shirley Temple played her first adult role and received her first screen kiss from real-life husband Agar. John Wayne also starred in Ford's *She Wore a Yellow Ribbon*, which featured Joanne Dru as the plucky daughter of a military man and Mildred Natwick as a military matron.

AFRICAN-AMERICAN WOMEN

In the years preceding the Civil War, there were very few African-Americans living on the frontier. Most of the African-Americans who were freed by their masters (or managed to escape enslavement) chose to live in Eastern cities such as New York, Philadelphia and Washington rather than migrate to the Western wilderness. The 1850 census reveals, however, that in the state of Missouri, which was considered quite far west for that time, there were 40 African-Americans among the 1,000 people of Cooper County. Seventeen of the 40 were women. These women were mainly employed as cooks and laundresses, but one became a schoolteacher in that county—a woman who had been freed by her master, went North and was educated in an educational normal school. In Howard County, Missouri, the African-American population was similar in number. Ten African-American women and 29 African-American men lived there between 1836 and 1861. Several African-Americans migrated further west; settlements as far west as Minnesota included blacks as far back as the early nineteenth century. In Mickilmackie Parish, Minnesota, a marriage license was recorded for Jean and Jeanne Bonga, both listed as "blacks," as early as 1794. A letter written by a white woman named Ann Ramsey, who lived in Minnesota in the early 1800s, told of "the deep affection" she felt for a black woman named Martha who worked for her as a domestic servant, but whom she claimed was her closest friend and confidante. A journal kept by settlers who migrated from Virginia to Missouri in 1822 recorded that they were accompanied by four black male servants and a black woman cook they called "Mammy." Another white Virginia family made the journey west in 1841, accompanied by 60 black slaves they planned to use as laborers once they established a farm in western Missouri. Unlike Missouri, where a large group of Southern-born settlers believed that owning slaves was their "God-given right," Iowa, Indiana and Minnesota prohibited slavery both before and after they became states. These areas were mostly inhabited by settlers from the Northeast.

The largest concentration of African-Americans west of the Mississippi was located in towns such as St. Louis and St. Paul, where they found employment as construction workers, barbers and domestic servants. During the first half of the nineteenth century, African-Americans tended to live in ghettos with people of their own race with whom they probably felt more comfortable. It is no wonder that they wanted no more contact with whites than necessary, considering their slavery backgrounds. Because of their relatively few numbers out West both before and immediately following the Civil War, it is difficult to determine what role black women played in their communities, but they frequently found employment as domestics in white homes.

One group of African-Americans who settled on the Kansas Plains in 1877 were led there by Benjamin "Pap" Singleton, who founded an all-black settlement he called "Nicodemus." By 1870, the black population of Kansas numbered 17,000, and by 1880, that number swelled to over 43,000. A white woman named Anne E. G. Bingham wrote in 1880 that she and her husband hired a black family of six to help them out on their farm, and that she was "very grateful to have their help." Mrs. Bingham also wrote about how "hard-working" these people were, and described one black woman who carried "a pail of water on her head with one hand to steady it, freeing her other hand to carry a basket of clothes that needed washing on her hip." Many black men found work as cowboys and "buffalo" soldiers. Black women who accompanied their menfolk found employment at military installations as laundresses and nursemaids. From 1867 until the early 1900s, two out of the ten regular cavalry army units were composed of African-Americans. These troops were first called "buffalo soldiers" by the Cheyenne Indians, who respected the black man's fighting ability as they respected the fighting nature of their beloved buffaloes. A *Harper's Weekly* magazine article of the late 1860s said that "Indians came to respect a black soldier with holy terror" because of their fearlessness.

One story that appeared in an Eastern newspaper was written by a white woman named Willa Hickman, who had gone to Nicodemus, Kansas, to perform missionary work with her husband. "The families lived in dugouts in the ground. The scenery to me was not at all living and I began to cry." In another account, written by an African-American schoolteacher who lived in Nicodemus, she said she taught a class of 45 black children in her dugout. Another black woman, Ava Daley, wrote a letter to a family member back east and described her experiences as a black woman growing up in the Wild West. Mrs. Daley's family raised cattle, mules and horses in the Dakotas, where she had been born. She married a black South Dakotan who was also a rancher, but admitted in the letter that her grandfather was a white man and her grandmother, black. "Color never made a difference to Grandpa. You were a person and a man and a lady." Mrs. Daley also reported that her neighbors seemed to feel pretty much the same way her grandfather did. "Everybody asked if you needed anything from town ... and brought it back to your house or left it at your gate." Another North Dakota black woman, Era Bell Thompson, had similar good feelings about her white neighbors: "I was very lucky to have grown up in North Dakota where families were busy fighting climate and soil, and there was little awareness of race." She wrote that her family was particularly close to a Norwegian family who often brought them supplies when they had difficulty getting into town themselves. Sudie Rone of Cheyenne, Wyoming, had a different opinion of her white neighbors. She wrote home that she felt "prejudice against blacks out West kept whites and blacks separated."

Several African-Americans who went west following the Civil War lived in some of the West's most celebrated towns (Tombstone, Deadwood, Dodge City, Wichita and Virginia City). One Deadwood woman, Estelline Bennett, wrote an excellent book (*Old Deadwood Days*) about her life as a girl in that infamous Western town. Estelline, who was white, met Calamity Jane as a child and saw many of Deadwood's most celebrated inhabitants. Estelline recalled that there were at least two African-American families living in Deadwood when it was at the peak of its notoriety. The two families lived in a section of town known as "Nigger Hill." Mrs. Goodrich, the matriarch of one of these families was, according to Estelline, "a kindly, mammy-like soul whose children went to school and slid down wintery hills" just like all the other town's youngsters. Mrs. Goodrich named one of her young sons "Sad," because, she said, he was "not a very happy baby when he was born, and he always had a sad look on his face." Another of Mrs. Goodrich's children, Laura, was a childhood friend of Estelline, and the two would often play together. Estelline described a time she and Laura were sliding down "Nigger Hill" on their sleds after a snowstorm and Estelline went over the side of the hill and landed in a deep pile of snow. She couldn't free herself from the snowdrift and began to panic, until she heard Laura's "soft velvety voice" calling out her name. Estelline shouted at the top of her lungs that she was stuck and Laura scurried down the hill and pulled her out. Sad and Laura's father was "not nearly as pleasant as the rest of the family." One evening, Estelline was asleep when she was awakened by the sound of gunfire under her second story bedroom window. Two men were shooting it out with six-shooters in the alley between Estelline's house and the house next door. One of the gunfighters was Mr. Goodrich, who was in the habit of getting drunk most nights and often "picked fights" with anyone who disagreed with him about practically anything at all. The sheriff eventually came upon the scene and convinced the two men to end the shooting. "Nobody was killed and nobody was arrested," according to Estelline, who had become so used to the sound of gunfire in town that she simply pulled the covers over her head and went back to sleep.

REAL LIFE AND FICTIONAL LADY SPORTS

Molly Monroe and Charlie Pankhurst, like Calamity Jane, were lady sports who were more like men than women. Molly (a.k.a. Mollie) Monroe, whose real name was Mary E. Sawyer, became a well-known real-life Western sport in Arizona. According to her obituary in the *Phoenix Herald*, "Molly was a girl cowboy who in her day would ride anything with four feet, chew more tobacco and swear harder than any man in America." Molly, despite her rough exterior, was known for being an extremely soft-hearted woman who freely gave away most of her money, and often spent time nursing sick miners and cowboys. This earned her the nickname the "Visiting Angel of Arizona." According to people who knew her, it was "a love affair gone bad" that brought Molly to Arizona from an unnamed Eastern state. The *San Francisco Mail* wrote about her, "For many years it was customary for Molly to accompany all the leading scouts against the common foe, the Apaches. Dressed in the uniform of the sports of that time—buckskin pants, the usual appendages of beads and fringes, broad-brimmed hat, armed with a Henry rifle, two six-shooters and a Bowie knife, she was ready for the fray. And when it came down to a good square Indian fight, Molly was there, as many a one of the Apache found to his cost."

In 1877 Molly was confined to the Clark and Langdon Sanitorium in Stockton, California, after being declared legally insane. In an interview that year, Molly told a reporter that she was "the meanest thing on earth" and intended to remain so until she was "turned out" to do as she pleased. Shortly after that interview, Molly died.

Until Charlotte Durkey Pankhurst died in 1879, no one knew she was a woman. For years, "Charlie" masqueraded as a man and it was not until a funeral director prepared her body for burial that the truth about her gender was revealed.

Charlotte was born in Lebanon, New Hampshire, in 1812. Abandoned by her desperately poor parents, Charlotte was placed in an orphanage to be raised by the state. Dressing herself in stolen boys' clothes, Charlotte ran away from the orphanage when she was in her early teens and went to Massachusetts, where she met a kind old man named Ebenezer Balch who took her under his wing believing she was a boy. When Balch moved to Providence,

Rhode Island, he took "Charlie" with him and from there they went to Georgia and then to California. Charlotte, who everyone thought was a man, got a job as a muleskinner and even voted in an election in Santa Cruz in 1868 (women had not yet been granted the right to vote). This made her the first woman in the United States to actually cast a vote, though no one knew it at the time. There was nothing in Charlie's demeanor to suggest that she was a woman. She stood five-foot-seven, had a deep voice, chewed tobacco, smoked cigars and (of course) always wore men's clothes. Amazingly, after the funeral director reported his discovery to the police, his autopsy revealed to everyone's surprise that not only was Charlie a woman, but she had at some time in her life given birth to a child.

Independent, high-spirited, tomboyish females were among the favorite characters of Western-action readers. The heroines of these simplistic dime novel adventures could ride, rope, shoot and "cuss" as well as any man, and were sometimes sexually attractive to men, but they were usually considered more like buddies or pals. One of the nineteenth century's most popular dime novel sports was Lola, the creation of pulp writer Joseph E. Badger. Several of Badger's books featured Lola as their central character. Lola "was a dark-eyed brunette" who "was pretty to look at, as she sits her piebald mustang 'savage' [Indian] style [without saddle] with her rifle balanced across her Mexican saddle and other weapons gleaming from the belt that encircled her round, compact waist." The heroine of such stories as *The Barranca Wolf, The Beautiful Decoy* and *A Romance of the Texas Border*, Lola was a sport whose father taught her to hate men and to use her feminine charms to lure men into traps so that he could rob them. Lola, however, did not approve of her father's criminal ways and was basically a "good girl." She fell in love with a cowboy named Ned and laid down her life saving him from death. This deeply disturbed Badger's readers, but put an end to Lola's career once and for all. Dime novelist E. L. Wheeler, who used Calamity Jane as the heroine of several adventure stories, also featured a sport named "Doll" in his books. In Wheeler's *The Detective Queen; or The Denver Doll's Devices*, Doll is "an elegant, lovely-to-look-at sport" who apprehends a band of desperadoes assisted by a Negro, a Dutchman and a Chinaman who serve as her deputies. Another Wheeler sport who proved popular with his readers was "Leadville Lil." In his book *The Girl Sport; or Jumbo Joe's Disguise*, Lil drinks whiskey, smokes cigarettes and uses a kiss as her stake in a poker game. Another lady sport in this same novel is a woman named "Sadie." Sadie and Lil fight over the love of a cowboy-hero named Joe, and Sadie is shot by Joe just as she is about to kill Lil. Lil and Joe become romantically involved and in the happy ending Lil reveals to Joe that she is actually an heiress to a large fortune.

Another fictional female sport, "Arietta Murdock," the creation of writer Cornelius Shea, became one of America's most popular fictional characters. Arietta was first introduced in 1901 as the major character in a story published in *Wild West Weekly* magazine. In it, Arietta was rescued from Sioux Indian captivity by a heroic character named "Young Wild West." Arietta was definitely "a cut above the average sport" and often rivaled "Young Wild West" in heroism and derring-do. Arietta became so popular with readers that she was featured on approximately 80 percent of the magazine's covers after her first appearance. Many other sports stories were written by St. George Rathbone (who used the pen name Ned Taylor) for *Wild West Weekly*, which before it ceased publication had released 175 issues.

The dime novelists laid the groundwork for later, more complex Western adventure novels. The novels of Louis L'Amour, for example, often featured sports as major characters. One of the most financially successful hard-cover novels published in 1908 was an adventure story called *Nancy MacIntyre, a Tale of the Prairies*, written by Lester Shepard Parker. In this novel, Nancy is the owner of a ranch and endures numerous hardships in the male-dominated West. The prestigious short story writer William S. Porter, who is better known by his pen name O. Henry, was a great admirer of all things Western and actually lived on a ranch for a time. In 1907, O. Henry wrote a series of stories called *Hearts of the West* which met with great critical and public acclaim. Several sports figure prominently in some of O. Henry's stories. In "The Marquis and Miss Sally," for example, a character named Sally disguises herself as a cowboy. Another successful writer of Western fiction was a woman named Berta "Buzzy" Sinclair, whose pen name was B. M. Bower. In one of her novels, *Rom o' the World*, heroine Belle Lorrigan is a ranching lady who refuses to ride horses (she considers it "unladylike") but is not opposed to tearing around the countryside in a buckboard wagon. She is described as "a golden-curled, pink-cheeked, honey-throated Amazon who shoots better than a man and sings like a bird." Short story writer Eugene Manlowe Rhodes, who rivaled O. Henry in popularity, used a lady sport as a character in his 1926 story "Paso Por Aqui." One of the sports featured in this story, lady rancher Eva Scales, also appeared in Rhodes' earlier story "Maid Most Dear" and was one of the Old West's staunchest defenders. Sports were also prominently featured in the novels of the celebrated writer Zane Grey. In books such as *The Hash Knife Outfit* (1929), he compares Eastern and Western girls and obviously favors the latter. "Strikes me," the hero tells an Eastern girl, "the Lord made you wonderful to look at, but left out any brains." The cowpoke then sings the praises of a woman of the West he calls "Gloriana."

Respectable Women of the West as Depicted in Films, on Stage and on Radio and Television

Women were featured in Western movies from the earliest days of the silent screen. One of the Edison Company's first films starred such Western celebrities as Buffalo Bill Cody and sharpshooter Annie Oakley, captured on film in 1893. Edison also produced the first story film in 1903, a Western short called *The Great Train Robbery*. In this eight-minute film, a group of outlaws rob a train and are subsequently brought to justice. A square dance sequence in the film features a group of dancing Western women.

Between 1910 and 1920, many silent films centered around female Western characters. Most of these films were serialized short subjects. *What Happened to Mary?* (1914) starred the film world's first female Western star, Helen Holmes, a former rodeo performer. Other early Western heroines such as Carol Holloway (*The Fighting Trail*), Betty Compson (*The Terror of the Range*) and Ethlyne Clair (*The Vanishing Rider*) proved extremely popular with the movie-going public. Another actress who became well known for starring in short Western adventure films was Texas Guinan, whose real name was Mary Louise Cecelia Guinan. According to Paul Sann's book *The Lawless Decade* (1957), Guinan was born and raised in Texas and was "one of the most authentic lady gunslingers on the celluloid prairie. In [the early 1900s] Texas Guinan had a mop of black hair menacing enough to scare off the villain even without a six-shooter." Other silent Westerns featuring women in major roles included *Frontier Days in the Early West* (1910), in which a woman dressed like a man rides in a horse race and wins, *Western Girls* (1912), in which two sisters disguise themselves as men and capture a bunch of stagecoach robbers, and *Rowdy Ann* (1919), which starred Fay Tincher as a rancher's daughter who wears her guns to class much to the amusement of her college classmates.

One of the brightest Western female stars of this early period was Ruth Delaney, whose most successful movie was *The Prairie Pirate*. Another popular film cowgirl was Edith Storey. ("Cowboy" was a term first used by President Theodore Roosevelt to describe a rodeo performer named Lucille Mulhall, an expert roper and trick horseback rider who appeared in the Mills Brothers' show at the turn of the century.) Edith Storey became America's first "cowgirl" film star and appeared in such motion pictures as *Scarlet Days* (1918) and *As the Sun Went Down* (1919).

In most silent Westerns, however, women played supporting roles opposite celebrated cowboy stars like G. M. "Bronco Billy" Anderson, Tom Mix and William S. Hart (Hollywood's first major Western superstars).

The popularity of Western films continued to grow when silent films gave way to "talkies" in the late 1920s. In these early sound features, women were usually portrayed as respectable and hard-working citizens. In 1945, the glamorous Loretta Young appeared in a low-key Western comedy called *Along Came Jones* with Gary Cooper as her co-star. Young played an independent frontier woman who meets and falls in love with a man she believes is a notorious outlaw, and sets out to reform him. A film with a similar plot, *The Angel and the Badman*, starred Gail Russell as a sweet young thing who tames a gunfighter played by Western superstar John Wayne. *Westward the Women* (1951) and *Westward Ho, the Wagons* (1956), were popular films about pioneer women traveling west. *Westward the Women* was interesting and somewhat unusual in that *most* of the characters in it *were* women. The plot of the film concerns a group of women headed west to California to meet their mail-order husbands.

Three films featuring respectable Western women stand head and shoulders above most of the other Westerns made in the 1930s, '40s, '50s and '60s: *Cimarron, The Harvey Girls* and *How the West Was Won*. These films were major releases (unlike most Westerns, which were usually second features) and were very successful at the box office. All three movies had big budgets and big name stars. There were actually two film versions of Edna Ferber's popular novel *Cimarron*. The first version was made in 1931 and was directed by Wesley Ruggles. It was critically acclaimed and won the Academy Award as "Best Film of the Year" in 1931. The film was about the much-publicized rush for free land when the Cherokee Strip in Oklahoma was opened for development in 1893. Irene Dunne, Richard Dix, Estelle Taylor and William Collier starred. A new version of *Cimarron* was made in 1961. Even though it was in Technicolor and was an epic production, it did not receive the critical acclaim of the first version. It did, however, prove popular with the movie-going public. This *Cimarron* was directed by Anthony Mann and starred Glenn Ford, Maria Schell, Anne Baxter, Arthur O'Connell, Mercedes McCambridge and Aline McMahon.

The Harvey Girls (1946) was a Technicolor musical comedy filmed at MGM. It starred Judy Garland as a respectable young lady from the East who travels West to work as a waitress in one of the Harvey restaurants located along the Atchison, Topeka and Santa Fe railroad line. The film co-starred John Hodiak (a gambler who falls in love with the high-spirited-but-pure Miss Garland) and Angela Lansbury (as a saloon girl).

A film of huge proportions, *How the West Was Won* (1963) was advertised as "the movie Western to end all Westerns." (It was indeed the most ambitious Western film ever made up until that time.) Directed by one of Hollywood's most prolific filmmakers, John Ford, this panoramic Technicolor saga covered a 60-year period (1830–1890) in the lives of a pioneer family out West. The film was divided into five segments: the family's covered wagon trip; their involvement in the California Gold Rush; their Civil War experiences; their participation in the building of the railroad; and their efforts to bring law and order to the frontier. The film's large cast included Debbie Reynolds, Carroll Baker, Lee J. Cobb, Henry Fonda, James Stewart, Carolyn Jones, Agnes Moorehead, Thelma Ritter, John Wayne, Gregory Peck, Eli Wallach and many others. Spencer Tracy narrated the film, but did not appear in it. Approximately 12,617 extras appeared in the film.

Paint Your Wagon was a Western musical comedy written for the stage by Alan J. Lerner

Judy Garland is a waitress and Angela Lansbury a saloon girl in *The Harvey Girls* **(1946). (Author's collection.)**

and Frederick Loewe, who a few years later gave the world *My Fair Lady*. *Paint Your Wagon* was presented on Broadway in 1954. Directed by Daniel Mann, with choreography by Agnes DeMille, the show focused on a grizzled old mining prospector (James Barton) and his young daughter (Olga San Juan). Some of its songs ("Wanderin' Star" and "They Call the Wind Maria") became popular hits. The musical ran for 289 performances and later became a film musical starring Lee Marvin and Clint Eastwood. In 1959, another Western musical comedy was presented on Broadway: *Destry Rides Again*. Based on the 1939 film starring

James Stewart and Marlene Dietrich, this stage version featured Andy Griffith as mild-mannered sheriff Tom Destry and Dolores Gray as Frenchy, a saloon girl whom Destry tames (along with the rest of the wild and woolly town). The show was choreographed by Michael Kidd and featured Scott Brady, Jack Prince and Libi Staiger. It ran for 473 performances.

One of Broadway's most celebrated musical comedies was *Oklahoma* by Richard Rodgers and Oscar Hammerstein II. Set on the Western frontier, *Oklahoma* was a precedent-setting production in many ways and broke many conventions when it premiered in 1943. Instead of the usual big production number that usually opened most Broadway musicals, the curtain rose on a dimly lit stage that revealed the front of a farmhouse with stretches of corn fields behind it. As the lights slowly came up, an offstage voice sang, "There's a bright golden sun in the meadow" and a cowboy slowly sauntered on stage enjoying the beautiful morning that was just dawning. In addition to this song ("Oh What a Beautiful Morning"), the first-night audience was treated to such numbers as "The Surrey with the Fringe on Top," "Many a New Day" and (of course) the rousing "Oklahoma." *Oklahoma* was the first Broadway musical to use its chorus of dancers and singers as individual, distinct characters, with unique personalities and mannerisms instead of the usual cut-out string of chorines and chorus boys. An enormous success, the play made Alfred Drake, Joan Roberts, Betty Garde, Marc Platt, Celeste Holm and others stage stars overnight. The musical was staged by Rouben Mamoulian, but it was the choreography of Agnes DeMille that gave it its unique look. DeMille's dance sequences included a dream ballet featuring various Western types (from dance hall girls to sweet and innocent farm girls). First night newspaper critics such as Lewis Nichols of the *New York Times*, Howard Barnes of the *New York Herald Tribune*, and Burns Mantle of the *New York Daily News* called *Oklahoma* "wonderful," "jubilant" and "enchanting ... the most thoroughly entertaining and attractive musical comedy since *Show Boat*." *Oklahoma* remained on Broadway for five years and ran for an unprecedented 2,212 continuous performances (a record first broken by *My Fair Lady*). In 1955, a film version of *Oklahoma* was made with Gordon MacRae, Shirley Jones, Rod Steiger, Gloria Grahame and Charlotte Greenwood in the major roles. The film, directed by Fred Zinnemann, failed to live up to the promise of the immensely popular Broadway version, and although it was successful enough at the box office, it did not become one of the screen's legendary films as expected.

In the mid-to-late 1930s, several popular radio dramatic programs featured women in prominent roles and involved Western themes. Two of the most successful radio Westerns were *A Woman of Courage* and *Prairie Folks*. These serials, which were presented five days a week, Mondays through Fridays, chronicled the everyday adventures of nineteenth-century families in the Great American West. The leading female character on *A Woman of America* was Prudence Dane, originally played by Anne Seymour and then by Florence Freeman. The program, which began with a Western setting, eventually became a modern-day drama set in a newspaper office. *Prairie Folks* told the story of settlers who went to Minnesota in the 1870s; Helen Warren played a stalwart pioneer wife and mother. Women were often featured as supporting characters on the western radio adventure series *The Lone Ranger*, *Gunsmoke*, *The Sheriff*, and many others in the 1930s, '40s and '50s.

Several successful television series centered around women of the West. The earliest TV series to depict the lives of ordinary Western women was *Death Valley Days* (1952–1975). One of television's longest-running syndicated series, *Death Valley Days* related stories of Western pioneers, ranchers, cowboys, trail blazers, settlers and adventurers. The program was hosted by Stanley Andrews for 13 years and then by Ronald Reagan (who hosted it until he was elected governor of California), Robert Taylor and Dale Robertson. The series' last host was country singer Merle Haggard. Guest stars included such performers as Fess Parker, Rudy Vallee, Gloria Talbott, Jane Russell, Guy Madison and many others. *Death Valley Days* was the brainchild of radio scriptwriter Ruth Woodman, who first wrote the series for radio in the 1930s.

The television series *The Big Valley* (1965–1969) starred Barbara Stanwyck as the widowed matriarch of the Barkley family who owned the vast Barkley ranch in California's San Joaquin Valley. Mrs. Barkley's four children were played by Richard Long (as Jarad), Peter Breck (as Nick), Lee Majors (as Heath) and Linda Evans (as Audra). *The Big Valley* was a thinly disguised imitation of the highly successful series *Bonanza*, which featured a ranch-owning widower and his three sons. One hundred twelve one-hour episodes were filmed before it finally departed the prime time airwaves. *Sarah* starred Brenda Vaccaro as Sarah Yarnell, a schoolteacher who left her eastern home to teach in Independence, Colorado, in the late 1800s. The show aired during the 1976 season and has seldom been seen in reruns.

The two most successful television series to feature law-abiding, respectable women as major characters are *Little House on the Prairie* and *Dr. Quinn, Medicine Woman. Little House on the Prairie* (1974–83) centered on the Ingalls family, Kansas farmers in the 1870s. Michael Landon played the family's patriarch Charles Ingalls, Karen Grassle played his wife Caroline, and Melissa Gilbert, Melissa Sue Anderson and the Greenbush twins played the Ingalls' three daughters Laura, Mary and Carrie (the Greenbush twins both playing the same part from time to time). The series was based on author Laura Ingalls Wilder's accounts of her family's actual experiences as farmers out West during the frontier days. It proved immensely popular with the viewing public.

The long-running television series *Dr. Quinn, Medicine Woman* made its debut in 1992. The series stars English actress Jane Seymour as a lady doctor named Michaela "Mike" Quinn, who moves from Boston to set up her practice in a small Western town in the late 1800s. The series also features Joe Lando as her husband Byron Sully, and Chad Allen, Erika Flores, and Shawn Toovey as orphaned youngsters adopted by Dr. Quinn shortly after her arrival out West.

CONCLUSION

That the women of the Western frontier managed to survive at all, in that vast, uncompromising, wild area west of the Mississippi is remarkable. That some went on to become legends and earn places in United States history is more remarkable yet. All were active participants in making the Western United States the vital and productive area it has become. But in spite of their amazing contributions to the development of the American West, the accomplishments of many of these women were never formally acknowledged until 1983, when the first *Women's West Conference* was held in Sun Valley, Idaho. This conference brought together from all over the country historians, educators, writers and others who shared a common goal: to make sure these remarkable women were given the recognition they deserved for their contributions to the expansion and development of the Western United States.

Selected Western Silent Films Featuring Women in Prominent Roles

1909   *The Mended Lute* (Biograph) Florence Lawrence
                    Conato the Sioux (Biograph) Marion Leonard

1910   *In Old California* (Biograph) Marion Leonard
                    A Romance of the Western Hills (Biograph) Mary Pickford

1911   Short subjects featuring Edith Storey
                    Fighting Blood (Biograph) Blanche Sweet

1912   *Bronco Billy Shorts* (Essanay) Marguerite Chapman
                    The Stranger at Coyote (American) Pauline Bush
                    Goddess of Sagebrush Gulch (Biograph) Dorothy Bernard

1913   *The Way of a Mother* (Biograph) Jane Novack

1914   *The Spoilers* (Selig) Bessie Eyton, Kathlyn Williams
                    The Squaw Man (Lasky) Winifred Kingston
                    The Virginian (Lasky) Winifred Kingston
                    Where the Trail Divides (Lasky) Winifred Kingston

1915   *Girl of the Golden West* (Lasky) Mabel Van Buren
                    The Great Divide (Lubin) Ethel Clayton

1916   *The Trail of the Lonesome Pine* (Lasky) Charlotte Walker
                    The Aryan (Triangle) Louise Glaum

1917   *The Big Trenoine* (Metro) May Allison
                    The Clodhopper (Triangle) Margery Wilson
                    Straight Shooting (Universal) Molly Malone
                    The Flame of the Yukon (Triangle) Dorothy Dalton
                    The Volunteer (World) Madge Evans

1918   *The Claw* (Select) Clara Kimball Young
                    The Gun Woman (Triangle) Texas Guinan

M'Liss (Artcraft) Mary Pickford
Riddle Gawne (Paramount-Artcraft) Katherine MacDonald

1919   *Told in the Hills* (Artcraft) Ann Little
The Outcasts of Poker Flats (Universal) Gloria Hope
The Knickerbocker Buckaroo (Artcraft) Marjorie Daw
Scarlet Days (Griffith) Clarine Seymour
Little Miss Deputy (Triangle) Texas Guinan
As the Sun Went Down (Metro) Edith Storey

1920   *The Marked Man* (Universal) Winifred Westover

1921   *Desperate Trails* (Biograph) Irene Rich

1923   *The Covered Wagon* (Paramount) Lois Wilson
Trail of the Lonesome Pine (Paramount) Mary Miles Minter
Wild Bill Hickok (First National) Ethel Grey Terry (as Calamity Jane)
The Bad Man (First National) Enid Bennett
Salomy Jane (Paramount) Jacqueline Logan
Tiger Rose (Warner Brothers) Leonore Ulrich

1924   *Wanderer of the Wasteland* (Paramount) Billie Dove
Mademoiselle Midnight (MGM) Mae Murray
The Iron Horse (Universal) Madge Bellamy

1925   *The Great Divide* (MGM) Alice Terry, Dorothy Mackaill
Zander the Great (Cosmopolitan) Marion Davies

1926   *The Flame of the Yukon* (PDC) Seena Owen
The Winning of Barbara Worth (United Artists) Vilma Banky
The Valley of Hell (MGM) Edna Murphy
The Desert's Trail (MGM) Anna May Wong

1927   *California* (MGM) Dorothy Sebastian
The Frontiersman (MGM) Claire Windsor
Spoilers of the West (MGM) Marjorie Daw
The Law of the Range (MGM) Joan Crawford

1929   *Tide of Empire* (MGM) Renee Adoree

Appendix B

Selected Western Sound Films Featuring Women in Prominent Roles

Included in this film listing are the actresses who played parts in these films, release dates, brief plot descriptions and the name of each film's director. Films in which at least one major character was a woman are preceded by an asterisk (*).

*Along Came Jones (1945) Loretta Young
A dignified frontier woman (Young) mistakes a cowboy-drifter (Gary Cooper) for a notorious outlaw and is determined to reform him. Director: Stuart Heisler

Ambush (1949) Arlene Dahl, Jean Hagen
Dahl and Hagen play western women caught up in a war between settlers and the Apaches. Robert Taylor and John Hodiak vow to protect the ladies. Director: Sam Wood

Ambush at Tomahawk Gap (1953) Maria Elena Marquis
A group of ex-convicts ward off an attack by hostile Indians and only one of them is left alive. Marquis plays a friendly maiden who tries to help them. Director: Fred Sears

*The Angel and the Badman (1947) Gail Russell
A sweet, respectable ranch girl (Russell) tames a gruff western gunslinger (John Wayne). Director: James E. Grant

*Annie Get Your Gun (1950) Betty Hutton
Irving Berlin's stage musical biography of sharpshooter Annie Oakley's (Hutton) show business career in Buffalo Bill Cody's Wild West Show is presented in glorious Technicolor. Howard Keel plays Frank Butler. Director: George Sidney

*Annie Oakley (1935) Barbara Stanwyck
This romanticized film biography of the life and times of Annie Oakley (Stanwyck) also features Preston Foster and Melvyn Douglas. Director: George Stevens

*Arizona (1940) Jean Arthur
An independent-minded woman (Arthur) battles corruption in old Arizona with William Holden's help. Director: Wesley Ruggles

Bad Men of Missouri (1941) Jane Wyman
The outlaw Younger brothers are the central characters in this film which features Wyman as the loyal girlfriend of one of the boys. Dennis Morgan and Wayne Morris co-star. Director: Ray Enright

Bad Girls (1994) Madeleine Stowe, Drew Barrymore, Mary Stuart Masterson, Andie Mac-Dowell
A group of prostitutes become outlaws after they kill a nasty customer at their brothel. Stowe looks up an outlaw from her past (Dermot Mulroney) to help them. Director: Jonathan Kaplan

Badlands of Dakota (1941) Ann Rutherford
Richard Dix plays Wild Bill Hickok in this film in which Robert Stack and Broderick Crawford both hope to win Rutherford's affections. Director: Alfred E. Green

Badman's Territory (1946) Ann Richards, Isabel Jewell
Richards plays a respectable woman who supports Sheriff Randolph Scott as he tracks down various well-known criminals including Belle Starr (Jewell). Director: Tim Whelan

Barbary Coast (1935) Miriam Hopkins
A saloon girl (Hopkins) challenges the despotic business practices of town tough guy Edward G. Robinson in 19th century San Francisco. Director: Howard Hawks

*The Beautiful Blonde from Bashful Bend (1949) Betty Grable
20th Century-Fox's blonde bombshell star of the '40s and '50s, Betty Grable, plays a saloon entertainer who is thought to be a schoolteacher when she arrives in a western town. Cesar Romero is Betty's love interest. Director: Preston Sturges

*Belle of the Nineties (1934) Mae West
Screen tough girl Mae West plays an entertainer out West in this comedy which also starred Roger Pryor. Director: Leo McCarey

*Belle Starr (1941/1980) Gene Tierney, Elizabeth Montgomery
"Bandit Queen" Belle Starr (Tierney) is portrayed as a victim of circumstance in the 1941 film biography of her life, but Montgomery plays her in a much more realistic light in the later (1980) made-for-television movie. Directors: Lesley Selander (1941) & John A. Alonzo (1980).

*Belle Starr's Daughter (1948) Ruth Roman, Isabel Jewell
Roman, the title character in this film, arrives in a tough town to avenge the death of her mother, Belle Starr (Jewell). Director: Lesley Selander

Billy the Kid (1930, 1941) Mary Howard
This highly romanticized version of the life of the young western outlaw (Johnny Mack Brown [1930], Robert Taylor [1940]) features Howard as his lover. Director: King Vidor (1930), David Miller (1941).

Blazing Saddles (1974) Madeline Kahn
Mel Brooks directed this hilarious spoof of Western films which starred Cleavon Little as a black cowboy and featured Kahn as a very funny saloon girl.

Bounty Hunter (1954) Marie Windsor, Dolores Dorn
The Pinkerton Detective Agency sends out a bounty hunter to track down three train robbers and recover money stolen from their clients. Marie is a saloon girl who sides with the bandits, then has a change of heart. Director: Andre de Toth

Brigham Young: Frontiersman (1940) Linda Darnell, Jane Darwell, Jean Rogers, Mary Astor
Dean Jagger plays the Mormon leader and Tyrone Power his disciple in this romanticized film biography. Darnell, Darwell, Rogers and Astor are the women in their lives. Director: Henry Hathaway

Buffalo Bill (1944) Maureen O'Hara, Linda Darnell
Joel McCrea plays "Buffalo Bill" Cody in this film biography that features Darnell as his wife and O'Hara as Annie Oakley. Director: William Wellman

Buffalo Bill and the Indians, or Sitting Bull's History Lesson (1976) Geraldine Chaplin
Even a star-studded cast including Paul Newman, Burt Lancaster, Joel Grey and Harvey Keitel could not save this rambling, often confusing film adaptation of a hit Broadway play (*Indians*) from being weighed down by an overabundance of improvised preaching in the usual Robert Altman manner. Chaplin plays a somewhat odd-looking Annie Oakley in this piece. Director: Robert Altman

*Buffalo Girls (1994) Anjelica Huston
The women who toured with the Buffalo Bill Wild West Show are the major characters in this made-for-TV adaptation of Larry McMurtry's popular novel. Huston plays a very sensitive Calamity Jane.

Butch Cassidy and the Sundance Kid (1969) Katharine Ross
Ross plays Etta Place, the Sundance Kid's girlfriend, in this first-rate Western that depicts the adventures of two of the West's most infamous criminals (Paul Newman and Robert Redford). Director: George Roy Hill

*Calamity Jane (1984) Jane Alexander
This down-to-earth, made-for-TV film stars Jane Alexander as Calamity and presents her as a much more pathetic victim of life than she actually was. Frederic Forrest is Alexander's co-star. Director: James Goldstone

*Calamity Jane (1953) Doris Day
Singer-actress Doris Day plays Calamity in this highly romanticized musical comedy version of her life. Howard Keel is Wild Bill Hickok and, of course, they have a serious romance. Director: George Sherman

*Calamity Jane and Sam Bass (1949) Yvonne DeCarlo
The central characters are Calamity Jane and outlaw Sam Bass, even though it is highly doubtful that the two ever met. DeCarlo is a far-too-glamorous-to-be-real Calamity and Howard Duff plays Bass. Director: George Sherman

*Cat Ballou (1965) Jane Fonda
One of the screen's most hilarious spoofs of Westerns, *Cat Ballou* stars Jane Fonda as a schoolteacher turned outlaw and Lee Marvin in a dual role as a drunk (one of Cat's band of inept outlaws) and as the film's black-hearted villain. Director: Elliot Silverstein

*Cattle Annie and Little Britches (1980) Amanda Plummer, Diane Lane
Plummer and Lane play teenage girls caught up in the criminal activities of the infamous
Bill Doolin gang. Director: Lamont Johnson

*Cattle Queen of Montana (1954) Barbara Stanwyck
A ranch-owning land baroness (Stanwyck) does what she must in order to protect her cattle from raiding Indians. Ronald Reagan is her co-star. Director: Allan Dwan

Cattle Town (1952) Amanda Blake, Rita Moreno
Blake and Moreno play the residents of a western town which Sheriff Dennis Morgan has
sworn to defend against outlaw bands who are trying to take it over. Director: Noel Smith

Cimarron (1931/1960) Irene Dunne (1931)/Maria Schell, Anne Baxter (1960)
The saga of an American family who travel west and settle there (as chronicled in Edna Ferber's
best-selling novel) was filmed twice. The first version stars Irene Dunne as the stalwart matriarch, and the second has Maria Schell in the role. Directors: Wesley Ruggles/Anthony Mann

Cincinatti Kid (1965) Ann-Margret
Gambling activities in the Old West are the focus of this film which features a wide variety of film actresses including Ann-Margret, Tuesday Weld and Joan Blondell. Director: Norman Jewison

Colorado Territory (1949) Virginia Mayo, Dorothy Malone
Mayo and Malone play good and bad Western women and Joel McCrea is a sheriff who is
the object of their affection. Director: Raoul Walsh

Colt .45 (1950) Ruth Roman
Randolph Scott, Zachary Scott and Ruth Roman received top billing in this film, but the
real star of the piece is the gun. Director: Edwin L. Marin

Comanche (1956) Linda Cristal
Dana Andrews plays a scout who is trying to make peace between the cavalry and the hostile Comanche tribes. Cristal provides some love interest. Director: George Sherman

Comanche Station (1960) Nancy Gates
Good girl Gates is rescued from her Indian captors by Randolph Scott in this action-packed
Western. Director: Budd Boetticher

Comanche Territory (1950) Maureen O'Hara
O'Hara is the wife of Jim Bowie, the knife designer and manufacturer, played by Macdonald
Carey, in this film biography. Director: George Sherman

The Comancheros (1961) Ina Balin
John Wayne, Lee Marvin and Stuart Whitman star in this better-than-average Western about
a Texas Ranger determined to apprehend a gang that has been selling liquor to Indians.
Director: Michael Curtiz

The Cowboys (1972) Colleen Dewhurst
A raw-boned female settler (Dewhurst) assists an aging rancher (John Wayne) when he takes
a group of youngsters on a cattle drive. Director: Mark Rydell

Marie Windsor as *Dakota Lil* **(1950). (Photofest.)**

Dakota Incident (1956) Linda Darnell
Darnell is a passenger on a stagecoach headed west when it is attacked by hostile Indians. She is defended by Dale Robertson. Director: Lewis R. Foster

Dakota Lil (1950) Marie Windsor
Windsor plays a female outlaw who helps a lawman (George Montgomery) track down a bunch of railroad thieves. Director: Lesley Selander

James Stewart and Marlene Dietrich in *Destry Rides Again* **(1939). (Author's collection.)**

Dallas (1950) Ruth Roman
When the Civil War ends, Gary Cooper returns to Texas and seeks revenge against Rebels he felt went beyond the law. He falls in love with Roman before becoming involved in a shootout with villain Steve Cochran. Director: Stuart Heisler

The Dalton Girls (1957) Merry Anders, Penny Edwards, Lisa Davis
A group of women who loved the infamous Dalton brothers turn outlaws themselves when their menfolk are killed by the law. Director: Reginald LeBorg

The Desperados (1943) Evelyn Keyes
A bandit (Glenn Ford) turns lawman and helps a sheriff (Randolph Scott) clean up a corrupt town and reform a bandit queen (Keyes). Director: Charles Vidor

Destry Rides Again (1939) Marlene Dietrich
When a saloon girl (Dietrich) encounters a mild-mannered lawman (James Stewart) and he attempts to tame her, sparks fly. Director: George Marshall

Dodge City (1939) Olivia deHavilland, Ann Sheridan
DeHavilland and Sheridan respectively play a good and bad girl in this Western that stars Errol Flynn as a devil-may-care Westerner loved by both of them. Director: Michael Curtiz

Jennifer Jones and Gregory Peck in *Duel in the Sun* (1946). (Author's collection.)

Duel in the Sun (1946) Jennifer Jones
David O. Selznick produced this expensive epic film hoping that it would be the *Gone with the Wind* of Westerns. It was not. Jones plays a half-breed Indian girl who is raised by a rich ranching family consisting of Lionel Barrymore, Lillian Gish, Joseph Cotten and Gregory Peck. Director: King Vidor

A Fistful of Dollars (1964) Marianne Koch
A wandering cowboy (Clint Eastwood) works both sides of the law in a divided Western town in this "spaghetti Western" which was produced in Italy and Spain but is set in the American West. Koch provides Eastwood with love interest. Director: Sergio Leone

Flame of Barbary Coast (1945) Ann Dvorak
A saloon girl (Dvorak) is the object of affection for tough guy John Wayne, who plays a heroic rancher, and Joseph Schildkraut, an oily businesman. Director: Joseph Kane

Flaming Star (1960) Barbara Eden
Elvis Presley plays a half Indian–half white young man who has to choose between his two backgrounds when Indians go on the warpath. Eden is the object of his affection. Director: Don Siegel

Follow the River (1995) Sheryl Lee, Ellen Burstyn
A female settler (Lee) is taken captive with her young son and sister by Shawnee Indians. She escapes with another captive (Burstyn) and is eventually reunited with her husband. Her

captor, a Shawnee warrior (Eric Schweig), returns her son and baby daughter to her because of her courage. Director: Martin Davidson

Fort Apache (1948) Shirley Temple, Anna Lee
A rigid U. S. Army commanding officer (Henry Fonda), a young officer (John Agar) and a scout (John Wayne) defend a fort and its womenfolk (Temple and Lee) during an attack by renegade Indians. Director: John Ford

Fort Dobbs (1958) Virginia Mayo
A former gunslinger (Clint Walker) fights the bad guys in an attempt to make a better, more law-abiding life for himself and the woman he loves (Mayo). Director: Gordon Douglas

Fort Massacre (1958) Susan Cabot
When a military leader (Joel McCrea) defends his fort, he finds himself desperately outnumbered by hostile Native American braves, but he manages to save the day and the residents of the fort, including Cabot. Director: Joseph Newman

Fort Utah (1968) Virginia Mayo
A familiar tale involving a gunfighter-turned-lawman (John Ireland) who fights a bad man (Scott Brady) stirring up trouble among the Indians. Mayo plays the girl both men love. Director: Lesley Selander

Fort Vengeance (1953) Rita Moreno
The Pacific Northwest is the setting for this film in which a Canadian Mountie (James Craig) tracks down a group of bandits who are encouraging Indians to attack an outpost so that they can get the spoils. Rita Moreno provides love interest. Director: Lesley Selander

Fort Worth (1951) Phyllis Thaxter
Another former gunslinger (Randolph Scott) turns in his guns and becomes a newspaper owner, but ultimately he has to rely on his guns to defend his town from outlaws. Phyllis Thaxter and Helena Carter play good and not-so-good women in this film. Director: Edwin L. Marin

Fort Yuma (1955) Joan Taylor
In this standard Western, Indians on the warpath menace Taylor, who is a young settler, and Joan Vohs, a more experienced western woman. Peter Graves defends them both. Director: Lesley Selander

Forty Guns (1957) Barbara Stanwyck
Stanwyck plays yet another cattle queen who ruthlessly defends her property against anyone who infringes upon it until a U. S. marshall (Barry Sullivan) sets her straight. Director: Samuel Fuller

Four Faces West (1948) Frances Dee
A fugitive from the law (Joel McCrea) is being unjustly pursued by a ruthless sheriff, but his girlfriend (Dee) remains loyal. Director: Alfred E. Green

Four Fast Guns (1959) Martha Vickers
Brothers who are at odds with each other (James Craig, Brett Halsey and Paul Richards)

eventually face each other in a gun duel in spite of Vickers' attempts to make peace between them. Director: Alfred E. Green

4 for Texas (1963) Anita Ekberg, Ursula Andress
Ekberg and Andress are just pretty scenery in this silly Western that starred Frank Sinatra and Dean Martin as soldiers of fortune. Director: Robert Aldrich

Four Guns to the Border (1954) Colleen Miller, Nina Foch
Outlaws face a band of renegade Indians in this better-than-average Western film that features Miller and Foch as women caught up in the fight. Director: Richard Carlson

*Frisco Sal (1959) Susanna Foster
Foster arrives in Frisco determined to find the man who killed her brother. Turhan Bey and Alan Curtis are her admirers. Director: George Waggner

*Frontier Gal (1945) Yvonne DeCarlo
A saloon girl toughie (DeCarlo) falls in love with a cowboy (Rod Cameron) who has been falsely accused of being an outlaw. Director: Charles Lamont

Frontier Hellcat (1966) Elke Sommer
European pioneers (including Sommer) cross the Rockies in covered wagons and encounter many difficulties in spite of a wagon master's (Stewart Granger) expert guidance. Director: Alfred Vohrer

The Furies (1950) Barbara Stanwyck
Barbara Stanwyck plays a strong-willed cattle rancher who squares off aginst her equally strong-willed father, played by Walter Huston. Director: Anthony Mann

Fury at Furnace Creek (1948) Coleen Gray
Victor Mature plays a lawman who tries to restore his dead father's good name with the help of Gray in this Western adventure. Director: H. Bruce Humberstone

The Gal Who Took the West (1949) Yvonne DeCarlo
Three cousins get together when they are old men and recall their feud over a beautiful New York singer (DeCarlo) in the Wild West. Charles Coburn, Scott Brady and John Russell co-starred. Director: George Sherman

*Girl of the Golden West (1938) Jeanette Macdonald
This MGM musical-operetta involves a western woman (Macdonald) who falls in love with a bandit (Nelson Eddy). Director: Robert Z. Leonard

*Go West, Young Girl (1978) Karen Valentine
In this made-for–TV Western comedy, a fiery young woman (Valentine) locks horns with a cavalry officer and tries to gain the affections of a lawman who helps her track down Billy the Kid. Director: Allan J. Levin

The Good, the Bad and the Ugly (1966) Rada Rassinov
This Italian-made Western stars Clint Eastwood as a post–Civil War fortune seeker searching for a government treasure chest. Director: Sergio Leone

A Good Day for a Hanging (1958) Maggie Hayes
Fred MacMurray plays a sheriff who apprehends a killer no one in town seems to want to punish. Hayes plays a schoolteacher who supports the sheriff. Director: Nathan Juran

Gun Battle at Monterey (1957) Mary Beth Hughes
A determined gunfighter sets out to avenge the death of a friend, as sweet Mary Beth Hughes tries to dissuade him from doing so. Director: Carl G. Hittelman

Gun Brothers (1956) Ann Robinson
Brothers Buster Crabbe and Neville Brand find themselves on opposite sides of the law. Robinson is Crabbe's supportive girlfriend. Director: Sidney Salkow

Gun Fury (1953) Donna Reed
A cowboy (Rock Hudson) sets out to track down his fiancée (Reed), who has been kidnapped by outlaws. Director: Raoul Walsh

The Gunfight at Dodge City (1959) Julie Adams
Sheriff Bat Masterson (Joel McCrea) cleans up an outlaw-infested town, as Adams prods him on. Director: Joseph M. Newman

The Gunfire at Indian Gap (1957) Vera Ralston
Saloon girl Ralston does what she can to prevent a gunfight in her westen town. Director: Joseph Kane

Gunfight at the O. K. Corral (1957) Rhonda Fleming, Jo Van Fleet
In this classic film about the Earp brothers' gunfight with the Clanton and McLaury brothers, Burt Lancaster is Wyatt Earp and Kirk Douglas plays his consumptive gunman-friend Doc Holliday. Rhonda Fleming plays a composite of several of Wyatt's women friends and Jo Van Fleet plays Holliday's female companion, Kate Fisher. Dennis Hopper is featured as young Billy Clanton. Director: John Sturges

The Gunfighter (1950) Helen Westcott, Jean Parker
Gregory Peck plays a gunfighter who is trying to forget his violent past but is persuaded by former enemies to become a lawman, in spite of protests by Westcott and Parker. Director: Henry King

Gunman's Walk (1958) Kathryn Grant
Two sons (Tab Hunter and James Darren) with very different personalities clash, as their father (Van Heflin) and the girl who loves them both (Grant) attempts to reconcile them. Director: Phil Karlson

*The Guns of Fort Petticoat (1957) Kathryn Grant, Hope Emerson
An army deserter (Audie Murphy) helps a group of women (Grant, Emerson, Jeff Donnell, Isobel Elsom and others) whose husbands have been killed by Indians. Director: George Marshall

*The Gunslinger (1956) Beverly Garland
Garland is a female marshall who tries to control an outlaw-infested town. Director: Roger Corman

Gunsmoke (1953) Susan Cabot
A reformed outlaw (Audie Murphy) works on a ranch and falls in love with the rancher's daughter (Cabot) but is forced to use his guns to defend against rival cattlemen. Director: Nathan Juran

The Half-Breed (1952) Janis Carter
A villainous profiteer encourages the Apaches to attack a white settlement which Robert Young, Janis Carter and others defend. Director: Stuart Gilmore

Hang 'Em High (1968) Inger Stevens
When Clint Eastwood, who is accused of murder, survives his own hanging, he sets out to avenge his wrongful punishment. Stevens plays Eastwood's devoted girlfriend, who believes in his innocence. Director: Ted Post

The Hanging Tree (1959) Maria Schell
A blind girl (Schell) is nursed back to health by a doctor (Gary Cooper) who has a checkered past. Director: Delmar Daves

Hangman's Knot (1952) Donna Reed
A former Southern rebel (Randolph Scott) robs a shipment of gold headed North, but is convinced by Reed, who knows the war is over, to make things right. Director: Roy Huggins

*The Harvey Girls (1946) Judy Garland, Angela Lansbury
Respectable waitresses (including Garland) are hired to work in the Harvey chain restaurants, and clash with saloon girls led by Lansbury. Garland and Lansbury also fight over the affections of a daring gambler (John Hodiak) in this colorful film musical. Director: George Sidney

*Heartland (1979) Conchata Ferrell
Ferrell plays a widowed woman with a child who goes west to marry a rancher (Rip Torn) she has never met and face hardships she never imagined. Director: Richard Pearce

*Heaven's Gate (1980) Isabelle Huppert
Kris Kristofferson, Christopher Walken and Jeff Bridges are involved in a conflict between power-hungry cattlemen and immigrant settlers in this confusing, overly produced epic that features Huppert as a rustler-prostitute who becomes involved in the proceedings. Director: Michael Cimino

*Hellfire (1956) Marie Windsor
A saloon girl-entertainer turned lady bandit (Windsor) has a change of heart when she falls in love with a gunfighter-turned-preacher (Wild Bill Elliott), but is killed by her brother-in-law sheriff. Director: Lesley Selander

High Noon (1952) Grace Kelly, Katy Jurado
This Oscar-winning film stars Gary Cooper as an aging sheriff who feels a responsibility to rid his town of outlaws even though its citizens refuse to help him. Grace Kelly plays Cooper's new bride, and Katy Jurado plays the Mexican girl who was his former flame. Director: Fred Zinnemann

Hombre (1967) Geraldine Page
A man raised by Indians (Paul Newman) tries to live in the white man's world, but finds his loyalties divided between whites and Native Americans. Director: Martin Ritt

The Horse Soldiers (1959) Constance Towers, Althea Gibson
In this Western, set during the Civil War, John Wayne plays a cattle driver who is trying to get beef South to feed the rebel troops and comes upon Southern aristocrat (Towers) during the journey. Director: John Ford

*How the West Was Won (1963) Debbie Reynolds, Carroll Baker, Thelma Ritter
This epic Western chronicles the lives of a family who travel west and settle the frontier. Agnes Moorehead, Reynolds, Baker and Ritter play women who head West. Also featured in major roles are such stellar performers as James Stewart, John Wayne, Gregory Peck and Henry Fonda. Director: Henry Hathaway

Hurry Sundown (1967) Faye Dunaway, Diahann Carroll, Jane Fonda
A ruthless cattleman cheats an English rancher out of his land and brings him to ruin, forcing him to avenge himself in this film that stars Michael Caine. Director: Otto Preminger

In Old California (1942) Binnie Barnes, Helen Parrish
When a cowboy (John Wayne) moves into a town ruled by an evil despot (Albert Dekker), he meets saloon girl Barnes and good girl Parrish and decides to rid the town of Dekker. Director: William McGann

Mercedes McCambridge in *Johnny Guitar* **(1954). (Author's collection.)**

Jesse James (1939) Nancy Kelly
The life and times of outlaw Jesse James (Tyrone Power) are depicted in this highly romanticized film biography. Kelly plays his lovely and loyal wife. Director: Henry King

Johnny Concho (1956) Phyllis Kirk
Kirk seems to be merely along for the ride in this Western which starred Frank Sinatra as a timid cowboy who has to find the strength and courage to fight a bully outlaw. Director: Don McGuire

*Johnny Guitar (1954) Joan Crawford, Mercedes McCambridge
A saloon owner (Crawford) fights the prejudice of self-righteous ranchers led by a mean-spirited ranch woman played by Mercedes McCambridge in this offbeat Western that features Sterling Hayden (as the title character), Royal Dano, Ward Bond and Ernest Borgnine. Director: Nicholas Ray

Kit Carson (1941) Lynn Bari
The legendary western hero (Jon Hall) joins forces with army officer Dana Andrews to fight the bad guys, but both men compete for the affections of Bari. Director: George B. Seitz

The Last Day (1975) Loretta Swit, Barbara Rush
Richard Widmark plays a former gunslinger who reluctantly joins the ambush of the outlaw Dalton brothers and their gang (Robert Conrad, Richard Jaekel, Tim Matheson, Tom Skerritt and Christopher Connelly) when they attempt to rob two banks in Coffeyville. Swit plays Bob Dalton's lover and Rush, Widmark's long-suffering wife. Director: Victor McEveety

The Last of the Comanches (1952) Barbara Hale
Cavalrymen fight off an attack by a band of renegade Indians. Broderick Crawford, Lloyd Bridges and Martin Milner defend their fort and the women in it. Director: Andre de Toth

The Last Wagon (1956) Felicia Farr
A condemned killer (Richard Widmark) saves wagon train pioneers (including Farr) from being slaughtered by the Indians and leads them to safety. Director: Delmer Daves

Law of the Lawless (1964) Yvonne DeCarlo
Dale Robertson plays an ex-gunman who has become a judge and runs a town with a strong hand, preventing a takeover by outlaws. DeCarlo plays a saloon girl. Director: William F. Claxton

The Lawless Breed (1952) Julie Adams
An ex-outlaw (Rock Hudson) tells his son about his days as a former gunfighter, hoping to prevent the young man from following in his footsteps. Adams plays Hudson's wife. Director: Raoul Walsh

Lawman (1971) Sheree North
When a lawman (Burt Lancaster) arrives in a western town to apprehend a favored citizen, the corrupt people of the town (except saloon girl North) turn against him. Director: Michael Winner

The Left Handed Gun (1958) Lita Milan
Billy the Kid's (Paul Newman) life and career in crime are probed in this pretentious psychological Western. Milan plays Billy's Mexican-American girlfriend. Director: Arthur Penn

The Life and Times of Judge Roy Bean (1971) Ava Gardner, Jacqueline Bisset
Paul Newman stars in this Western about a saloon owner who builds his own town and names it after his favorite performer, Lilly Langtry (Ava Gardner), whom he has never met. Director: John Huston

Little Big Man (1970) Faye Dunaway, Amy Eccles
The entire saga of 19th century Indians out West seems to be chronicled in this story which is told by an old man (Dustin Hoffman) who has seen it all in his 121 years. Dunaway plays a prostitute who seduces Hoffman when he is a young man and Eccles plays his sister who is, like him, abducted by Indians when they are young. Director: Arthur Penn

Julie Christie and Warren Beatty in *McCabe and Mrs. Miller* **(1971). (Author's collection.)**

*Lola Montes (1955) Martine Carol
The life and times of the legendary actress Lola Montez (Carol), including her tour of the Old West, is chronicled in this biographical film. Director: Max Ophuls

Lone Star (1952) Ava Gardner
Gardner plays a tired, experienced woman of the West who is torn between loyalties for two gunfighters (Clark Gable and Broderick Crawford). Director: Vincent Sherman

The Lonesome Trail (1955) Adele Jurgens
A ranch owner (Wayne Morris) combats a group of men who are trying to take over his spread, but uses a bow and arrow instead of a rifle and six-shooter. Director: Richard Bartlett

The Long Riders (1980) Pamela Reed
The Younger brothers (Keith, David and Robert Carradine) and Belle Starr (Reed) are the major characters in this film which also features real-life brothers Stacy and James Keach and Randy and Dennis Quaid. Director: Walter Hill

*McCabe and Mrs. Miller (1971) Julie Christie
A gritty, realistic, decidedly unromantic look at the Old West, this film is about an opportunistic pimp (Warren Beatty) who joins forces with a more experienced madam (Christie) hoping to become rich in a primitive mining town. Director: Robert Altman

The Man Behind the Gun (1952) Patrice Wymore
An undercover army officer (Randolph Scott) combats Californians who want to make that state an independent country. Director: Felix E. Feist

A Man Called Horse (1970) Judith Anderson
Richard Harris plays an Englishman who is taken captive by Sioux Indians and learns the real value of life as he is tested for bravery by his captors. Judith Anderson plays an old Indian woman who adopts him. Director: Elliot Silverstein

The Man from Colorado (1948) Ellen Drew
A disillusioned law enforcer (Glenn Ford) is appointed Federal Judge and ruthlessly cleans up a western community. Director: Henry Levin

Man or Gun (1958) Audrey Totter
A sheriff (Macdonald Carey) is hired to straighten out a lawless town. In the process, he also tames tough saloon girl Totter. Director: Albert Gannaway

The Man Who Loved Cat Dancing (1973) Sarah Miles
When a defiant young woman (Miles) runs away from her elderly husband (Lee J. Cobb), she takes up with a band of outlaws led by Burt Reynolds. Director: Richard C. Sarafin

Many Rivers to Cross (1955) Eleanor Parker
An independent woman (Parker) matches a wagonmaster (Robert Taylor) in courage when their wagon train is attacked by Indians. Director: Roy Rowland

*The Marshall's Daughter (1953) Laurie Anders
In this comedy, Anders plays a girl whose father was the marshall and replaces him to help Ken Murray rid the town of a nasty element. Director: William Berke

Massacre (1956) Marta Roth
Unscrupulous men sell guns to renegade Indians, and settlers (Dane Clark, James Craig and Roth) are left to combat the Indians. Director: Louis King

Massacre River (1949) Cathy Downs, Carole Matthews
While they are not fighting outlaws, three cowboys (Guy Madison, Rory Calhoun and Johnny Sands) find themselvers fighting over Downs and Matthews. Director: John Rawlins

*Maverick (1994) Jodie Foster
Mel Gibson plays the nephew of former big-time gambler Bart Maverick (James Garner) and Foster is the spirited lady gambler he encounters. Director: Richard Donner

*The Maverick Queen (1956) Barbara Stanwyck
A female outlaw (Stanwyck) goes straight when she falls in love with lawman Barry Sullivan. Director: Joseph Kane

Montana (1950) Alexis Smith
Errol Flynn plays a gunslinger and Smith a respectable lady who tries to make him give up the gunfighting game. Director: Ray Enright

*Montana Belle (1952) Jane Russell
This fictional film, which features Russell as a much-too-glamorous Belle Starr, has Belle encountering the infamous Dalton brothers, which in all probability never actually happened. Director: Allan Dwan

Linda Darnell plays Doc Holliday's lady friend in *My Darling Clementine* **(1946). (Author's collection.)**

My Darling Clementine (1946) Linda Darnell
In this fictionalized film depicting the famous gunfight at the O.K. Corral Henry Fonda plays
Wyatt Earp and Victor Mature plays Doc Holliday. Darnell plays Holliday's shady lady
friend. Director: John Ford

My Little Chickadee (1940) Mae West
This comedy stars two of filmdom's most celebrated comedy stars, W. C. Fields and Mae West, who meet on a train headed west. Director: Edward Cline

The Naked Spur (1953) Janet Leigh
Considered by film buffs to be one of Hollywood's best, this film tells the story of a bounty hunter (James Stewart) who is tracking down a bad guy (Robert Ryan). Leigh offers a bit of love interest. Director: Anthony Mann

Nevada (1944) Anne Jeffreys
Robert Mitchum plays a lawman and Jeffreys a saloon girl in this formula Western, adapted from a Zane Grey story. Director: Edward Kelly

Oklahoma Annie (1952) Judy Canova
Comedienne Canova appears in this spoof that also stars John Russell. It was yet another film about cleaning up a corrupt town, but it has an amusing twist. Director: R. G. Springsteen

Oklahoma Territory (1960) Gloria Talbott
When an Indian agent is murdered, a lawman (Bill Williams) sets out to track down his killers. Talbott is a hard-boiled gal who helps him out. Director: Edward L. Cahn

Oklahoma Woman (1956) Peggie Castle
Castle plays the title character in this film that starred Richard Denning as a lawman who must fight the "outlaw queen" (Castle) and her gang. Director: Roger Corman

The Oklahoman (1957) Barbara Hale
An outcast Indian (Brad Dexter) regains his rights with the help of Joel McCrea and Barbara Hale. Director: Francis D. Lyon

The Oregon Trail (1959) Gloria Talbott
A newspaper reporter (Fred MacMurray) finds adventure in Oregon, as well as a beautiful girl (Talbott), while investigating Indian attacks on settlers. Director: Gene Fowler, Jr.

The Outlaw (1943) Jane Russell
Howard Hughes produced and directed this Western about Billy the Kid (Jack Buetel). The most memorable thing about the film, however, was the buxom Miss Russell's physical attributes and a wonderful performance by character actor Walter Huston.

Outlaw's Daughter (1954) Kelly Ryan
Ryan is the daughter of a notorious outlaw who is falsely accused of robbing a stagecoach. Lawman Bill Williams tries to help her prove her father innocent. Director: Wesley Barry

Outlaw's Son (1957) Lori Nelson
An outlaw (Dane Clark) tries to make things better for his son (Ben Cooper) and his wife (Nelson) but becomes embroiled in a gun battle. Director: Lesley Selander

The Outlaws Is Comin' (1965) Nancy Kovack
The Three Stooges are the unlikely leading men in this Western comedy which also features Adam West and Kovack in the cast. Director: Norman Maurer

Paint Your Wagon (1969) Jean Seberg
This expensive, misguided film musical was adapted for the movies from a hit Broadway play. It features Clint Eastwood (singing badly) as a cowboy and Lee Marvin and Jean Seberg as a prospector and his daughter who have headed west to find gold. Director: Josh Logan

The Paleface (1948) Jane Russell
Bob Hope is a timid hero in this comedy which features curvaceous Jane Russell as the object of his affection and Iris Adrian as a quintessential tough-talking saloon girl. Director: Norman McLeod

Pat Garrett and Billy the Kid (1973) Katy Jurado
The man who killed Billy the Kid, Pat Garrett (Kris Kristofferson), is the major focus of this film that features Jurado as Billy's girlfriend. Singer Bob Dylan, who also wrote the score for the movie, has a minor role. Director: Sam Peckinpah

Pawnee (1957) Lola Albright
A white settler (George Montgomery) who has been raised by Indians finds himself in conflict when redmen and white settlers clash. Director: George Waggner

*Pioneer Woman (1973) Joanna Pettet
The difficulties of homesteading in Wyoming in the 1860s, especially those endured by a single woman on her own (Pettet), are the subject of this film. Director: Buzz Kulik

*The Plainsman (1936) Jean Arthur
This fictitious but well-produced film spectacular stars Arthur as a cute, tomboyish Calamity Jane and Gary Cooper as Wild Bill Hickok. The two fall in love as they face many dangers together. Director: Cecil B. DeMille

*The Plainsman and the Lady (1946) Vera Ralston
Ralston starred in several Westerns for Republic Pictures and this film, which also starred Wild Bill Elliott, was one of them. Elliott is a soft-spoken cowboy and Ralston the woman he saves from criminal types. Director: Joseph Kane

Poker Alice (1987) Elizabeth Taylor, Liz Torres, Susan Tyrrell
This made-for-TV film is a totally fictitious account of the famous lady gambler of Deadwood's life. Tom Skerritt plays a bounty hunter who wins Alice's heart and George Hamilton her parasite-cousin. Director: Arthur Allan Speidelman

Powder River (1953) Corinne Calvet
A sheriff (Rory Calhoun) clears up the murder of a friend and tames a fiery Gallic beauty (Calvet) in the bargain. Director: Louis King

Quantrill's Raiders (1958) Diane Brewster
Brewster plays one of the women caught up in the Rebel renegade activities of Quantrill (Leo Gordon) and his infamous rebel raiders. Director: Edward Bernds

The Quick and the Dead (1995) Sharon Stone
A woman intent on vengeance (Stone) arrives in the town of Redemption seeking justice against the corrupt despot (Gene Hackman) who ruined her family. Director: Sam Raimi

*Rachel and the Stranger (1948) Loretta Young
When a cowboy (Robert Mitchum) is hired by a spinster (Young) to help her fight a band of land grabbers, the inevitable happens and she falls in love with him. Director: Norman Foster

Raiders of Old California (1957) Arlene Whelan
Set during the California gold rush in the 1850s, this film featured Jim Davis and Lee Van Cleef as prospector-cowboys and Whelan as a good girl trying to keep them on the straight and narrow. Director: Albert Gannaway

Rawhide (1951) Susan Hayward
A group of settlers (including a high-spirited Hayward) are held captive in a stagecoach station by outlaws and eventually become involved in a gunfight to the death. Director: Henry Hathaway

The Rawhide Trail (1958) Nancy Gates
Two men accused of being outlaws (Rex Reason and Richard Erdman) set out to prove themselves innocent by helping settlers fight off an attack by hostile Indians. Director: Robert Gordon

Red Canyon (1949) Ann Blyth
Adapted from a novel by Zane Grey, this film depicts the problems of rounding up wild horses out West. Director: George Sherman

Red River (1948) Joanne Dru
One of the finest Westerns ever made, *Red River* stars John Wayne as a rancher who with the help of his foster son (Montgomery Clift) drives a herd of cattle to market. The two clash, but Dru makes them behave. Director: Howard Hawks

*Red Garters (1954) Rosemary Clooney
A musical spoof of Westerns, this movie stars singer Rosemary Clooney as a saloon hall entertainer and features Jack Carson and Guy Mitchell in the cast. Director: George Marshall

Red Tomahawk (1967) Joan Caulfield
An army officer (Howard Keel) saves a town from hostile Sioux Indians and wins the heart of Caulfield. Director: R. G. Springsteen

*The Redhead and the Cowboy (1950) Rhonda Fleming
Fleming is a spy for the South living out West during the Civil War but falls in love with a loyal Union officer (Glenn Ford). Director: Leslie Fenton

*The Redhead From Wyoming (1952) Maureen O'Hara
A fiery, independent woman of the West (O'Hara) falls in love with a sheriff (William Bishop) while trying to fight off a treacherous land baron (Alexander Scourby). Director: Lee Sholem

*Renegades (1949) Evelyn Keyes
A girl bandit (Keyes) rides the range with a group of outlaws called the Dembrows, but she is eventually reformed by a sheriff (Willard Parker). Director: George Sherman

Requiem for a Gunfighter (1965) Olive Sturgess
In order to make sure that justice prevails, a gunfighter (Rod Cameron) pretends to be a judge. Director: Spencer Bennet

The Restless Breed (1957) Anne Bancroft
A tough guy bandit (Scott Brady) sets out to find his father's killer, aided by Bancroft. Director: Allan Dwan

Return of a Man Called Horse (1976) Gale Sondergaard
An Englishman (Richard Harris) returns West to help Native Americans fight for their rights. Sondergaard plays the Indian woman who adopted him while he was previously in captivity. Director: Irvin Kershner

The Return of Frank James (1940) Gene Tierney
Frank James (Henry Fonda) sets out to avenge his brother Jesse's death, in spite of Tierney's plea to let the matter rest. Director: Fritz Lang

The Return of Jesse James (1950) Ann Dvorak
John Ireland plays Jesse James in this fictionalized film biography and Dvorak plays his loyal wife. Director: Arthur Hilton

The Return of the Bad Man (1948) Anne Jeffreys
Jeffreys is a female outlaw convinced by a lawman (Randolph Scott) to go straight. Director: Ray Enright

The Return of the Frontiersman (1950) Julie London
A sheriff's son (Jack Holt) is falsely accused of murder and the sheriff (Gordon MacRae) and London try to prove his innocence. Director: Richard Bare

The Return of the Gunfighter (1967) Ana Martin
Lawman (Robert Taylor) helps a fugitive (Chad Everett) who has been falsely accused of killing his girlfriend's (Martin) parents. Director: James Nielson

The Return of the Texan (1952) Joanne Dru
Rancher Dale Robertson fights to save his spread from being taken over by land barons, and is aided by Dru and Walter Brennan. Director: Delmer Daves

Ride Lonesome (1959) Karen Steele
While a lawman (Randolph Scott) is bringing in an outlaw (Lee Van Cleef), he comes upon a stagecoach whose passengers (including Steele) are being attacked by a band of hostile Indians. Director: Budd Boetticher

Ride the High Country (1962) Mariette Hartley
Two over-the-hill gunfighters (Randolph Scott and Joel McCrea) are reunited when they are hired by Hartley to guard a gold delivery. Director: Sam Peckinpah

Ride Vaquero (1953) Ava Gardner
A border war between Mexico and the United States erupts and Gardner is caught up in the fracas. Robert Taylor, Howard Keel and Anthony Quinn also appear in the film. Director: John Farrow

Rio Bravo (1959) Angie Dickinson
Dickinson is just a pretty face with little to do in this adventure film that stars John Wayne as a sheriff trying to prevent a killer from getting out of jail. Director: Howard Hawks

Rio Grande (1950) Maureen O'Hara
The Civil War over, frictions between cowboys and the Apache Indians increase. John Wayne and O'Hara do their best to end the skirmishes. Director: John Ford

Rio Lobo (1970) Jennifer O'Neill
Although she is pretty, O'Neill does not contibute more than her good looks to this Western that stars John Wayne, Jorge Rivero, Jim Davis and Bill Williams. Director: Howard Hawks

River of No Return (1954) Marilyn Monroe
Monroe hires Robert Mitchum to help her track down her fiancée who has deserted her and gone west, and the two fall in love. Director: Otto Preminger

Rodeo Girl (1980) Katharine Ross
A bored bronco buster's wife (Ross), decides she can do as well as her husband in the rodeo arena and eventually becomes a cowgirl-star. Director: Jackie Cooper

Rooster Cogburn (1975) Katharine Hepburn
In an obvious rehashing of Hepburn's hit film *The African Queen*, she plays a similar role as a spinster out West, rather than in Africa, who encounters a gruff, uncouth cattleman (John Wayne, repeating his *True Grit* role). Director: Stuart Miller

The Rounders (1965) Sue Ane Langdon
Glenn Ford and Henry Fonda compete for the affections of Langdon, but join forces to combat evildoers. Director: Burt Kennedy

Saddle Tramp (1950) Wanda Hendrix
A westerner (Joel McCrea) adopts four kids (including Hendrix) and tries to teach them right from wrong in an outlaw-infested West. Director: Hugo Fregonese

Salome, Where She Danced (1945) Yvonne DeCarlo
An exotic dancer (DeCarlo) takes her act west and entrances woman-starved audiences. Rod Cameron, David Bruce, Walter Slezak and Albert Dekker are a few of the men she conquers. Director: Charles Lamont

San Antonio (1945) Alexis Smith
Errol Flynn stars as a lawman who falls in love with a saloon hall entertainer (Smith) but ends up fighting her "protector." Director: David Butler

Sea of Grass (1947) Katharine Hepburn
Farmers and ranchers clash in this epic film that stars Hepburn, Spencer Tracy, Robert Walker and Melvyn Douglas. Director: Elia Kazan

The Searchers (1956) Vera Miles, Natalie Wood
John Wayne plays a man who seachers for his niece (Wood) who has been held captive by Indians for many years. Director: John Ford

*Seven Brides for Seven Brothers (1954) Jane Powell
A musical set in the Pacific Northwest, this film features incredible dance sequences and is about brothers who are seeking wives in the woman-scarce northwestern United States. Powell plays one of the girls hoping to find a husband. Howard Keel, Russ Tamblyn, Jeff Richards, Virginia Gibson and Julie Newmar co-star. Director: Stanley Donen

Shane (1953) Jean Arthur
A former gunfighter (Alan Ladd) helps homesteaders (Van Heflin and Jean Arthur) who are being harassed by land barons. He becomes their young son's (Brandon DeWilde) hero, and this concerns his parents. Director: George Stevens

She Wore a Yellow Ribbon (1949) Joanne Dru
John Wayne plays an army officer who is about to retire, but cannot leave his post when he hears that Indians are about to go on the warpath. Director: John Ford

The Sheriff (1971) Linda Dey, Ruby Dee
A controversial rape case in a California town divides black and white settlers. Ossie Davis and Dee play a black couple caught up in the controversy. Director: David Lowell Rich

Shoot the Sun Down (1981) Margot Kidder
An odd group, including Kidder as an indentured servant and Christopher Walken as a gunfighter, go on a quest for gold. Director: David Leeds

Shooting High (1940) Jane Withers
A spirited teenager (Withers) helps cowboy Gene Autry bring a rancher's family under control. Director: Alfred E. Green

The Shootist (1976) Laureen Bacall
A gunfighter dying of cancer teaches Bacall's son (Ron Howard) about the value of life. Director: Don Siegel

Shootout (1971) Pat Quinn
Gregory Peck plays a cowboy who tries to help a young girl (Quinn) and ends up in a gunfight. Director: Henry Hathaway

Shootout in a One Dog Town (1974) Stefanie Powers
Richard Crenna is a banker who battles Richard Egan and his outlaw gang, who are attempting to steal $200,000 from his bank. Director: Burt Kennedy

Shotgun (1955) Yvonne DeCarlo
A half breed Indian girl (DeCarlo) becomes the cause of friction between a sheriff and an outlaw (Sterling Hayden and Zachary Scott). Director: Lesley Selander

Showdown (1963) Kathleen Crowley
Audie Murphy and Charles Drake are escaped convicts, one who is innocent and one who is guilty, who become involved in a shootout. Director: R. G. Springsteen

Showdown at Abilene (1956) Martha Hyer
A retired sheriff (Jock Mahoney) returns from the Civil War and tries to reestablish law and order in a western town. Director: Charles Haas

Showdown at Boot Hill (1958) Carole Matthews
Tomstone's Boot Hill cemetery is the final resting place of outlaws who become involved in a shootout with Charles Bronson. Director: Gene Fowler, Jr.

Siege at Red River (1954) Joanne Dru
Dru is one of the stars of this second feature film that is set during the Civil War years out West. Director: Rudolph Mate

Sierra Passage (1951) Lola Albright
An honest gunfighter (Wayne Morris) intervenes when a former outlaw he knows is innocent is about to be lynched. Director: Frank McDonald

Sierra Stranger (1957) Gloria McGhee
A mild mannered lawman (Lloyd Bridges), who has vowed never to use his six-shooters again, is forced out of retirement by warring settlers and rancher, in spite of McGhee's protests. Director: Lee Sholem

Silver City (1951) Yvonne DeCarlo
Miner Edmond O'Brien gets into a feud with Richard Arlen over DeCarlo's affections. Director: Byron Haskin

Silver River (1948) Ann Sheridan
Married settlers (Sheridan and Errol Flynn) become estranged when Flynn unwittingly becomes involved in a shady land deal, but he eventually ends up fighting for what is right. Director: Raoul Walsh

Singing Guns (1950) Ella Raines
Vaughn Monroe sings cowboy love songs to Raines in between gunfights in this dull film. Director: R. G. Springsteen

Sitting Bull (1954) Mary Murphy
Sitting Bull (J. Carrol Naish) is a minor character in this film, which is mainly about an army officer (Dale Robertson) and his wife (Murphy) who befriend the Sioux and attempt to avoid an Indian attack. Director: Sidney Salkow

Six Black Horses (1962) Joan O'Brien
O'Brien hires two men (Audie Murphy and Dan Duryea) to lead her safely across Indian lands so that she can kill the man who murdered her husband. Director: Harry Keller

Small Town in Texas (1976) Susan George
An evil sheriff frames a young man (Timothy Bottoms) and sends him to jail, but Bottoms escapes and plots his revenge. Director: Jack Starrett

The Son of Belle Starr (1953) Dona Drake, Peggie Castle
This highly fictionalized biographical film has Ed Reed, Belle Starr's son, avenge his mother's death, which most certainly never happened in real life. Director: Frank McDonald

Son of Paleface (1952) Jane Russell
Bob Hope repeats his cowardly–Easterner-out–West character which he first played in *The*

Paleface. Russell is once again on hand to offer Hope support and provide visual interests. Director: Frank Tashlin

The Spoilers (1942) Marlene Dietrich
Dietrich plays a tough saloon girl in this Western film set in the Yukon. Randolph Scott and John Wayne are her co-stars. Director: Ray Enright

Springfield Rifle (1952) Phyllis Thaxter
An upright female settler (Thaxter) convinces a lawman (Gary Cooper) to join forces with a group of outlaws in order to find out where they have been hiding stolen rifles. Director: Andre de Toth

Stage to Thunder Rock (1964) Marilyn Maxwell
Barry Sullivan plays a sheriff who reluctantly arrests the family of outlaws who raised him. Maxwell plays his sympathetic lady friend. Director: William F. Claxton

Stagecoach (1939) Claire Trevor
This Western film which is considered a classic is set almost entirely in a stagecoach that is headed west. Trevor plays a woman of experience who is a passenger on the stagecoach. Director: John Ford

Stagecoach to Dancer's Rock (1962) Jody Lawrence
Stagecoach passengers are stranded in the Badlands when the driver of the coach discovers that one of them has smallpox. Martin Landau and Lawrence are two of the passengers. Director: Earl Bellamy

Stagecoach to Fury (1956) Mari Blanchard
Outlaws hold up a stagecoach and a sheriff, played by Forrest Tucker, tracks them down. Director: William Claxton

The Stalking Moon (1969) Eva Marie Saint
When an army scout (Gregory Peck) rescues a woman who has been held captive by Indians (Saint), he encounters various problems in their flight to freedom. Director: Robert Mulligan

Stampede (1949) Gale Storm
The range wars between homesteaders and ranchers is the focus of this film which stars Rod Cameron and Storm as two people caught in the middle of the struggle. Director: Lesley Selander

Stand at Apache River (1953) Julie Adams
A group of settlers (including Adams, Stephen McNally and Hugh Marlowe) make a stand against Indians on the rampage. Director: Lee Sholem

Star in the Dust (1956) Mamie Van Doren
The "star" in this film's title refers to a sheriff's badge in this tale of a lawman (John Agar) who fights corrupt townspeople in order to restore law and order to his town. Van Doren is a sympathetic supporter. Director: Charles Haas

Claire Trevor and John Wayne in the 1939 classic *Stagecoach*. (Author's collection.)

The Stranger and the Gunfighter (1976) Patty Shepard, Julie Upgate
A hard-drinking cowboy (Lee Van Cleef) joins forces with a Chinese kung fu expert to recover a missing fortune out West. Director: Anthony Dwan

Stranger on Horseback (1955) Jaclyne Greene
A judge (Joel McCrea) who had been a gunfighter in his younger days puts on his guns again to bring a murderer to justice. Director: Jacques Tourneur

The Stranger Wore a Gun (1953) Claire Trevor
A law-abiding settler (Randolph Scott) becomes involved with a bandit and his saloon girl companion (Trevor) and is tricked into participating in a holdup. Director: Andre de Toth

Sugarfoot (1951) Adele Jergens
A former Rebel captain (Randolph Scott) comes across an old adversary from his Civil War days in Arizona, but is reluctant to get into a fight with him. Director: Edwin L. Marin

Support Your Local Sheriff (1969) Joan Hackett
This Western spoof stars James Garner as a good guy who outsmarts the bad guys by using his brain instead of his guns while romancing a somewhat addle-pated Hackett. Director: Burt Kennedy

Taggart (1964) Jean Hale
A young gunfighter (Tony Young) is set on revenge and pursues outlaws into Indian Territory. Director: R. G. Springsteen

Tall in the Saddle (1944) Ella Raines
Cowboy John Wayne is woman-shy until he goes to work for a rancher and falls in love with his daughter (Raines) and ends up fighting a bunch of rustlers. Director: Edwin L. Marin

Tall Man Riding (1955) Peggie Castle, Dorothy Malone
Greedy ranchers are outsmarted by Randolph Scott and Dorothy Malone when they try to grab up all of the good grazing land in Montana. Director: Lesley Selander

The Tall Men (1955) Jane Russell
Clark Gable and Robert Mitchum fight the elements, Indians and eventually each other for Jane Russell's affections. Director: Raoul Walsh

The Tall Stranger (1957) Virginia Mayo
Mayo is a settler traveling west on a wagon train that is being guarded by a gunfighter (Joel McCrea). Director: Thomas Carr

*The Tall Women (1966) Anne Baxter
Seven women (including Baxter) make their way by wagon train across hostile Indian territory. Director: Sidney Pink

Ten Wanted Men (1955) Jocelyn Brando
Cattleman Randolph Scott and his wife (Brando) hope they will prevail when they are threatened by a ruthless and greedy rancher (Richard Boone). Director: H. Bruce Humberstone

*The Texan Meets Calamity Jane (1950) Evelyn Ankers
Ankers is much too ladylike as Calamity Jane in this film which centers around the celebrated western character's attempt to prove she is the owner of a saloon. Director: Andre Lamb

The Texans (1938) Joan Bennett
This film, which is about post–Civil War settlers in Texas, stars Bennett and Randolph Scott. Director: James Hogan

Texas (1941) Claire Trevor
A cattleman (William Holden) and a rustler (Glenn Ford) clash and compete for the love of a saloon girl (Trevor). Director: George Marshall

Texas Across the River (1966) Rosemary Forsythe
Dean Martin plays a lawman, Joey Bishop a deadpan Indian, Forsythe a female settler and Tina Marquand a pretty Indian girl in this Western comedy. Director: Michael Gordon

Texas Rangers (1951) Gale Storm
Texas lawmen (including George Montgomery) are pitted against a gang of outlaws who threaten ranchers (including Storm). Director: Phil Karlson

The Texican (1966) Dianna Lorys
When Lorys seeks his help, Audie Murphy enforces the law and makes a group of no-gooders led by Broderick Crawford behave. Director: Lesley Selander

They Died with Their Boots On (1941) Olivia deHavilland
Custer's last stand is the finale in this film biography of General Custer's life, which stars Errol Flynn as Custer and deHavilland as his loving and loyal wife. Director: Raoul Walsh

They Rode West (1954) Donna Reed
A young surgeon (Robert Francis) is ordered not to treat Indians during a devastating epidemic, but ignores his commanding officer (Phil Carey) to the delight of Reed. Director: Phil Karlson

This Savage Land (1963) Kathryn Hays
An Ohio family sells their farm and migrates west, where they become involved in a vigilante dispute. Barry Sullivan and Hays are members of the family. Director: Vincent McEveety

Thunder of Drums (1961) Luana Patten
A young lieutenant (George Hamilton) has a difficult time adjusting to army life out West. Patten, Richard Boone and Richard Chamberlain are in the supporting cast of this slow-moving Western. Director: Joseph M. Newman

A Ticket to Tomahawk (1950) Anne Baxter
This Western spoof is about a drummer touring with a theatrical troupe in the Wild West. Director: Richard Sale

The Tin Star (1957) Betsy Palmer
A novice sheriff (Anthony Perkins) becomes a bounty hunter and enlists the aid of a more experienced lawman (Henry Fonda) to fight the desperadoes who are terrorizing his town. Palmer owns the town's newspaper. Director: Anthony Mann

Tomahawk (1951) Yvonne DeCarlo
The cavalry and Native Americans clash in the action-packed Western that stars Van Heflin, DeCarlo and Preston Foster. Director: George Sherman

Tombstone (1994) Dana Delany, Joanne Pacula
Kurt Russell and Sam Elliott play Wyatt and Virgil Earp, Val Kilmer plays Doc Holliday and Delany plays Josie Marcus (later Earp) in this excellent retelling of the Earp family's adventures in Tombstone. Director: George P. Cosmatos

Top Gun (1953) Karin Booth
When a gunman (Sterling Hayden) is cleared of murder charges, he is elected marshall and sets about to find the real killer. Director: Ray Nazarro

Toughest Gun in Tombstone (1958) Beverly Tyler
George Montgomery plays an expert gunfighter who is hired to defend a town against corrupt and greedy men. Director: Earl Bellamy

Town Tamer (1965) Terry Moore
Predictably, as the title suggests, this Western is about a lawman (Dana Andrews) who cleans up a corrupt town with Moore's help. Director: Lesley Selander

Trail of the Vigilantes (1940) Peggy Moran
An Eastern lawman (Franchot Tone) travels west and becomes involved in hunting down an outlaw gang. Director: Allan Dwan

Trail Street (1947) Anne Jeffreys
A saloon entertainer (Jeffreys) has two suitors (Randolph Scott and Robert Ryan), one good and one bad. Director: Ray Enright

Tribute to a Bad Man (1956) Irene Papas
Film tough guy James Cagney plays a hard-boiled land owner who uses any means at his disposal to get what he wants. Papas plays an unhappy settler who opposes him. Director: Robert Wise

True Grit (1969) Kim Darby
An over-the-hill gunman (John Wayne) helps a 14-year-old girl (Darby) track down her father's killer in this classic Western. Director: Henry Hathaway

The True Story of Jesse James (1957) Hope Lange, Agnes Moorehead
Lange plays the famous outlaw's wife and Moorehead his mother in this fictionalized film version of Jesse's life. Robert Wagner plays Jesse. Director: Nicholas Ray

Tumbleweed (1953) Lori Nelson
Audie Murphy is a soldier who tries to prove he didn't desert his post as accused, and Nelson is the girl who believes him. Director: Nathan Juran

Two Flags West (1950) Linda Darnell
This Western takes place during the Civil War and is about the divided loyalties which existed in the West. Among the many stars who appear are Darnell, Joseph Cotten, Jeff Chandler, Cornel Wilde and Dale Robertson. Director: Robert Wise

*Two Gun Lady (1956) Peggie Castle
A gunslinging lady bandit (Castle) and a lawman (William Talman) track down her father's killer. Director: Richard Bartlett

Two Guns and a Badge (1954) Beverly Garland
An ex-convict (Wayne Morris) is hired as a deputy sheriff and proves himself an excellent lawman. Garland plays his girlfriend. Director: Lewis D. Collins

Two Rode Together (1961) Linda Cristal, Shirley Jones
James Stewart and Richard Widmark play a sheriff and a cavalry officer who set out to rescue pioneers kidnapped by Comanche Indians. Director: John Ford

Under Western Skies (1945) Martha O'Driscoll
A somewhat silly Western comedy, this film starred O'Driscoll, Noah Beery, Jr., and Leon Errol. Director: Jean Yarbrough

*Union Pacific (1939) Barbara Stanwyck, Evelyn Keyes
In this epic film, Stanwyck and Joel McCrea, Robert Preston, Brian Donlevy, Anthony Quinn and Evelyn Keyes are involved in the Union Pacific Railroad's coast-to-coast development. Director: Cecil B. DeMille

Untamed Breed (1948) Barbara Britton
Cattle breeders in Old Texas are the central characters in this film. Sonny Tufts, Britton and William Bishop star. Director: Charles Lamont

Untamed Frontier (1952) Shelley Winters, Rita Moreno
Winters and Moreno play two women who are caught in the middle when Texas cattle raisers (Joseph Cotten and Scott Brady) become involved in a range war. Director: Hugo Fregonese

Valley of the Sun (1942) Lucille Ball
A dishonest white man (Dean Jagger) provokes an Indian uprising to distract a lawman (James Craig) from investigating his questionable activities. Ball plays Jagger's daughter, who becomes Craig's girlfriend. Director: George Marshall

The Vanquished (1953) Jan Sterling
A crooked town is set right by an honest sheriff (John Payne) with the help of Sterling. Director: Edward Ludwig

Vigilante's Return (1947) Margaret Lindsay
A marshall (Jon Hall) is hired to bring law and order to an out-of-control town which has become overrun by outlaws and bawdy ladies. Director: Ray Taylor

The Virginian (1929/1946) Mary Brian/Barbara Britton
Owen Wister's best-selling novel was adapted for films two times. In the earlier version, Gary Cooper is the title character; in the second version Joel McCrea plays the part of the gunfighter. Brian and Britton are the fair ladies in these two films. Directors: Victor Fleming/Stuart Gilmore

Wagonmaster (1950) Joanne Dru
Two roving cowboys join a group of Mormons which includes Jane Darwell, Joanne Dru, Ward Bond and Alan Mowbray. Director: John Ford

Wagons East (1994) Ellen Greene
An inept wagonmaster (John Candy) leads an odd assortment of characters who are sick of living in the wild and woolly West and want to go back east in this spoof. Comedian Richard Lewis plays a disillusioned doctor and Green a delightfully dizzy prostitute. Director: Peter Markle

Walk the Proud Land ((1956) Anne Bancroft, Pat Crowley
Audie Murphy is an Indian agent who tries to control trouble that is growing between white settlers and disgruntled Indians. Bancroft and Crowley play women who live at the agency. Director: Jesse Hibbs

*Wanted—The Sundance Woman (1976) Katharine Ross
Ross reprises her *Butch Cassidy and the Sundance Kid* role of Etta Place in this film sequel, which did not feature Paul Newman or Robert Redford. In this film, Ross runs guns for Pancho Villa, an event that certainly never happened. Director: Lee Phillips

The War Wagon (1967) Joanna Barnes
Cowboy John Wayne gets even with bad man Bruce Cabot by stealing the evil rancher's cattle. Barnes plays a western sport in this film. Director: Burt Kennedy

Warpath (1951) Polly Bergen
Edmond O'Brien tracks down an outlaw who has killed his girlfriend and with Bergen manages to survive an Indian attack. Director: Byron Haskin

Way Out West (1936) Sharon Lynn
Laurel and Hardy act as messengers delivering a mining deed to a prospector's daughter (Lynn). Director: James W. Horne

The Way West (1967) Lola Albright
This adaptation of A. B. Guthrie, Jr.'s best-selling novel about life in the Wild West stars Kirk Douglas, Richard Widmark, Albright and Sally Field in her first major film role. Director: Andrew V. McLaglen

Wells Fargo (1937) Frances Dee
While building his successful mail express delivery service, the founder of the Wells Fargo company (Joel McCrea) loses the support of his wife, before his ambition subsides. Director: Frank Lloyd

Western Union (1941) Virginia Gilmore
A Union officer (Robert Young) helps bring telegraph lines to California during the Civil War. Director: Fritz Lang

The Westerner (1940) Lillian Bond
Land wars between cattlemen and farmers has Walter Brennan as Judge Roy Bean settling disputes with an iron hand. Gary Cooper co-stars. Director: William Wyler

Westward Ho, the Wagons (1956) Kathleen Crowley
Walt Disney produced this tale of pioneers that featured his television Mousketeers Karen, Cathy, Tommy and Doreen, but the real star of the film was Fess Parker (who had become well known as Davy Crockett on TV) as a wagonmaster. Director: William Beaudine

Westward the Women (1951) Denise Darcel, Beverly Dennis, Hope Emerson, Julie Bishop, Marilyn Erskine
Robert Taylor leads a wagon train full of women westward and they face numerous hardships. Director: William Wellman

When the Daltons Rode (1940) Kay Francis
This fictionalized account of the Dalton brothers' criminal careers stars Randolph Scott as a lawman who tracks them down. Francis provides a bit of love interest. Director: George Marshall

The White Buffalo (1977) Kim Novak
Buffalo Bill Cody is the central character of this abstract film which is about Bill's search for a legendary white buffalo. Charles Bronson plays Bill; Novak and Jack Warden are seen in supporting roles. Director: J. Lee Thompson

Wild Bill (1995) Ellen Barkin
Barkin plays Calamity Jane and Jeff Bridges plays Wild Bill Hickok in this gritty version of the life of Wild Bill and his relationship with Calamity, which is depicted as more romantic than it probably was. Director: Walter Hill

Wild Rovers (1971) Lynn Carlin
Two cowboys rob a bank on a whim, and become fugitives from the law. William Holden, Ryan O'Neill, Karl Malden and Carlin star. Director: Blake Edwards

The Wild Westerners (1962) Nancy Kovack
A marshall's daughter (Kovack) goes along for the ride when her husband (James Philbrook) takes gold eastward to aid the Southern cause during the Civil War. Director: Oscar Rudolph

Wild Women (1970) Anne Francis
A group of female convicts are recruited to masquerade as the wives of road builders in order to distract Mexicans fighting a border war with the United States. Hugh O'Brian is the leader of the expedition; Francis, Marie Windsor, Marilyn Maxwell, Sherry Jackson and Cynthia Hall play some of the women. Director: Don Taylor

Will Penny (1968) Joan Hackett
This big-budget Western stars Charlton Heston as a strong-willed drifter who encounters the eccentric Hackett, who enlists his aid to help her fight some bad guys. Director: Tom Gries

Winchester 73 (1967) Joan Blondell
A man recently released from prison (John Saxon) seeks revenge for his imprisonment. Lawman Tom Tryon brings him to justice after he goes on a crime spree. Director: Herschel Daugherty

The Wistful Widow of Wagon Gap (1947) Marjorie Main
Abbott and Costello are the stars of this comedy Western that features Main as a coarse Calamity Jane–type of widow. Director: Charles Barton

Woman They Almost Lynched (1953) Audrey Totter, Joan Leslie
When a proper Southern lady (Leslie) goes west, she learns to tote a gun and saves lady bandit Totter from being lynched. Director: Allan Dwan

Wyatt Earp (1994) Catherine O'Hara, Jobeth Williams, Mare Winningham, Isabella Rossellini
Kevin Costner and Dennis Quaid play Wyatt Earp and Doc Holliday in this film about the famed gunmen and Wyatt's brothers' infamous careers as lawmen. Catherine O'Hara plays Josie Marcus (later Earp), Mare Winningham plays Mattie Earp, Jobeth Williams plays Allie Earp and Isabella Rossellini plays "Big Nose" Kate Fisher, Doc Holliday's mistress. Director: Lawrence Kasdan

Wyoming (1940) Vera Ralston
Ranch owner Ralston and homesteaders fight it out, but lawman Wild Bill Elliott eventually restores law and order. Director: Joseph Kane

Wyoming Renegades (1955) Martha Hyer
An ex-outlaw (Phil Carey) and his girlfriend (Hyer) cannot start their lives together until he helps the local sheriff track down outlaw Butch Cassidy. Director: Fred Sears

Yellow Tomahawk (1954) Peggie Castle
An Indian guide (Rory Calhoun) tries to prevent an attack by hostile Indians. When he fails to do so, he joins the fight to protect settlers (including Castle). Director: Lesley Selander

Young Fury (1965) Virginia Mayo
A weary gunslinger (Rory Calhoun) returns home and finds that his son has turned to crime. Mayo plays a sympathetic western woman. Director: Christian Nyby

The Young Guns (1956) Gloria Talbott
A young man (Russ Tamblyn) tries to erase all memories of his gunslinger-father (Scott Marlowe) and lead a normal life. Talbott is a saloon girl-friend of his father, who tells him the truth about his father's heroism. Director: Albert Band

Young Guns (1988) Sharon Thomas
An English aristocrat (Terence Stamp) hires six young punks including Billy the Kid (Emilio Estevez) and others (Kiefer Sutherland, Lou Diamond Phillips) to guard his New Mexico ranch. This was one of the few films to attempt to accurately depict Billy's affection for Mexican-Americans, especially young Hispanic girls. A sequel (*Young Guns II*, 1990) also starred Estevez, Sutherland and Phillips. Director: Christopher Cain

The Young Guns of Texas (1962) Alana Ladd
James Mitchum (Robert Mitchum's son), Alana Ladd (Alan Ladd's daughter) and Jody McCrea (Joel McCrea's son) are the leading characters in this story of a search to find gold in the Old West. Director: Maury Dexter

The Young Land (1959) Yvonne Craig
Life in Texas immediately following the Mexican-American War is explored in this film that stars Pat Wayne (John Wayne's son), Dennis Hopper and Craig. Director: Ted Tetzlaff

Zaccariah (1971) Pat Quinn

This unusual spoof, which is not as funny as it wants to be, takes an offbeat look at life out West in the nineteenth century. John Rubenstein plays a young bandit and Pat Quinn is a glamorous Belle Starr. Director: George Englund

Appendix C

Western Television Series Featuring Women in Prominent Roles

Alias Smith and Jones (1971–1973)
Sally Field was featured as a character named Clementine Hale on this western series about two outlaws who make a deal with the governor to go straight for a year in order to have criminal charges against them dropped. Peter Deuel, and then Roger Darn, and Ben Murphy played the outlaws; Roger Davis later replaced Deuel (an apparent suicide).

Annie Oakley (1954–1956)
Former rodeo performer-turned-actress Gale Davis was the star of this syndicated Saturday morning series, playing sharpshooter Annie Oakley. Brad Johnson and Jimmy Hawkins were also featured as Deputy Sheriff Lofty Craig and Tagg Oakley.

The Big Valley (1965–1969)
Film star Barbara Stanwyck was ranch-owning cattle queen Victoria Barkley on this hour-long, weekly series that also starred Richard Long, Peter Breck, Lee Majors and Linda Evans as her children.

Brave Eagle (1955–1956)
Native American actress Kim Winona was featured as a character named Morning Star on this syndicated series, which starred Keith Larsen in the title role.

Cimarron City (1958–1960)
Audrey Totter, who played many saloon girl roles in films, was one of the stars of this western series that was set in Cimarron City when Oklahoma was called "Indian Territory." George Montgomery and John Smith co-starred.

Dirty Sally (1974)
Veteran character actress Jeanette Nolan played hard-drinking muleskinner Sally Fergus on this western series that was set during the California gold rush days.

Dr. Quinn, Medicine Woman (1992–present)
English actress Jane Seymour plays a female physician from Boston, Dr. Michaela Quinn, who goes west and sets up her medical practice in a small frontier town. Joe Lando is featured

Gale Davis starred on the TV series *Annie Oakley* (Photofest.)

as Byron Sully, Dr. Quinn's love interest, and Chad Allen, Erika Flores and Shawn Toovay play three orphaned youngsters adopted by Dr. Quinn.

Empire (1962–1964)
Set in contemporary New Mexico, this series featured Terry Moore and Anne Seymour as ranch women and starred Richard Egan as a character named Jim Redigo. When *Empire*

was canceled, Egan became the star of a series called *Redigo*. In addition to Egan, Elena Verdugo and Mina Martinez were also featured in *Redigo*.

Gunsmoke (1955–1975)
One of television's longest-running and most popular westerns, *Gunsmoke* was originally a half-hour, weekly radio program and became a one-hour, weekly TV series in 1955. Amanda Blake was featured as Miss Kitty Russell, and is probably one of the most famous saloon girl characters of all time. James Arness played Sheriff Matt Dillon, and Milburn Stone and Dennis Weaver were featured as Doc Adams and Chester Goode.

Hotel De Paree (1959–1960)
This television series was a situation comedy set in a fictitious hotel in the Colorado town called Georgetown in the mid–1800s. The hotel of the show's title was owned and operated by Judi Meredith and Jeanette Nolan. Earl Holliman also starred as Sundance, the town's sheriff.

How the West Was Won (1978–1979)
When *Gunsmoke* left the air, James Arness played frontiersman Zeb Macahan on this series, which was about a family that settles on the western frontier. Fionnula Flanagan and Kathryn Holcomb were featured as Aunt Molly Culhane and Laura Mecahan.

Johnny Ringo (1959–1960)
Although the real-life Johnny Ringo was a notorious outlaw, he was portrayed as a bandit-turned-sheriff on this series. Karen Sharpe played Ringo's female friend Laura Thomas and Don Durant starred as Ringo.

The Legend of Jesse James (1965–1966)
Ann Doran played Mrs. James, the mother of outlaws Frank and Jesse James, on this series which glorified the early days of Frank and Jesse and the Younger brothers. Christopher Jones and Allan Case played Jesse and Frank and John Milford and Tim McIntire played Cole and Bob Younger.

The Life and Times of Wyatt Earp (1955–1961)
Gloria Talbott played a fictional character, Abbie Crandall, who was a compilation of several women who were in the actual Earp brothers' lives. Hugh O'Brian starred as Wyatt on this long-running series and Douglas Fowley played his friend Doc Holliday.

Little House on the Prairie (1974–1983)
One of television's most successful long-running series, *Little House on the Prairie* was the episodic story of the Ingalls family who settled on the Kansas prairie. Based on Laura Ingalls Wilder's popular books, the one-hour, weekly series starred Michael Landon as patriarch Charles Ingalls, and featured Karen Grassle as his wife Caroline and Melissa Sue Anderson, Melissa Gilbert, and Lindsay and Sidney Greenbush as their daughters.

The Monroes (1966–1967)
Barbara Hershey and Tammy Locke appeared as Kathy and Amy, the female members of the Monroe family on this series. Michael Anderson, Jr., and Keith and Kevin Schultz played their brothers. These five siblings run their family ranch in the Wyoming Territory in the 1870s after their parents are killed by Indians.

The Nichols (1971–1972)
After his hit series *Maverick* left the air, James Garner starred in this short-lived western series that featured Neva Patterson, Margot Kidder and Alice Ghostley in major supporting roles.

The Oregon Trail (1977)
Darleen Carr played Margaret Devlin, a pioneer woman headed west in a covered wagon, and Rod Taylor played wagon master Evan Thorpe on this western series that was only on the air for a single season.

Pistols and Petticoats (1966–1967)
This sitcom set in the Old West featured film star Ann Sheridan as Henrietta Hanks, who lives in a Colorado town called Wretched with her daughter. Douglas Fowley played Grandpa Hanks and Carole Wells played Henrietta's daughter, Lucy.

The Roy Rogers Show (1951–1964)
One of filmdom's best-known cowboy stars, Roy Rogers was the star of one of the most popular children's adventure and western variety series. Roy's real-life wife, actress-singer Dale Evans, was Roy's co-star, and Pat Brady was his comic sidekick. In 1962, Dale received equal billing when the show was called *The Roy Rogers–Dale Evans Show* and was seen on Saturday evenings on ABC.

Sara (1976)
A schoolteacher (Brenda Vaccaro) migrates west to Independence, Colorado, in the 1870s. Also featured are Bert Kramer as Emmet Ferguson, Albert Stratton as Martin Pope and Mariclare Costello as Julia Bailey.

Sky King (1953–1966)
For 13 years, the syndicated children's adventure series *Sky King* was a popular Saturday morning program. Formerly a radio series, *Sky King* was about an airplane pilot–ranch owner (Kirby Grant) and featured Gloria Winters and Ron Haggerty as his niece and nephew, Penny and Clipper.

The Virginian (1962–1971)
This series, set at the fictitious Shiloh Ranch in Wyoming, quite remarkably remained on the air in the same time slot for eight continuous years. Lee J. Cobb played Judge Henry Garth from 1962 until 1966, James Drury played the Virginian for the entire run of the series and Doug McClure played a popular character named Trampas. Pippa Scott, Roberta Shaw, Sara Lane and Jeanette Nolan were leading female characters on the series at various times.

The Yellow Rose (1983–1984)
Cybill Shepherd played Colleen Champion on this western soap opera series set on a 200,000-acre Texas ranch called "The Yellow Rose." Also featured were Sam Elliott, Chuck Connors, Susan Anspach, Kerrie Keane, and Caryn Cabrera.

Appendix D

Twelve Celebrated Locales
of the Western Frontier

Several locations are regularly mentioned as the settings for factual, as well as fictional, events that occurred in the Old West. It is altogether appropriate, therefore, that these locations be profiled in the appendix of this book, since they were the places where so many of the West's women's real-life adventures took place.

Abilene, Kansas: Texas ranchers drove their livestock to Abilene for distribution to the East by rail. Between 1867 and 1872, the town was the major shipping point for over one and a half million longhorn steers which were bound for Kansas City, Chicago and other eastern stockyards. Joseph McCoy, a middleman who bought herds from ranchers and then sold them to eastern beef buyers, founded Abilene because it was west of "The Quarantine Line" which preserved vast areas of open Kansas grassland to graze herds which were soon to be shipped east. The town also had a good water supply from the Smokey Hill River and, of course, was at the terminal point of the existing railway line. Fort Riley, which was located nearby, was a deterrent from renegade Indian attacks. The town had a hotel, "Drover's Cottage," where cowboys could bathe and sleep after long, dusty days on the trail. Abilene also had large fenced-in areas for steers, barns, livery stables, several dance halls and, of course, saloons. Cowboys could enjoy more "intimate" entertainment with ladies of ill repute on the outskirts of town in an area called "Devil's Addition." When the quarantine line was moved further west, the town of Newton (which was also on the railway line 60 miles south of Abilene) became the major shipping center for cattle.

The Cherokee Strip: This was an area that had been reserved as "native land" for the Five Civilized Indian Tribes in a treaty of 1866. The region was in the northwestern corner of what was called "The Indian Territory" in Oklahoma. In 1889, certain tribes began to sell their tracts of land and this eventually led to the Oklahoma Land Rush of 1893, when white settlers made a dash across the countryside to claim land as their own. Many outlaws hid out from the law in the Cherokee Strip because it was not under anyone's jurisdiction until the land rush officially made it part of the United States.

Deadwood, South Dakota: Established in a gulch in the Black Hills, Deadwood was founded in 1876 when gold was discovered there. Basically a mining town, Deadwood became famous as the playground of such celebrated westerners as Calamity Jane, Wild Bill Hickok and Poker Alice Tubbs. The town was nearly burned to the ground in 1879, and in 1883 a flood carried away almost half the town's buildings. Deadwood has been restored to

Deadwood, South Dakota, in 1876. (Author's collection.)

look as it did during its heyday, and is now one of the West's most popular tourist attractions.

Denver, Colorado: At the spot where the Great Plains meet the Rocky Mountains, the town of Denver was first established when gold was discovered in Cherry Creek and the Silver River in 1858. A major mining center, Denver became a boom town that had over 5000 inhabitants by 1870, and it eventually became one of the first cultural centers in the western United States. A severe blow was dealt to the city when the Union Pacific Railroad elected to take their line to Cheyenne, Wyoming, instead of to Denver. The Kansas Pacific, however, did bring its railroad line to Denver in 1870, connecting the city to the rest of the country by rail; this caused its population to soar.

Dodge City, Kansas: A cattle town from which 250,000 steers were shipped east each year between 1876 and 1886, Dodge City was founded in 1872 to service the Fort Dodge army post. Originally Dodge City was called "Buffalo City" in honor of famous buffalo hunter William Cody. The Atchison, Topeka and Santa Fe Railroad brought its line to Buffalo City in order to ship out the one million or so buffalo hides that were gathered there. The town was renamed Dodge City in 1876 because, as the buffalo hide business ended due to diminishing numbers of buffalo, Fort Dodge had become its major attraction. In 1876, the town had 1,200 citizens and sported 20 saloons to quench the thirst of the residents, visiting cowboys and soldiers on leave from Fort Dodge. Dodge City developed a reputation for being one of the West's wildest towns and such legends of the West as Wyatt Earp, Doc Holliday and Bat Masterson took up residence there at one time or another.

Helena, Montana: Before it became well known as a western frontier town, Helena was called "Last Chance Gulch." First settled in 1864 by a prospector named John Cowan,

Dodge City, Kansas, in 1878. (Author's collection.)

Helena became a boom town when Cowan discovered a vein of gold that eventually yielded $16 million. It became the capital of Montana when the territory became a state in 1889.

Leadville, Colorado: Another Colorado gold boom town, Leadville (established in 1867) was originally named Oro City (Gold City) because of all of the ore found there. The rich gold deposits ran out by 1877, but silver was discovered in the area soon after and the town's boom years continued. The town became prosperous enough to have a large opera house constructed on its main street, and the Irish-English author Oscar Wilde lectured there on the "ethics of art" in 1882. Over $100,000,000 worth of gold, silver, lead and other metals were taken from Leadville mines between 1879 and 1885. The town's boom days ended when the depression of 1893 saw the price of silver dropping to an all-time low.

Salt Lake City, Utah: Founded by the leader of the Mormon Church, Brigham Young, this city on the Great Salt Lake was first settled in 1857. The railroad brought ever-increasing numbers of inhabitants to Utah when the Civil War ended and in 1869 the population was soaring. The city has continued to increase in size steadily ever since.

San Francisco, California: Originally called Yerba Buena (good herbs), the city was renamed San Francisco in 1857 for the Mission of San Francisco de Asis (Mission Dolores), which had been founded in 1776 by Spanish missionaries. San Francisco became an American settlement when the United States defeated Mexico in the Mexican-American War in 1846. Located on San Francisco Bay, the city proved to be a natural West Coast harbor for shippers who crossed the Pacific Ocean or traveled to America from Europe around the South American cape. When gold was discovered near San Francisco in 1848, the town's population suddenly rose from 459 people to 35,000 in two years' time. Although the earthquake and fire of 1906 were the city's most publicized disasters, its wooden buildings were destroyed by fire several times before. But the city was always rebuilt and it continues to prosper.

Tombstone, Arizona: One of the West's most famous towns, Tombstone was named by prospector Ed Schieffelin who was warned that all he would find there was a tombstone for himself. Schieffelin, his clothes worn and torn and his health very poor indeed, discovered silver which brought many other fortune-seekers to the area. The town they built became a mecca for other prospectors as well as the usual assortment of gamblers, prostitutes and adventurers. Familiar western characters like the Earps, Johnny Ringo and Bat Masterson joined the swelling population of over 7000 inhabitants at one time or another, and such notorious watering holes as "The Oriental Saloon" and "The Crystal Palace" whore house operated on a 24-hour basis. In addition to the town's numerous saloons and bawdy houses, many churches and schools also thrived, supported by a heavy gambling tax. "Shieffelin Hall," named after the town's founder, presented theatrical plays and concerts. The town also boasted several newspapers, the most prominent being *The Tombstone Epitaph*, founded by John P. Clum, who believed that "every *tombstone* needed an *epitaph*." Eight million dollars' worth of silver was mined in Tombstone between 1878 and 1886, but operations ended when the mines were flooded in 1891 and Tombstone eventually became a ghost town. Today, the town has been restored and, like Deadwood, is a popular tourist attraction.

Virginia City, Nevada: The Comstock Lode, which contained the largest deposits of silver ever discovered in the West, led to the establishment of Virginia City, which was founded as the central mining town of that area in 1859. The town had one of the largest populations in the developing west and by 1879, about 25,000 people lived there. As with so many other famous mining towns, gold and silver deposits eventually diminished to the point that mining became unprofitable; by 1890, Virginia City had become a ghost town. At its peak, the town was a cultural center like Denver, and there were numerous theaters, fashionable homes, richly appointed houses of prostitution, banks, churches and even a stock exchange. A young writer named Samuel Clemens, who became better known as Mark Twain, once worked for a Virginia City newspaper as a reporter.

Wichita, Kansas: Wichita was a major cattle town from 1871 until 1875 when Dodge City replaced it as the railroad's major cattle shipping center. During its peak years, Wichita shipped 200,000 head of cattle to cities all across the United States. Earlier it had been an Indian trading post, but the Indians were relocated to reservations in 1867 and Wichita became a cattle boom town because the railroad line was brought to its doorstep. After the cattle industry deserted Wichita, it became a center for agriculture and industry.

Bibliography

Adams, Les, and Buck Rainey. *Shoot-Em-Ups: The Complete Reference Guide to Westerns of the Sound Era*. Waynesville, N.C.: World of Yesterday, 1978.

Adams, Ramon F. *Burns Under the Saddle: A Second Look at Books and Histories of the West*. Norman: University of Oklahoma Press, 1989.

_____. *A Fitting Death for Billy the Kid*. Norman: University of Oklahoma Press, 1960.

Aikman, Duncan. *Calamity Jane and the Lady Wildcats*. New York: Holt, 1927.

Alexander, Kent. *Heroes of the Wild West*. New York: Millard, 1992.

Anderson, Charles D., comp. and ed. *Outlaws of the West*. Los Angeles: Markland, 1973.

Armitage, Susan, and Elizabeth Jameson, eds. *The Woman's West*. Norman: University of Oklahoma Press, 1987.

Baker, Pearl. *The Wild Bunch at Robber's Roost*. Lincoln: University of Nebraska Press, 1989.

Bataille, Gretchen M., and Kathleen Multen Sands. *American Indian Women*. Lincoln: University of Nebraska Press, 1984.

Bartholomew, E. *Wyatt Earp: The Man and the Myths*. Fort Davis, Tex.: Frontier, 1964.

_____. *Wyatt Earp: The Untold Story*. Fort Davis, Tex.: Frontier, 1964.

Beachy, E. B. "The Saga of Cattle Kate." *Frontier Times*, 1964.

Beck, Warren A., and Ynez D. Hasse. *Historical Atlas of the American West*. Norman: University of Oklahoma Press, 1966.

Bennett, Estelline. *Old Deadwood Days*. Lincoln: University of Nebraska Press, 1982.

Bird, Isabella. *A Lady's Life in the Rocky Mountains*. Norman: University of Oklahoma Press, 1960.

Blackstone, Sarah J. *Bullets, Buckskins and Business: A History of Buffalo Bill's Wild West*. Westport, Conn.: Greenwood, 1986.

Blevins, Winfred. *Dictionary of the American West*. New York: Facts on File, 1993.

Booker, Anton S. *Wildcats in Petticoats: A Garland of Female Desperados*. Girard,Kans.: Halderman-Julius, 1951.

Botkin, Benjamin A. *A Treasury of Western Folklore*. New York: Bonanza, 1975.

Boyer, Glenn. *I Married Wyatt Earp: The Recollections of Josephine Sarah Marcus Earp*. University of Arizona Press, 1976 (reprint).

Breihan, Carl W. *The Complete and Authentic Life of Jesse James*. New York: Fell, 1953.

_____, and Charles A. Rosamond. *The Bandit Belle*. Seattle: Hangman/Superior, 1970.

Brown, Dee. *The Gentle Tamers: Women of the Old Wild West*. Lincoln: University of Nebraska Press, 1968.

Bullington, Ray A. *America's Frontier Heritage*. New York: Holt, Rinehart and Winston, 1966.

Bunton, Mary Taylor. *A Bride on the Old Chisholm Trail*. San Antonio, Tex.: 1939.

Burns, Walter Noble. *Tombstone: Gun-Toting, Cattle Rustling Days in Old Arizona*. New York: Grosset and Dunlap, 1929.

Carrington, Frances. *My Army Life*. Philadelphia: 1911.

Castel, Albert. *William Clarke Quantrill: His Life and Times*. New York: Fell, 1962.

"Cattle Queen of Wyoming Must Serve Sentence." *Denver Post*, October 23, 1921.

Cawelti, John. *The Six-Gun Mystique*. Bowling Green, Ohio: Bowling Green University Press, 1971.

Chona, Maria. *Papago Woman*. Edited by Ruth M. Underhill. New York: Holt, Rinehart and Winston, 1979.

Chum, John P. *It All Happened in Tombstone*. Flagstaff, Arizona: Northland, 1965.

Claimonte, Glenn. *Calamity Was the Name for Jane*. Denver: Sage, 1943.

Cleveland, Agnes Morley. *No Life for a Lady*. Boston: Houghton-Miflin, 1941.

Coates, Robert M. *The Outlaw Years: The History of Land Pirates*. Lincoln: University of Nebraska Press, 1986

Cody, William F. *The Life of Hon. William F. Cody, Known as Buffalo Bill, the Famous Hunter, Scout and Guide*. Lincoln: University of Nebraska Press, 1978 (reprint).

Commager, Henry Steele, ed. in chief. *The Story of America: The Age of the West*. New York: Torstar, 1975.

Constable, George, ed. *The Gamblers: Old West Series*. Alexandria, Va.: Time-Life, 1978.

"Cowgirls." *Texas Monthly*, November 1978, October 1987.

Cunningham, E. *Triggernometry: A Gallery of Gunfighters*. New York: Press of the Pioneers, 1934.

Curry, Larry, ed. *The American West*. New York: Viking, 1972.

Cusic, Don. *Cowboys and the Wild West*. New York: Facts on File, 1994.

Custer, Elizabeth. *Following the Guidons*. Lincoln: University of Nebraska Press, 1994 (reprint).

_____. *Tenting of the Plains*. New York: 1887.

De Voto, Bernard, ed. *The Journals of Lewis and Clark*. Boston: Houghton-Mifflin, 1953.

Dick, Everett. *Tales of the Frontier*. Lincoln: University of Nebraska Press, 1963.

Dippie, Brian W. *Custer's Last Stand*. Lincoln: University of Nebraska Press, 1994.

Drago, Henry Sinclair. *Outlaws on Horseback*. New York: Dodd, Mead, 1964.

Durham, Philip, and Everett L. Jones. *The Negro Cowboys*. Lincoln: University of Nebraska Press, 1983.

Dykstra, Robert R. *The Cattle Towns*. Lincoln: University of Nebraska Press, 1983.

Faulk, Odie B. *Dodge City*. New York: Oxford University Press, 1977.

_____. *Tombstone: Myth and Reality*. New York: Oxford University Press, 1972.

Flanagan, Mike. *Out West*. New York: Abrams, 1987.

Frizzle, Lodisa. "Accounts of a Trip Across the Plains in 1855." *Society of California Pioneers Quarterly* 6, 1929.

Garrett, Pat F. *The Authentic Life of Billy the Kid*. Norman: University of Oklahoma Press, 1954.

Gordon, Mike. *I Arrested Pearl Starr and Other Stories of Adventure as a Policeman in Fort Smith, Arkansas for 40 Years*. No publisher; no date..

Hanes, Colonel Bailey C. *Bill Doolin, Outlaw*. Norman: University of Oklahoma Press, 1968.

Herman, Samuel W. *Belle Starr, the Female Desperado—From Hell on the Border*. Houston: Frontier Press of Texas, 1954.

Hicks, Edwin P. *Belle Starr and Her Pearl*. Little Rock, Ark.: Pioneer, 1963.

Holmes, Kenneth L. *Covered Wagon Women*. Lincoln: University of Nebraska Press, 1995.

Horan, James D. *Desperate Women*. New York: Bonanza, 1952.

Howard, Harold P. *Sacajawea*. Norman: University of Oklahoma Press, 1971.

Jackson, Joseph Henry. *Bad Company*. Lincoln: University of Nebraska Press, 1977.

Jones, Daryl. *The Dime Novel Western*. Bowling Green, Ohio: Bowling Green University Popular Press, 1978.

Jordan, Teresa. *Cowgirls*. Lincoln: University of Nebraska Press, 1992.

Lamar, Howard, ed. *The Reader's Encyclopedia of the American West*. New York: Harper and Row, 1977.

Larson, T. A. "Dolls, Vassals and Drudges: Pioneer Women in the West." *Western Historical Quarterly*, January 1972

Lloyd, Everett. *Law West of the Pecos*. San Antonio, Tex.: Naylor, 1967.

Logsdon, Guy. *The Whorehouse Bells Were Ringing*. Chicago: University of Illinois Press, 1989.

Lovejoy, Julia L. *Letters. Kansas Historical Quarterly* 16, 1948.

McLoughlin, Denis. *Wild and Woolly: An Encyclopedia of the Old West*. Garden City, N.Y.: Doubleday, 1975.

Maltin, Leonard, ed. *TV Movies*. New York: New American Library, 1982.

Martin, Douglas D. *The Earps of Tombstone*. Tombstone Epitaph, 1959.

Mercer, A. S. *The Banditti of the Plains: On the Cattlemen's Invasion of Wyoming in 1892*. Norman: University of Oklahoma Press, 1954.

Miller, Ronald Dean. *Shady Ladies of the West*. Los Angeles: Western-lore, 1964

Murphy, Virginia (Reed). "Across the Plains in the Donner Party." *Century*, 1891.

Myers, John. *Doc Holliday*. Lincoln: University of Nebraska Press, 1973.

_____. *Tombstone's Early Years*. Lincoln: University of Nebraska Press, 1995.

Myers, Sandra L. *Westering Women and the Frontier Experience, 1800–1915*. Albuquerque: University of New Mexico Press, 1982.

Nix, Evett Dumas. *Oklahombres*. Lincoln: University of Nebraska Press, 1993.

O'Neal, Bill. *Encyclopedia of Western Gunfighters*. Norman: University of Oklahoma Press, 1979.

Perkins, Col. Henry Mercedes. "Sallie Skull." *Frontier Times*, November, 1928.

Phillips, Charles. *Heritage of the West*. New York: Crescent, 1992.

Poling-Kempes, Lesley. *The Harvey Girls*. New York: Paragon, 1989.

Preece, Harold. *The Doolin Gang: End of an Outlaw Era*. New York: Hastings, 1963.

Rankin, M. Wilson. "The Meeker Massacre." *Annals of Wyoming* 16, 1944.

Ray, Grace Ernestine. *Wily Women of the West*. San Antonio, Tex.: Naylor, 1972.

Reiter, Joan Swallow. *Women of the West*. Alexandria, Va.: Time-Life, 1978, 1979.

Riley, Glenda. *Frontierswomen: The Iowa Experience*. Ames: Iowa State University Press, 1981.

_____. *The Frontier Female: A Comparative View of Women on the Prairie and the Plains*. Lawrence: University of Kansas Press, 1988.

Roach, Joyce. *The Cowgirls*. Denton: University of North Texas Press, 1977, 1990.

Rosa, Joseph G. *The Gunfighter: Man or Myth*. Norman, University of Oklahoma Press, 1989.

Ryland, Lee. "Skirts, Powder Puffs and Rodeos." *Big West*, April 1968.

Sann, Paul. *The Lawless Decade*. New York: Crown, 1957.

Shackleford, William Yancy. *Belle Starr, The Bandit Queen: The Career of the Most Colorful Outlaw the Indian Territory Ever Knew*. Girard, Kans.: Haldeman-Julius, 1943.

Shirley, Glenn. *Belle Starr and Her Times: The Literature of Facts and the Legends*. Norman: University of Oklahoma Press, 1982.

Sonnichsen, C. L. *Roy Bean: Law West of the Pecos*. New York: 1943.

Sprague, William Forrest. *Women of the West*. Boston: Christopher, 1946.

Spring, Agnes Wright. *Good Little Bad Man: The Life of Colorado's Charlie Utter*. Boulder, Colo.: Pruett, 1987.

Steffen, Jerome. *The American West: New Perspectives, New Dimensions*. Norman: University of Oklahoma Press, 1977.

Stratton, R. B. *Captivity of the Oatman Girls*. Lincoln: University of Nebraska Press, 1983.

Summerhayes, Martha. *Vanished Arizona; Recollections of My Army Life*. Chicago: 1939.

Tighman, Zoe. "I Knew Rose of the Cimarron." *True West*, May-June 1958.

Trachtman, Paul. *The Gunfighters*. Alexandria, Va.: Time-Life, 1974.

Tuska, Jon. *Billy the Kid: A Handbook*. Lincoln: University of Nebraska Press, 1986.

Utley, Robert M. *Billy the Kid*. Lincoln: University of Nebraska Press, 1989.

Velasquez, Loreta. *The Woman in Battle*. Hartford: no date.

Vestal, Stanley. *Queen of the Cowtowns: Dodge City, 1972–1886*. New York: Harper, 1952.

Waters, Frank. *The Earp Brothers of Tombstone: The Story of Mrs. Virgil Earp*. Lincoln: University of Nebraska Press, 1976.

Wellman, Paul. *A Dynasty of Western Outlaws*. New York: Bonanza, 1966.

The West: A Collection from Harper's *Magazine*. New York: Gallery, 1990.

Wheeler, Homer. *Buffalo Days, Forty Years in the Old West: The Personal Narrative of a Cattleman, Indian Fighter, and Army Officer*. Indianapolis: Bobbs-Merrill, 1925.

"Woman Rancher Alleged Rustler, Dead." *Denver Post*, August 20, 1956.

"Women Who Helped Make the West Wild." *Bent County Democrat* July 15, 1938.

Index

Abbott, Bud 183
Abilene Town 101, 102
Adams, Antoinette 69
Adams, Charles, 134
Adams, Julie 162, 165, 172
Adoree, Renee 152
Adrian, Iris 170
"The Adventures of Ozzie and Harriett" 33
Agar, John 141, 160, 176
Ah Tay 97
Ailen, Duncan 2, 6, 15, 23, 24, 27, 28, 35, 63, 64, 87, 88, 92
Al Swerringer's Lady Entertainers 29
Albright, Lola 170, 175, 182
Aldrich, Robert 161
Alexander, Jane 35, 155
Alexander, Kent 57
Alkire, Assenath 129–130
Alkire, Frank 129, 130
Allen, Chad 149, 187
Allen, "Prairie Lillie" 74
Allen, Steve 20
Allison, May 151
Along Came Jones 146
Alonzo, John A. 19, 154
Altman, Robert 103, 155, 166
America Illustrations of Today 1
The Angel and the Badman 146
Anders, Laurie 167
Anders, Merry 158
Anderson, G. M. ("Broncho Billy") 146
Anderson, Judith 167
Anderson, Melissa Sue 149, 188
Anderson, Michael, Jr. 188
Andress, Ursula 161
Andrews, Dana 18, 156, 165, 180
Andrews, Stanley 148
Ankers, Evelyn 178
Ann-Margret 156

Annie Get Your Gun 72
Annie Oakley (film) 72
"Annie Oakley" (TV) 72, 187
Anspach, Susan 189
Antony and Cleopatra 80
Antrim, Kid *see* Billy the Kid
Appell, George 19
"Arietta Murdock" 144
Arista, William 97
Arlen, Richard 175
Armitage, Susan 69, 106
Arness, James 188
Arthur, Jean 33, 34, 35, 153, 170, 174
As the Sun Went Down 146
Astor, John Jacob 85
Astor, Mary 155
Astors 129
Austin, Sadie 124
Autry, Gene 73, 174
Averill, James "Jim" 50, 51, 52

Bacall, Lauren 174
Badger, Joseph E. 144
Badman's Territory 19
Baker, Carroll 146, 164
Baker, Pearl 40
Balch, Ebenezer 143
Baldwin, Tillie 74
Balin, Ina 156
Ball, Lucille 181
Bancroft, Anne 172, 182
Band, Albert 184
Banky, Vilma 152
Barchus, Eliza 118
Barde, Frederick 13
Bare, Richard 172
Bari, Lynn 165
Barkin, Ellen 35, 183
Barnes, Barbara 79
Barnes, Binnie 164
Barnes, Clive 148
Barnes, Jane 85–87
Barnes, Joanna 182

Barnum, Phineas T. 71
Barranca Wolf 144
Barry, Wesley 169
Barrymore, Drew 154
Barrymore, Lionel 159
Bartholomew, E. 57
Bartlett, Richard 166, 180
Barton, Charles 183
Barton, James 147
Bass, Sam 33, 34, 155
Bassett, Ann 45
Battle of Little Big Horn 24, 106, 138, 140
Baxter, Anne 146, 156, 178, 179
Baylor, Hal 57
Beadle, Ernest 27
Bean, Judge Roy 76, 77, 118, 182
Beatty, Warren 106, 166
Beaudine, William 40, 183
The Beautiful Blonde from Bashful Bend 66, 67
The Beautiful Decoy 144
Becker, Fritz 124
Becker Sisters 124
Beecher, Henry Ward 115
Beery, Noah, Jr. 181
Beery, Wallace 40
Behan, John 53, 55, 56, 58
Bella Union 100
Bellamy, Earl 180
Bellamy, Madge 152
Belle of the Nineties 100
Belle Starr (film) 15, 18
Belle Starr (musical comedy) 20
Belle Starr's Daughter 19, 20
Belle's Castle 20
Bennett, Enid 152
Bennett, Estelline 21, 30–32, 142
Bennett, Joan 179
Bennett, Spencer 172
Bergen, Polly 182
Berke, William 167

Berlin, Irving 72, 153
Bernard, Dorothy 151
Bernard, H. H. 127
Bernds, Edward 38, 170
Bernhardt, Sarah 81
Beutel, Jack 40, 129
Bey, Turhan 161
Bierstadt, Albert 1
Big Nose Kate *see* Elder, Kate
"The Big Valley" 149
Bignon, "Big Minnie" 89, 90–91
Billy the Kid 9, 38–40, 161, 169, 170, 184
Billy the Kid (film) 149
Billy the Kid (play) 40
Billy the Kid vs. Dracula 40
Bingham, Anne E. G. 142
"Bird Cage Theater" 69
Bird Woman *see* Sacajawea
Bishop, Joey 179
Bishop, Julie 183
Bishop, William 171, 181
Bisset, Jacqueline 81, 165
Blake, Amanda 103, 156, 188
Blanchard, Mari 176
Blanchett, Berta 74
Blonde Marie (Dubonnet, Dubarry or Durrant) 89–90
Blondell, Joan 156, 183
Blue, Teddy 30
Blue Duck 10, 11
Blyth, Ann 171
Boatright, Mody C. 13
Boerticher, Budd 156, 172
Bond, Lillian 182
Bond, Ward 141, 164, 181
Bonga, Jean and Jeanne 141
Bonney, William *see* Billy the Kid
Boone, Richard 178, 179
Boot, Joe 63, 64
Boot Hill 95, 175
Booth, Edwin 69
Booth, John Wilkes 69
Booth, Junius 69
Booth, Karen 180
Borgnine, Ernest 42, 164
Bothwell, Albert 50, 51, 52
Bottoms, Timothy 175
Bowdre, Manuella 38
Bower, B. M. (Berta "Muzzy" Sinclair) 145
Bowie, Jim 156
Brady, Scott 19, 148, 160, 161, 172, 181
Brand, Neville 162
Brando, Jocelyn 178
Breck, Peter 149
Breiham, W. W. 15
Brennan, Walter 172, 182

Brent, George 19
Brewster, Diane 38, 170
Brian, Mary 181
Bridges, Jeff 35, 52, 163, 183
Bridges, Lloyd 33
Bright, Abbie 106, 123
Bright Star 73
Britton, Barbara 181
Brodt, Helen 118
Broncho Sue 64
Bronco Billy 146
Bronson, Charles 175, 183
Brook, Peter 186
Brooks, Mel 154
Brown, Angie 130–131
Brown, Dr. Charlotte 116
Brown, George Waldo 115
Brown, James 128, 129
Brown, Johnny Mack 40
Brown, Molly 128–129
Bruce, David 173
Bryant, William Cullen 115
Buffalo Bill Cody *see* Cody, William S.
Buffalo Bill Cody's Rocky Mountain and Prairie Exhibition 70
Buffalo Bill's Congress of Rough Riders 22
Buffalo Bill's Wild West Exhibition 21, 22, 115
Buffalo Bill's Wild West Show 32, 33, 70, 71, 73, 135, 153, 155
Buffalo Girls 35
Bullette, Julia C. 93–94
Bullion, Laura ("Della Rose") 37, 40, 42, 44
Burke (or Burk), John (or Clinton) 30
Burke, Pearl 30
Burroughs, John Rolfe 127
Burstyn, Ellen 159
Bush, Pauline 151
Butch Cassidy and the Sundance Kid 42, 43, 182
Butler, David 35, 173
Butler, Frank 70, 72, 153

Cabot, Bruce 182
Cabot, Susan 160, 163
Cabrera, Caryn 189
Cagney, James 180
Cahill, F. P. 39
Cahn, Edward L. 169
Cain, Christopher 184
Caine, Michael 164
Calhoun, Rory 167, 170, 184
Calamity Jane *see* Canary, Martha Jane
Calamity Jane 34

Calamity Jane and Sam Bass 33, 34
Calamity Jane, the Heroine of Whoop Up 27
Callan, Michael 65, 66
Calvet, Corinne 170
Cameahwait 109
Cameron, Evelyn Jephson 119
Cameron, Rod 19, 81, 161, 172, 173, 176
Camille 81
Canary, Charlotte 21
Canary, James 21
Canary, Martha Jane ("Calamity Jane") 2, 3, 5, 21–36, 88, 89, 90, 91, 113, 142, 143, 144, 155, 170, 178, 183, 190
Canary, Robert "Bob" 21
Canary, Thornton 21
Candy, John 182
Canova, Judy 169
Carey, Macdonald 156, 167
Carey, Phil 35, 179, 184
Carlin, Lynn 183
Carlson, Richard 161
Carol, Martine 76, 166
Carr, Darlene 189
Carr, Thomas 178
Carradine, David 166
Carradine, John 40
Carradine, Keith 19, 103, 166
Carradine, Robert 166
Carrington, Henry 137
Carrington, Frances *see* Grummond, Frances
Carroll, Diahann 164
Carson, Jack 100
Carson, Kit 5
Carter, Helena 160
Case, Allan 188
Casey, R. J. 35
Cashman, Nellie 113–115
Cashman-Cunningham, Frances 114
The Casper Weekly Mail 50
Cassakas 86
Cassidy, Butch 40, 41, 42, 45, 184
Castle, Peggy 169, 175, 178, 180, 184
Cat Ballou 65, 66
Catlin, George 1
Cattle Annie *see* McDougal, Annie
Cattle Annie and Little Britches 47
Caulfield, Joan 171
Cavanaugh, Michael 19
Chamberlaine, Richard 179
Chandler, Jess 180

Chanslor, Roy 66
Chaplin, Geraldine 155
Chapman, Caroline 78–79
Chapman, Marguerite 151
Chapman, William 78, 79
Charbonneau, Toussaint 109
Cherokee Strip 190
Cheyenne Daily Leader 51
Chisholm Trail 126
Chona, Maria 109–111
Christie, Julie 103, 166
Cimarron 146
Ciminio, Michael 163
Claiborne, Billy 53, 54, 57, 162
Claimont, Glenn 36
Clair, Ethlyne 145
Clanton Brothers 53, 56, 57, 95, 162
Clark, Dane 167, 169
Clark, William 109
Claxton, William F. 165, 176
Clayton, Ethel 151
Clemens, Samuel *see* Twain, Mark
Clift, Montgomery 171
Cline, Edward 169
Clooney, Rosemary 171
Clum, John P. 193
Cobb, Lee J. 146, 167, 189
Coburn, Charles 161
Cochran, Steve 38
Cody, William S. ("Buffalo Bill") 5, 26, 27, 32, 70, 71, 72, 73
Cole, Nat "King" 66
Collier, William 146
Collins, Lewis D. 181
Collins, Ray 10
Colt, Miriam 134–135
Compson, Betty 15, 145
Comstock Lode 94, 193
Congressional Record 135
Connelly, Christopher 165
Connor, Bob 51
Connors, Chuck 189
Conrad, Michael 47
Conrad, Robert 165
"Contrary Mary" 83
Cooper, Ben 169
Cooper, Gary 33, 34, 146, 153, 158, 163, 170, 176, 181, 182
Cooper, Jackie 173
Corman, Roger 162, 169
Corpus Christi Caller 60
Cosmatos, George P. 180
Costello, Lou 183
Costello, Mariclaire 189
Costner, Kevin 56, 184
Cotten, Joseph 52, 159, 180, 181
Coues, Elliott 85
Court Martial 15

Courtney, Chuck 40
Cowan, John 191
Cox, Ross 86
Crabbe, Buster 162
Crabtree, Charlotte "Lotta" 77–78, 79
Crabtree, John 78
Crabtree, Mary Ann 77, 78
Craig, James 160, 167, 181
Craig, Yvonne 184
Crawford, Broderick 154, 165, 166, 179
Crawford, Joan 152, 164
Crazy Horse (Chief) 137
"Crazy Horse Lil" 94
Crenna, Richard 174
Cristal, Linda 156, 181
Crittenden, Alexander 61
Crockett, Davy 183
Crowley, Kathleen 174, 182
Crowley, Pat 182
Crystal Palace 193
Cummings, George M. 58
Cummings, Irving 15
Curry, Kid *see* Logan, Harvey
Curry, Orrin 45
Curtis, Alan 161
Curtiz, Michael 156, 158
Cusic, Don 2, 42, 57
Custer, Elizabeth 106, 135, 138–141, 179
Custer, George Armstrong 24, 106, 135, 138, 139, 140, 141, 179
Custer's Last Stand 24, 138

Dahl, Arlene 153
Dakota Lil 101
Daley, Ava 142
Dalton, Dorothy 151
Dalton, Emmett 45
Dalton, Grattan (or Grat) 45, 46
Dalton, Robert (or Bob) 45, 46, 165
Dalton Brothers 45, 46, 90, 158, 165, 167, 183
Dano, Royal 164
Dante (Dante Alighieri) 83
Darby, Kim 180
Darcel, Denise 183
Darling, Amanda 76
Darling, Lucia 76, 131
Darn, Roger 186
Darnell, Linda 56, 155, 157, 168, 180
Darren, James 162
Darwell, Janer 155, 181
Daugherty, Herschel 183
Daves, Delmer 163, 165, 172
Davidson, Martin 160

Davies, Marion 152
Davis, Albert 45
Davis, Gail 72, 186, 187
Davis, Jim 171, 173
Davis, Lisa 158
Davis, Maude 40, 45
Davis, Ossie 174
Davis, Roger 186
Daw, Marjorie 152
Dawes Act 120
Dawson, General 21, 31, 33
Day, Doris 35, 155
Day, Mabel Doss 128
Day, William 128
Day Cattle Ranch Company 128
Deadwood Dick in Leadville 28
Deadwood Dick on Deck 27
Deadwood Dispatch 24, 92
"Death Valley Days" 148
deBathe, Sir Hugh Gerald 76
DeCarlo, Yvonne 33, 34, 81, 155, 161, 165, 173, 174, 175, 179
Dee, Frances 160, 182
Dee, James L. 120
Dee, Ruby 174
deHavilland, Olivia 158, 179
Dekker, Albert 164, 173
Delany, Dana 56, 180
Delany, Ruth 145
Della Rose *see* Bullion, Laura
DeMille, Agnes 147
De Mille, Cecil B. 33, 170, 181
Denning, Richard 169
Dennis, Beverly 183
Denny, Reginald 66
Denver Dolls Devices 144
Denver Post 52
The Desperados 38
The Desperados Are in Town 38
Destry Rides Again (film) 33, 100, 158
Destry Rides Again (musical comedy) 147
The Detective Queen 144
deToth, Andre 155, 165, 176, 178
Deuel, Peter 186
Devil's Addition 190
Devine, Andy 19
Dewhurst, Colleen 156
DeWilde, Brandon 174
Dexter, Brad 169
Dexter, Maury 184
Dey, Linda 174
"Diamond Lil" *see* Powers, Lillian
Dickenson, Angie 173

Dietrich, Marlene 83, 100, 148, 158, 176
Dime Novels 1, 21, 27–28
Disney, Walt 182
"The Divine Sarah" *see* Bernhardt, Sarah
Dix, Richard 146, 154
"Dr. Quinn, Medicine Woman" 116, 149
"Doll" 144
Donen, Stanley 174
Donlevy, Brian 40, 181
Donnell, Jeff 162
Donner, George 107
Donner, Richard 167
Donner Party 106, 107
Doolin, William "Bill" 45, 46, 47, 48
Doolin Gang 45, 46, 156
Doran, Ann 188
Dorn, Delores 155
"Douglas" 134
Douglas, Gordon 160
Douglas, Kirk 56, 162, 182
Douglas, Martin 57
Douglas, Melvin 153, 173
Dove, Billie 152
Downs, Cathy 56, 167
Drake, Alfred 148
Drake, Charles 174
Drake, Donna 175
Drew, Ellen 167
Dru, Joanne 141, 171, 172, 174, 175, 181
Drury, James 189
Dubarry, Marie *see* Blonde Marie
Dubonnet, Marie *see* Blonde Marie
Duff, Howard 33, 34, 155
Duffield, Mr. 91
Duffy, Mrs. George 71
Dumas, Alexander 75
Dumont, Eleanora ("Madame Mustache") 23, 26, 35, 87–89, 92, 98
Dunaway, Faye 164, 165
Dunn, Bill 46
Dunn, Irene 146, 156
Dunn, Rose (or Rosa) 45, 47–49, 65
Dunn Brothers 48, 49
Durant, Don 188
Durbin, John 51
Durrant, Marie *see* Blonde Marie
Duryea, Dan 175
Duvall, Shelley 103
Dvorak, Anne 101, 102, 159, 172
Dwan, Alan 19, 156, 167, 172, 177, 180, 184

Dwyer, Mary Ann "Molly" 125
Dylan, Bob 170

Earp, Alvira "Allie" 53, 54, 55, 57, 58, 114, 184
Earp, Bessie 52, 53, 56, 90, 95, 193
Earp, Hattie 54
Earp, James 53, 54, 57
Earp, Josephine Sarah Marcus "Josie" 53, 54, 55–56, 114, 180, 184
Earp, Lou 53, 54
Earp, Matilda "Mattie" 54, 55, 114, 184
Earp, Morgan 52, 53, 54, 57
Earp, Newton 52
Earp, Virgil 52, 53, 54, 57, 114
Earp, Warren 52, 54, 57
Earp, Wyatt 5, 52, 53, 54, 55, 56, 57, 58, 114, 119, 162, 168, 180, 188, 191
Earp Brothers 52, 53, 56, 90, 95, 193
East India Company 87
Eastwood, Clint 147, 159, 161, 163, 170
Eccles, Amy 165
Eddy, Nelson 161
Eden, Barbara 159
Edison Company 145
Edward VII, King of England 76
Edward, Prince of Wales 76
Edwards, Blake 183
Edwards, Penny 158
Egan, Richard 174, 187, 188
Ekberg, Anita 161
Elder, Kate ("Big Nose Kate") 54, 55, 56, 57–59, 162, 184
Elliott, Sam 189
Elliot, "Wild Bill" 68, 163, 170, 184
Ellis, Georgia 103
Elsom, Isabelle 161
"Em Straight Edge" 83
Emerson, Hope 162, 183
Emerson, Ralph Waldo 120
Engle, Flora Pearson 105
Englund, George 185
Enright, Ray 153, 167, 172, 176, 180
Erback, Arthur 15
Erdman, Richard 171
Errol, Leon 181
Erskine, Marilyn 183
Evans, Dale 189
Evans, Laura 98, 99
Evans, Linda 149, 186
Evans, Madge 151
Eyton, Bessie 151

Fair, Laura 59, 60–62
Fair, William 61
Farnham, Elizabeth 115–116
Farnham, Thomas 115
Farr, Felicia 165
Farrow, John 172
Feist, Felix E. 166
Fenton, Leslie 171
Ferber, Edna 156
Ferrell, Conchata 163
Ferrell, Dell 71
Field, Sally 182, 186
Fields, W. C. 169
The Fighting Kentuckians 101
The Fighting Trail 145
Fisher, Kate *see* Elder, Kate
Flame of the Barbary Coast 101, 102
Flanagan, Fionnuala 188
Fleming, Rhonda 171
Fleming, Victor 181
Flores, Erika 149, 187
Flynn, Errol 158, 167, 173, 175, 179
Foch, Nina 161
Fonda, Henry 56, 141, 146, 160, 164, 168, 172, 173, 179
Fonda, Jane 65, 66, 155, 164
Forbis, William 124
Ford, Glenn 146, 158, 167, 171, 173, 179
Ford, John 56, 141, 146, 160, 164, 168, 173, 174, 176, 181
Ford, Robert "Bob" 12
Forrest, Frederick 155
Forrest, Nola 69
Forrest, Steve 42
Forsythe, Rosemary 179
Fort Apache 141
Fort Smith Elevator 10
Foster, Jodie 167
Foster, Lewis R. 157
Foster, Norman 171
Foster, Preston 153, 179
Foster, Susanna 161
Fowler, Gene, Jr. 169, 175
Fowley, Douglas 57, 188, 189
Fox, Richard 15, 16, 17
Francis, Anne 68, 188
Francis, Kaye 183
Francis, Robert 179
Frank Leslie's Magazine 125
Freeman, Agnes 124
Fregonese, Hugo 181
French, Jim 9
Frenchie 101
Frontier Days 60
Frontier Days in the Early West 145
The Frontier Scout 1
Fuller, Samuel 160

Gable, Clark 81, 166, 178
Gannaway, Albert 167, 171
Garcia, Abrana 38
Garde, Betty 148
Gardner, Abbie 131
Gardner, Ava 81, 165, 166, 172
Garland, Beverly 162, 181
Garland, Judy 72, 146, 147, 163
Garner, James 167, 178, 189
Garrett, Pat 39, 40, 170
Gates, Nancy 156, 171
Gentry, Elizabeth 20
George, Susan 175
Ghostly, Alice 189
Gibson, Althea 167
Gibson, Mel 167
Gibson, Virginia 174
Gilbert, Melissa 149, 188
Gilbert, Marie *see* Montez, Lola
Gilmore, Stuart 163, 181
Gilmore, Virginia 182
Gilmore, William 6
Girl of the Golden West 65
Girl Sport 144
Gish, Lillian 159
Glaum, Louise 151
Glenn, Scott 47
"Gloriana" 145
Go West, Young Man 100
Goldstone, James 155
Gone with the Wind 68
Goodnight, Charles 125
Goodnight, Molly 125
Goodrich, Laura 143
Goodrich, "Sad" 143
Gordon, Leo 38
Gordon, Michael 179
Gordon, Robert 171
Grable, Betty 20, 66, 67, 154
Graham, Anne 129
Graham, Gloria 148
Graham, Tom 129
Granger, Stewart 161
Grant, Alexander 112
Grant, Bridget 111–113
Grant, Ignatius 112
Grant, James 112
Grant, James E. 153
Grant, Kathryn 162
Grant, Kirby 189
Grant, Peter 111
Grant, Ulysses S. 5, 140
Grant, William 112
Grassle, Karen 149, 188
Graves, Peter 160
Gray, Colleen 161
Gray, Dolores 148
Grayson, Thomas 61

Grayson, Watt 7
The Great Train Robbery 145
Greeley, Horace 115
Green, Alfred E. 154, 160, 161, 174
Green, Emma 118
Greene, Ellen 182
Greene, Jaclyne 178
Greenbush Twins 149, 188
Greenwood, Charlotte 148
Grey, Joel 155
Grey, Zane 145, 169, 171
Gries, Tom 183
Griffith, Andy 148
Grimes, Tammy 128
Grummond, Frances 106, 135, 136–138
Grummond, George 136, 137
Guinan, "Texas" 145, 151, 152
Guiterrez, Celsa 38, 39, 40
Guiterrez, Sabal 38
Gunfight at the O.K. Corral 56
"Gunsmoke" 103
Guthrie, A. B. 182

H.M.S. Pinafore 55
Haas, Charles 174, 176
Hackett, Joan 178, 183
Hackman, Gene 170
Hagan, Jean 153
Haggard, Merle 149
Haggerty, Ron 189
Haines, Joanne Harris 122
Hale, Barbara 165, 169
Hale, Jean 178
Haley, Ora 127
Hall, Cynthia 183
Hall, George Riley 19
Hall, Jon 165, 181
Hall, Sarah 116
Hall, Sharlot 119–120
Halsey, Brett 160
Hamilton, George 92, 170, 179
Hamlet 80
Hammerstein, Oscar II 148
Hancock, J. C. 57
Hand, Dora 95, 96
Hardcastle, Stoney 20
Hardy, Oliver 182
Harney, Colonel W. S. 111
Harper's Weekly Magazine 27, 142
Harris, Richard 167, 172
Harrison, Will 14
Hart, Dorothy 33
Hart, Eliza 105
Hart, John 62, 63
Hart, Lt. 21
Hart, Mrs. Charlie 129
Hart, Pearl 62–64

Hart, William S. 146
Hartley, Mariette 172
Harvey, Fred 117, 118
Harvey Girls 117–118
The Harvey Girls 83, 146, 147
Haskin, Byron 175, 182
Hathaway, Henry 155, 164, 171, 174, 180
Havinghurst, Walter 72
Hawkins, Jimmy 186
Hawks, Howard 154, 171, 173
Hayden, Sterling 164, 174, 180
Hayes, George "Gabby" 19
Hayes, Maggie 162
Hayes, Kathryn 179
Hays Office 100
Hayward, Susan 171
Hazlitt, Frederick 57
Hearts of the West 145
Heaven's Gate 52
Heflin, Van 162, 179
Heisler, Stuart 153, 158
Hellfire 68, 101
Henderson, Alice Stillwell 126
Henderson, "Prairie Rose" 74
Hendrix, Wanda 173
Henry, Alexander 85, 86
Henry, O. 145
Hepburn, Katharine 173
Herbert, Hugh 67
Herman, Samuel 15
Hershey, Barbara 188
Hervey, Irene 100
Heston, Charlton 183
Hibbs, Jesse 182
Hickman, Dwayne 65, 66
Hickman, Willimina 142
Hickok, Alice *see* Lake, Alice
Hickok, Emma Lake 71
Hickok, James "Wild Bill" 5, 26, 27, 28, 29, 30, 32, 33, 34, 35, 71, 90, 91, 154, 155, 170, 185, 190
Hicks, E. P. 15
Hildegarde, Evelyn *see* Powers, Lillian
Hill, George Roy 42, 155
Hill, Walter 166, 183
Hilliard, Harriet 33
Hilton, Arthur 172
Historical Wild West Show 43
Hittelman, Carl G. 162
Hodiack, John 146, 153, 163
Hoffman, Dustin 131, 165
Hogan, James 179
Holcomb, Kathryn 188
Holden, William 42, 153, 179, 183
Holliday, John Henry "Doc"

53, 54, 55, 56, 57, 58, 95,
  162, 168, 180, 184, 191
Holliman, Earl 188
Holloway, Carol 145
Holloway, Sterling 67
Holm, Celeste 148
Holmes, Helen 145
Holt, Jack 172
"Hopalong Cassidy" 72
Hope, Bob 170, 175
Hope, Gloria 152
Hopkins, Miriam 154
Hopper, Dennis 162, 184
Horan, James 48
Horne, James W. 182
How the West Was Won 146
Howard, Mary 154
Howard, Ron 174
Howe, Ed 81
Huckert, George 91
Hudson, Rock 162, 165
Huggins, Roy 163
Hughes, Howard 169
Hughes, Mary Beth 162
Humberstone, H. Bruce 161,
  178
Hunter, Jeffrey 131
Hunter, Tab 81, 162
Huppert, Isabelle 52, 163
Hurt, John 52
Huston, Anjelica 35, 155
Huston, John 81, 165, 169
Huston, Walter 40, 161
Hutton, Betty 72, 153
Hyer, Martha 174, 184

Ileff, Elizabeth 124
Indian Territory 9, 10, 14, 15,
  186, 190
Ingalls, Nancy 45
Ireland, John 160, 170
Ivers, Alice *see* Tubbs, Alice
  Ivers

Jackson, Helen Hunt 120
Jackson, Sherry 68, 183
Jaeckel, Richard 165
Jagger, Dean 155, 181
James, Frank 5, 6, 8, 19, 188
James, Jessie 5, 6, 8, 10, 11, 13,
  19, 26, 17, 172, 180, 188
James-Younger Gang 8, 10
Jameson, Elizabeth 64, 106
Jeffreys, Anne 169, 172, 180
Jenny Leatherlungs 78
Jersey Lil *see* Langtry, Lilly
Jewell, Isabelle 19, 154
Jewison, Norman 156
Johnson, Brad 186
Johnson, Kay 40
Johnson, Lamont 47, 156

Johnson County Wars 51, 52
Jones, Carolyn 146
Jones, Christopher 188
Jones, Emma 8
Jones, Jennifer 159
Jones, Shirley 148, 181
Josephson, Berta 123
"Julia's Place" 94
July, Jim *see* Starr, James
Jurado, Katy 163, 170
Juran, Nathan 162, 163, 180
Jurgens, Adele 166, 178

Kaepernick, Berta *see* Blan-
  chett, Berta
Kahn, Madeline 154
Kane, Joseph 159, 162, 167, 170,
  184
Kansas-Pacific Railroad 191
Kaplan, Joanthan 154
Karlson, Phil 162, 179
Kasdan, Lawrence 184
Katzenberger, Charlie 70
Kaye, Stubby 66
Kazan, Elia 173
Keach, James 19, 166
Keach, Stacy 19, 166
Keane, Kerrie 189
Keel, Howard 35, 72, 153, 155,
  171, 172, 174
Keller, Harry 175
Kelly, Edward 169
Kelly, Fanny Wiggins 131,
  132–133
Kelly, Grace 163
Kelly, Mary 21, 22
Kelly, Nancy 164
Kendrick, Eula 124
Kennedy, Burt 173, 174, 178,
  182
Kershner, Irvin 172
Keyes, Evelyn 67, 68, 158, 171,
  181
Keyes, "Granny" 105, 107
Kid Antrim *see* Bonney,
  William
Kid Curry *see* Logan, Harvey
Kidd, Michael 148
Kidder, Margot 174, 189
Kilmer, Val 56, 180
Kinchlow, Ben 60
King, Henry 162, 164
King, Louis 167, 170
Kingston, Winifred 151
Kirk, Phyllis 164
Kirkpatrick, Ben 40, 42, 44
"Kitty the Schemer" *see*
  LeRoy, Kitty
Klondike Annie 100
Koch, Marianne 159
Koener, W. H. D. 106

Kohl, Edith Ammona 106
Kohrs, Augusta 124
Kovack, Nancy 169, 183
Kramer, Burt 189
Kristofferson, Kris 52, 163, 170
Kulick, Buzz 170

Ladd, Alan 174, 184
Ladd, Alana 184
Lady Windermere's Fan 76
Lake, Alice 27, 126
Lake, Stuart 53, 57
Lamb, Andre 178
Lamont, Charles 161, 173, 181
L'Amour, Louis 144
Lancaster, Burt 47, 56, 155,
  162, 165
Landau, Martin 176
Lane, Diane 47, 156
Lane, Sara 189
Lando, Joe 149, 186
Landon, Michael 149, 188
Lang, Fritz 172, 182
Langdon, Sue Ane 173
Lange, Hope 180
Langtry, Lilly ("Jersey Lil")
  76–77, 81, 118
Lansbury, Angela 83, 146, 147,
  163
Larimer, Sarah 132
Larsen, Keith 186
Latter-Day Saints *see* Mor-
  mons
Laurel, Stan 182
Lawrence, Florence 151
Lawrence, Jody 176
Lay, William Ellsworth "Elzy"
  40, 42, 44, 45
Lea, Joseph C. 128
Leadville Chronicle 93
"Leadville Lil" 144
Lease, Mary E. 122
LeBord, Reginald 158
Lee, Anna 141, 160
Lee, Polly 74
Lee, Robert E. 37, 138
Lee, Sheryl 159
Leeds, David 174
Leigh, Janet 169
Leighton, Caroline 106
Leonard, Marion 40, 151
Leonard, Robert A. 161
Leone, Sergio 159, 161
Lerner, Alan J. 161
LeRoy, Kitty ("Kitty the
  Schemer") 26, 92–93
Leslie, Joan 184
Levin, Allan J. 161
Levin, Henry 167
Lewis, Geoffrey 19
Lewis, Meriwether 109

Lewis, Richard 182
Lewis and Clark Expedition 108
The Life and Legend of Wyatt Earp 57
The Life and Times of Judge Roy Bean 81
Lillie, Gordon William ("Pawnee Bill") 73
Lillie, May 73
Lincoln, Abraham 69, 138
Lincoln, Mary Todd 107
Lincoln, Robert 107
Lincoln County Wars 39
Lind, Jenny 71, 78
Lindsay, Margaret 181
Liszt, Franz 75
Little, Ann 152
Little, Cleavon 154
Little Big Horn, Battle of 24, 106
Little Big Man 131
"Little Britches" *see* Metcalf, Jennie
"Little Gold Dollar" 83
"Little House on the Prairie" 148
Lloyd, Frank 182
Lockhart, Matilda 132
Locke, Tammy 158
Logan, Harvey ("Kid Curry") 42, 43, 44
Logan, Jacqueline 152
Logan, Josh 190
"Lola" 144
Lola Montez 76
London, Julie 172
"The Lone Ranger" 148
Long, Richard 149, 186
The Long Riders 19
Longabaugh, Harry *see* Sundance Kid
Lopez, Juan 129
Lorys, Dianna 179
Louis I, King of Bavaria 75, 76
Lowe, Frederick 147
Lucas, "Tad" 74
Ludwig, Edward 181
Lummis, Charles 129
Lynn, Sharon 182
Lyon, Francis D. 169

McCabe and Mrs. Miller 102, 103, 166
McCall, Jack 28
McCambridge, Mercedes 146, 164
McCann, William 164
McCarey, Leo 154
McCarty, Patrick Henry *see* Bonney, William

McClelland, General 138
McClure, Doug 189
McCoy, Joseph 190
McCrea, Jody 184
McCrea, Joel 155, 156, 160, 162, 163, 172, 173, 178, 181, 182, 184
McCullough, John 80
McDonald, Frank 175
MacDonald, Jeanette 81, 161
MacDonald, Katherine 152
McDougal, Annie ("Cattle Annie") 45–47, 156
McDowall, Roddy 81
McDowell, Andie 154
McEveetty, Tim 165, 179
McGhee, Gloria 175
McGinnis, Vera 74
McGuire, Don 164
McIntire, Nancy 144
McIntire, Tim 165, 179
Mackaill, Dorothy 152
Mackay, "Darling Bob" 23
McLaglen, Andrew V. 182
McLaglen, Victor 141
McLain, Edward 51
McLaury, Frank 53
McLaury Brothers 53, 56, 57, 95
McLeod, Norman 170
McLerie, Allyn 35
McMahon, Aline 146
MacMurray, Fred 162, 169
McMurtry, Larry 35, 155
McNally, Stephen 176
McPherson, Jim 45
MacRae, Gordon 148, 172
McTavish, Donald 85, 86
Madame Mustache *see* Dumont, Eleanora
Madison, Guy 149, 167
Magoffin, Susan Shelby 105
Mahoney, Jock 174
Main, Marjorie 183
Majeska, Helena 80–81
Majors, Lee 149, 186
Malden, Karl 183
Malone, Dorothy 156, 178
Mann, Anthony 146, 156, 161, 169, 179
Mann, Daniel 147
Marcus, Josephine *see* Earp, Josephine Sarah Marcus "Josie"
Marin, Edwin L. 156, 160, 178
Markham, Pauline 55
Markle, Peter 182
Marlowe, Hugh 176
Marlowe, Scott 184
Marquand, Tina 179
Marquis, Maria Elena 153

Marshall, George 100, 158, 162, 161, 179, 181, 183
Martin, Ana 172
Martin, Dean 161, 179
Martinez, Tina 188
Marvin, Lee 65, 66, 147, 155, 156, 170
Masterson, Bat 5, 55, 56, 90, 97, 191, 193
Masterson, Mary Stuart 154
Mate, Rudolph 175
Matheson, Tim 165
Matthews, Carole 167, 175
Mature, Victor 56, 161, 168
Maurer, Norman 169
Maxwell, Deluvina 40
Maxwell, James 118
Maxwell, Marilyn 68, 176, 183
Maxwell, Martha 118
Maxwell, Paulita 38, 40
Maxwell, Pete 38, 39
May, Molly *see* May, Rosa
May, Rosa 92, 98
Mayo, Virginia 156, 160, 178, 184
Mazeppa or The Wild Horse of Tartary 79
Meeker, Arvella 134
Meeker, Josephine 105, 133–134
Meeker, Nathan 134
Menken, Adah Isaacs 79–80
Meredith, Judi 188
Merkle, Una 100
Merman, Ethel 72
Metcalf, Jennie ("Little Britches") 45–47, 156
Michael of Russia, Grand Duke 71
Middleton, John 5, 9
Milan, Lisa 165
Miles, Sarah 167
Miles, Vera 131, 173
Milford, John 188
Millain, John 94, 95
Miller, Colleen 161
Miller, David 40, 154
Miller, Joaquin 79
Miller, Stuart 173
Mills Brothers' 101 Wild West Show 146
Milner, Martin 165
Milton, John 83
Minter, Mary Mil 152
"Miss Kitty" 103
"Miss Leslie" 81
The Missouri Legend 20
Mitchell, Guy 171
Mitchum, James 184
Mitchum, Robert 171, 173, 178
Mix, Tom 146, 184

Modjeska, Helena *see* Majeska, Helena
"Molly b'Damned" 83
Monahseetah 140
Monroe, Marilyn 173
Monroe, Molly (Mollie) *see* Sawyer, Mary E.
Monroe, Vaughn 175
Montana Belle 19
Montez, Lola 2, 35, 74–75, 77, 79
Montgomery, Elizabeth 19, 154
Montgomery, George 19, 157, 170, 179, 180, 186
Moore, Eugenia 46
Moore, Terry 180, 187
Moorehead, Agnes 146, 164, 180
Moran, Jack 48
Moran, Peggie 180
Moran, Sadie 45
Moran, Thomas 1
Moreno, Rita 156, 160, 181
Morgan, Dennis 154, 156
Morgan, Speer 20
Mormons 105, 120, 121, 155, 181, 192
Morrell, Dorothy 74
Morris, J 70
Morris, Wayne 154, 166, 175, 181
Moses, Phoebe Ann *see* Oakley, Annie
Mouchanoff, Madame 80
Mousketeers 182
Mowbray, Alan 181
Mulhall, Lucille 74, 145
Mulligan, Richard 176
Mulroney, Dermott 154
Moses, Jacob 70
Moses, Susan 70
Murat, Henri 113
Murat, Katrina 113
Murphy, Audie 162, 163, 174, 175, 179, 180, 182
Murphy, Ben 186
Murphy, John 107, 108
Murphy, Mary 175
Murphy, Michael 103
Murray, Ken 167
Murray, May 152
Muscle Shells War 19
Muscogi Daily Phoenix 19
Mustache, Madame *see* Dumont, Eleanora
My Darling Clementine 56, 168
My Fair Lady 147
My Little Chickadee 100
Naish, J. Carrol 175

"Nancy" 144
Nardini, Tom 65, 66
Natwick, Mildred 141
Nazzaro, Ray 180
Nelson, Lori 169, 180
New York Daily News 148
New York Herald Tribune 148
New York Police Gazette see *Police Gazette*
New York Times 8, 14, 76, 135, 148
New York Weekly 1
Newcomb, George "Bitter Creek" 47, 48
Newman, Joseph M. 160, 162, 179
Newman, Paul 42, 43, 81, 155, 164, 165, 182
Newmar, Julie 174
Newton, Grace 52
Newton, Orlando 52
Nichols, Clarina Irene 122
Nicodemus 142
Nielson, James 172
Nix, Evrett 48
Nolan, Jeanette 186, 188, 189
North, Major Frank 73
North Sheree 165
Northern Pacific Railroad 30
Northwest Lumber Company 85
Novack, Jane 151
Novak, Kim 183
Nyby, Christian 184

O.K. Corral 52, 53, 54, 55, 56, 95, 114
Oakley, Annie 2, 70–73, 145, 153
Oatman, Lorenzo 131
Oatman, Mary Ann 131
Oatman, Olive 131
O'Brian, Hugh 56, 68, 183, 188
O'Brien, Edmond 42, 182
O'Brien, Joan 175
O'Connell, Arthur 146
O'Driscoll, Martha 181
O'Hara, Catherine 56, 184
O'Hara, Maureen 155, 156, 171, 173
Oklahoma (film) 148
Oklahoma (musical comedy) 148
The Oklahombres 45
Olcott, Sidney 40
"Old Bet" 108
Old Birdcage Theater 90, 119
O'Neal, Ryan 183
O'Neill, Jennifer 173
Ophuls, Max 76, 166

O'Quinn, Terry 52
Oriental Hall 193
O'Shea, Con 95
The Outlaw 40
Outlaw Woman 101
Owen, Seena 152
Owens, Dr. Bethenia 116–117

Pacula, Joanna 180
Page, Geraldine 164
Paint Your Wagon 146
Palmer, Betsy 179
Pankhurst, Charlotte "Charlie" 143
Pappas, Irene 180
Parker, Eleanor 167
Parker, Fess 149, 182
Parker, George Leroy *see* Cassidy, Butch
Parker, "Hanging Judge" Isaac 12, 14, 15, 50
Parker, Jean 162
Parker, Lester Shepherd 144
Parker, Robert *see* Cassidy, Butch
Parker, Willard 68, 171
Parks, Larry 68
Parrish, Helen 164
Patterson, E. 8
Patterson, Elizabeth 18
Patterson, Neva 189
Patton, Luana 179
"Pawnee Bill" *see* Lillie, Gordon William
Payne, John 181
Pearce, Richard 163
Peck, Gregory 146, 158, 162, 164, 174, 176
Peckinpah, Sam 42, 170, 172
"Peg Leg Annie" 83
Penn, Arthur 165
Perkins, Anthony 81, 179
Persune 134
Petitt, Joanna 170
Philbrook, James 183
Phillips, Lee 182
Phillips, Lou Diamond 184
Pickford, Mary 151, 152
"Pickhandle Kate" 26
Pierce, Mary 48
Pink, Sidney 178
Pinkerton Detective Agency 12, 155
Pitts, Charlie 8
Place, Etta 40, 41, 42, 43, 44, 45, 155, 182
The Plainsman 33, 34, 35
Platt, Marc 148
Pleasant Valley Wars 129
Plummer, Amanda 47, 156

Pocahontas 108
"Poker Alice" *see* Tubbs, Alice Ivers
Poker Alice 92
Police Gazette (*New York Police Gazette*) 1, 14, 15, 39, 79
Pony Express 32
Porter, Fanny 97–98
Porter, William S. (O. Henry) 145
Post, Ted 163
Potts, Cliff 19
Powell, Jane 174
Power, Tyrone 155, 164
Powers, Lillian ("Diamond Lil") 84, 98–99
Powers, Stephanie 174
Prairie Folks 148
Prairie Pirate 145
Preminger, Otto 164, 173
Presley, Elvis 154
Preston, Robert 18
Price, Mrs. 134
Prince, Jack 148
Principal, Victoria 81
Pryor, Roger 154
Puccini, Giacomo 65
Pyle, Denver 57

Quaid, Dennis 56, 166, 184
Quaid, Randy 166
Quantrill, William Clark 6, 7, 37–38
Quantrill's Raiders 6, 37, 38, 170
Quarantine Line 190
Quinn, Anthony 172, 181
Quinn, Pat 174, 185

Raimi, Sam 170
Raines, Ella 175, 178
Ralston, Vera 162, 170, 184
Rambeau, Marjorie 81
Ramona 120
Ramsey, Ann 141
Rascoe, Burton 15
Rassinov, Rada 161
Rathbone, George *see* Taylor, Ned
Rawlins, John 167
Ray, Nicholas 164, 180
Reagan, Ronald 148, 156
Reason, Rex 171
Red Cloud (Chief) 137
"The Red Skelton Show" 32
Redford, Robert 42, 43, 155, 182
Reed, Donna 162, 163, 179
Reed, Ed 7, 19, 175
Reed, James Frazier 105, 107
Reed, James "Jim" 5, 7

Reed, Margaret 105, 107
Reed, Pamela 19, 166
Reed, Pearl 7, 12, 14–15
Reed, Rosa *see* Reed, Pearl
Reed, Virginia 105, 107, 108
Remington, Frederick 1
Renegades 67, 68
The Return of Jesse James 101
Reynolds, Burt 167
Reynolds, Debbie 146, 164
Rhodes, Eugene Manlowe 145
Rich, David Lowell 174
Rich, Irene 152
Richards, Ann 19, 154
Richards, Jeff 174
Richards, Paul 160
Richey, Anne 52
Riker, Janette 123
Ringo, Johnny 193
Ritt, Martin 164
Ritter, Thelma 146, 164
Rivero, Jorge 173
Roach, Joyce Gibson 13, 64
Roach, Ruth 74
Robbins, Gale 35, 38
Roberts, Joan 148
Robertson, Dale 148, 157, 165, 172, 175, 180
Robinson, Ann 162
Robinson, Edward G. 154
Robinson, Jesse 60
Rocky Mountain Museum 118
Rocky Mountain News 98
Rodeo Hall of Fame 74
Rodgers, Richard 148
Roe, Frances 135
Rogers, Annie 40, 43, 44
Rogers, Jean 155
Rogers, Jennie 98
Rogers, Roy 189
Roman, Ruth 19, 154, 156, 158
Romance of Rosie Ridge 101
Romeo and Juliet 80
Romero, Cesar 67, 154
Rone, Sudie 142
Roosevelt, Theodore 145
Rose, Isabelle 76
Rose of the Cimarron *see* Dunn, Rose
Ross, Katharine 42, 155, 173, 182
Ross, Shirley 76
Rossellini, Isabella 56, 59, 184
Roth, Marta 167
Rowdy Anne 145
"Rowdy Kate" 26
Rowland, Roy 167
Rowlandson, Mary 131
Rubenstein, John 184
Rudolph, Oscar 183
Ruggles, Charles 153, 156

Rush, Barbara 145
Russell, Gail 146, 153
Russell, Jane 19, 40, 149, 167, 169, 170, 175, 178
Russell, John 161, 169
Russell, Kurt 56, 180
Rutherford, Ann 154
Ryan, Kelly 169
Ryan, Robert 42, 169, 180
Rydell, Mark 156

Sacajawea 108–108
Sacramento Union 88
"Sadie" 144
Saint, Eva Marie 176
Sale, Richard 179
Salkow, Sidney 162, 175
Salome Where She Danced 81
San Francisco 81
San Francisco Chronicle 80
San Francisco Examiner 74
San Francisco Mail 143
San Juan, Olga 65, 147
Sann, Paul 145
Sands, Johnny 167
Santa Fe Railroad 117
Sarafin, Richard C. 167
Sarah 149
Savage, John 47
Sawyer, Mary E. 143
Saxon, John 183
Scarlet Days 145
Schell, Maria 146, 156, 163
Schieffelin, Ed 193
Schildkraut, Joseph 159
Schuck, John 103
Schultz, Keith 188
Schultz, Keven 188
Schweig, Eric 160
Scott, Pippa 189
Scott, Randolph 18, 19, 154, 156, 160, 163, 166, 172, 176, 178, 179, 180, 183
Scott, Zachary 156, 174
Scourby, Alexander 171
The Searchers 131
Sears, Fred S. 153, 184
Sebastian, Dorothy 152
Seberg, Jean 170
Seitz, George B. 165
Selander, Leslie 154, 157, 160, 163, 174, 176, 178, 179, 180, 184
Selznick, David O. 159
"Señorita Rosalie" 73
Seymour, Anne 187
Seymour, Clarine 152
Seymour, Jane 149, 186
Shakespeare, William 69, 83
Sharp, Karen 188
Shaw, Roberta 189

She Done Him Wrong 100
She Stoops to Conquer 79
She Wore a Yellow Ribbon 141
Shelton, Mary E. 122
Shepard, Patty 177
Shepherd, Cybill 189
Sheridan, Ann 158, 175, 189
Sherman, George 57, 68, 155, 156, 161, 171, 179
Sherman, Philip Henry 138
Shirley, Cravens 7
Shirley, Edwin "Ed" 6
Shirley, Eliza 5, 6
Shirley, Glenn 6, 9, 15, 20
Shirley, John 5, 6
Shirley, John Allison 7
Shirley, Myra Maybelle *see* Starr, Belle
Sholem, Lee 171, 176
Show Boat 148
Sichel, Pierre 76
Sidney, George 72, 153, 163
Siegel, Don 159, 174
Silk, Mattie 98
The Silver Belt 55
Silver Star 101
Silverstein, Elliot 66, 155, 167
Sinatra, Frank 161, 164
Sinclair, Berta "Muzzy" 145
Singleton, Benjamin "Pap" 142
Sitting Bull 32, 71
Skelton, Enid Jones 125
Skerrit, Tom 92, 165
Skull, Sally 59–60, 127
Slaughter, John 129
Slaughter, Viola 129
Slezak, Walter 81, 173
Smith, Alexis 167, 173
Smith, John 186
Smith, Lillian 71
Smith, Noel 156
Smoke, David 113
Snyder, Jesse 61
Snyder, John 107
Sokalski, Annie Blanche 105, 138
Sokalski, George 138
Soldier's Aid Society of Iowa 122
Solomon, Edward 80
Sommers, Elke 161
Sondergaard, Gale 172
Southwestern Historical Quarterly 125
Spaniard, Jack 9
"Spanish Queen" 88
Speidelman, Arthur Allan 170
Sperber, Madame 57, 59

Springsteen, R. G. 169, 171, 174, 175, 178
Stack, Robert 154
Stagecoach 177
Staiger, Libi 148
Stamp, Terrence 184
Stanley, Joseph 40
Stanwyck, Barbara 71, 72, 149, 153, 156, 160, 161, 167, 181, 186
Starr, Belle 2, 3, 5–21, 32, 35, 46, 50, 65, 88, 154, 166, 167, 175, 185
Starr, James ("Jim July") 9, 10, 14
Starr, Sam (Samuel) 9, 10, 11, 12
Starr, Tom 9
Starrett, Jack 175
Steele, Karen 172
Steiger, Rod 47, 148
Stenhouse, "Fanny" 61, 120, 121–122
Stenhouse, Thomas 121
Sterling, Jan 181
Stevens, George 153, 174
Stevens, Inger 163
Stevens, Stella 42
Stewart, James 100, 146, 148, 158, 164, 169, 181
Stillwell, Hallie 126
Stoecker, Martha 106
Stone, Carol 57
Stone, Milburn 188
Stone, Sharon 170
Storey, Edith 145, 146, 151, 152
Storm, Gale 176, 179
Stowe, Madeleine 154
Stratton, Albert 189
Strudwick, Shepperd 18
Stuart, Awbonnie 124
Stump, John 99
Sturges, John 162
Sturges, Preston 56, 57, 154
Sturgess, Olive 172
Sullivan, Barry 160, 167, 176, 179
Summerhayes, Martha 105, 136
Sundance Kid 40, 41, 42, 45
Sutherland, Kiefer 184
Sutter's Mill 88
Swan, Dr. 87
Sweet, Blanche 151
Swit, Loretta 165

Talbott, Gloria 57, 149, 169, 184, 188
Talman, William 180
Tamblyn, Russ 174, 184
Tashlin, Frank 176
Taylor, Don 68, 183

Taylor, Elizabeth 92, 170
Taylor, Estelle 146
Taylor, Joan 160
Taylor, Mort 78
Taylor, Ned 144
Taylor, Ray 181
Taylor, Robert 40, 148, 153, 154, 167, 172, 183
Taylor, Rod 189
Teller, Henry Moore 134
Temple, Shirley 141, 160
The Terror of the Range 145
Terry, Alice 152
Terry, Ethel Grey 152
Tetzlaff, Ted 184
Thaxter, Phyllis 160, 176
Thomas, Sharon 184
Thompson, Era Bell 142
Thompson, J. Lee 183
Thompson, Joan 117
Thorp, Jack 64
Three Stooges 169
Tierney, Gene 15, 18, 154, 172
Tincher, Fay 145
Titanic 129
Tobin, David 89
Tobin, Maggie *see* Brown, Molly
Tombstone 56
The Tombstone Epitaph 57, 193
Tone, Franchot 180
Toovay, Shawn 149, 187
Torn, Rip 163
Torres, Liz 92, 170
Totter, Audrey 167, 184, 186
Tourneur, Jacques 178
Towers, Constance 164
Townsend, E. E. 127
Tracy, Spencer 173
Trevor, Claire 176, 177, 178, 179
Tryon, Tom 183
Tubbs, Alice Ivers ("Poker Alice") 28, 84, 91–92
Tucker, Forrest 19, 68, 176
Tufts, Sonny 181
Twain, Mark 80, 193
Tyler, Beverly 180
Tyrrell, Susan 92, 170
Two Gun Lady 101

Ulrich, Lenore 152
Underhill, Ruth 109, 110, 111
Union Pacific Railroad 29, 181, 191
Union Protestant Church 56
The Unsinkable Molly Brown 128
Upgate, Julie 177
Ustinov, Peter 76
Utter, Charlie 27, 90, 91

Vaccaro, Brenda 149, 189
Valentine, Karen 161
Vallee, Rudy 67
Van Buren, Mabel 151
Van Cleef, Lee 171, 172, 177
Van Doren, Mamie 176
Van Dyke, D. W. S. 81
Van Fleet, Jo 56, 59, 162
Vanderbilts 129
The Vanishing Rider 145
Vann, H. J. 10
Velasquez, Loreta 111
Verdugo, Elena 188
Vickers, Martha 160
Vidor, King 40, 158
Villa, Pancho 42
Vint, Jesse 19
*Virginia City Territorial Enter-
prise* 80
Vohrer, Alfred 161
Vohs, Joan 160

Waggner, George 161, 170
Wagner, Robert 180
Walbrook, Anton 76
Walken, Christopher 163, 174
Walker, Charlotte 151
Walker, Clint 160
Walker, Robert 173
Wallach, Eli 146
Walsh, Raoul 156, 162, 165,
175, 178, 179
Wanted: The Sundance Woman
42
Ward, Fred 19
Warden, Jack 183
Warhol, Andy 95
Warner, Phoebe Kerrick 125
Warren, Helen 148
Waters, Frank 53, 54, 57
Waterston, Sam 52
Watson, Edgar 14
Watson, Ella "Cattle Kate"
49–52
Way Out West 101
Wayne, John 102, 131, 141, 146,
153, 156, 159, 160, 164, 171,
173, 174, 176, 177, 178, 180,
182, 184
Wayne, Pat 184
Weaver, Dennis 188

Weaver, John F. 10
Weld, Tuesday 156
Wellman, William 155, 183
Wells, Carole 189
Werner, Oscar 76
West, Adam 169
West, John 12
West, Mae 99, 154, 169
West Point Military Academy
138
Westcott, Helen 162
Western Girls 145
Westover, Winifred 152
Westward Ho the Women 146
Westward the Women 146
What Happened to Mary? 145
Wheeler, E. L. 27, 28, 144
Whelan, Arlene 171
Whelan, Edmund 21
Whelan, Tim 19, 154
White, Laura 117
Whitman, Narcissa 105
Whitman, Stuart 156
Whitneys 129
Whittaker, Mary Ann 74
Wichita Wildlife Refuge 73
Widmark, Richard 165, 181,
182
Wilbaux, Nellie 124
Wild Bill 35
Wild Bunch 37, 40, 41–43,
44, 45, 98
The Wild Bunch 42, 43
Wild West Weekly 144
Wild Women 68
Wilde, Cornel 180
Wilde, Oscar 96, 192
Wilder, Laura Ingalls 149, 188
William of Germany, Crown
Prince 71
Williams, Bill 169, 173
Williams, Hezekiah 125
Williams, JoBeth 56, 184
Williams, Kathlyn 151
Williams, Lizzie Johnson 125,
126
Willis, Ann Bassett 127–128
Willis, Frank 128
Wilson, Lois 152
Wilson, Marjorie 151
Willson, Meredith 128

Windsor, Claire 152
Windsor, Marie 68, 83, 101,
155, 157, 163, 183
Winner, Michael 165
Winniger, Charles 100
Winningham, Mare 184
Winona, Kim 186
Winters, Gloria 189
Winters, Shelley 181
Wise, Robert 180
Wister, Owen 181
Witcher, John Stamp 99
Withers, Jane 174
Wittenmeyer, Annie Turner
122
A Woman of Courage 148
Women's West Congress 149
Wong, Anna May 152
Wood, Natalie 131, 173
Wood, Sam 153
Woodman, Ruth 149
Woods, Leah J. *see* Rogers,
Jennie
Woodworth, John 20
World Columbia Exhibition 62
World Industrial Cotton Exhi-
bition 70
Wyatt Earp 56
Wyler, William 182
Wyman, Jane 154
Wymore, Patrice 166
Wyoming Stock Growers Asso-
ciation 51

Yarbrough, Jean 181
Yerby, Narsaria 38
Young, Ann Eliza 105, 120–121,
122
Young, Brigham 120, 121, 192
Young, Clara Kimball 151
Young, Loretta 146, 153, 171
Young, Robert 163, 182, 188
Young, Tony 178
Younger, Cole 7, 8, 10, 14, 19,
188
Younger, Pearl *see* Reed, Pearl
Younger Brothers 5, 6, 8, 10,
46, 154, 188
Younger's Bend 9, 10, 12

Zinnemann, Fred 148, 163

ml

12/06